A **LIGHT** THROUGH **THE** CRACKS

A LIGHT THROUGH THE CRACKS

A CLIMBER'S STORY

BETH RODDEN

Little
a

Published by Little A, New York

www.apub.com

Amazon, the Amazon logo, and Little A are trademarks of Amazon.com, Inc., or its
affiliates.

ISBN-13: 9781503903814 (hardcover)
ISBN-13: 9781503903791 (paperback)
ISBN-13: 9781503958791 (digital)

Cover design by Tree Abraham
Cover illustration by Alexandria Neonakis

Printed in the United States of America

First edition

This book is dedicated with all my love to Mom, Dad, Randy, and Theo.

AUTHOR'S NOTE

This book, many, many years in the making, was written about a specific time in my life. I know the story I'm telling would have been vastly different if I had been remotely close to meeting my deadlines and ended it five years, three years, or even six months ago. But just like with my life, these stories, how I feel about them, how they impacted me and my role in this world, have changed drastically over the years, and will inevitably continue to change. I'm keenly aware that a book is a snapshot in time and, in turn, that how I reflect on and understand what happened during that time is also a snapshot. I'm certain that I will think differently, that these stories will hold different meanings to me, the day after I turn it in to the publisher, the week after, and one, five, ten, twenty years down the line. But perhaps there's some beauty in that, remembering what it meant to me at the time, seeing how that evolved over the years, and being open and curious to how I feel about it—how that will later grow and expand and contract and probably even reverse itself in some cases.

Memories are fallible, but this is, to the best of my ability, a work of nonfiction. Some names of individuals have been changed.

PART ONE

CHAPTER ONE

Amsterdam, August 2000

By the time Tommy and I made it to Amsterdam's gleaming, sterile airport, we had been passed along a half dozen times, like an important but increasingly well-worn package. Military helicopters had brought us and our other two climbing partners from base to base. We'd endured a surreal ride on a private jet from the last military base to the capital, Bishkek, traveling alongside the tipsy and jovial president of Kyrgyzstan. He'd patted us on the shoulders like a grandfather and claimed us long enough for a photo op and a speech to local media in a language we couldn't understand. Then he handed the four of us off to the American embassy, which scrambled to find us flights home. A few days later, Tommy and I drove across the Kazakhstan border, in a hired car with a diplomatic escort, to the international airport in Almaty, and finally a commercial jet took us from Central Asia to the edge of the Atlantic. Now we had just one more flight to go.

Our tickets were a last-minute mess, and we needed to check on our connection. As we crossed the terminal, I carried a brown paper gift bag from the airport candy shop—despite what we'd been through, I still wanted to bring my older brother a present from this trip. I watched the families clustered around the gates, the lone business travelers perched at the bars, scanning, scanning each face around me. I'd been on edge through practically every step of the journey: the embassy in Bishkek had felt almost safe, but at the hotel where they'd sent us to get some sleep, I'd felt vulnerable and stayed vigilant.

In the airport, I was hungry again. When we'd made it to the second army base, the one that felt like a cluster of portable classrooms set down on a vast brown plain, we'd stuffed ourselves with barley and warm buttered bread, but I could not stay full. I had just eaten two chocolate croissants. Still, my stomach felt like a cavern. My brother didn't really need a present, did he?

I ate half the chocolate in the bag before we got to our gate.

The line at the KLM counter felt so orderly. The whole airport did. Just existing there felt like getting a big, soothing hug. When we'd boarded the flight in Kazakhstan, the passengers had formed no line. Everybody just pushed in a scrum toward the plane. Tommy and I stood frozen, like the good, shocked scouts that we were, and got lost in the flood. I felt so fragile, so extremely fragile, and so resigned to that fragile state.

We weren't safe. That was obvious to me. No line, no order, no rule of law. I loved rules. People smoked openly on that first plane.

"Next . . . ," the flight attendant said as we arrived at the counter. Her voice was as professionally cheerful as her uniform: light blue skirt, light blue jacket, white blouse underneath.

"We're here to check in for our flight," I said.

"Wonderful. May I please have your boarding passes?"

I mumbled something apologetic and handed her a few crumpled, dirty sheets of paper. "I think we have to get our seats and stuff from you."

She pinched her brow as she read our mess of documents. She typed vigorously. I was sure this meant we weren't going to make it home.

"Can you wait one second?" she asked, flashing a strained smile. She disappeared behind a wall.

I looked at Tommy. He stared into the blank space where the woman had just been. I couldn't tell if he was as scared as I was, if he was also monitoring the people pooling and flowing around us for any threat. I felt like I had grown an invisible antenna that vibrated continually, never at rest. Never letting me rest. A memory tried to surface inside me: A body in silhouette, sailing off a dark cliff. A crunch, and an exhale. I forced it back down.

Two blond attendants now appeared where there had been one.

"Can you tell me: Was it something KLM did?" the new flight attendant asked.

I looked back at Tommy. Did he know what she was talking about? Did she know what had happened? Tommy shrugged.

"Wait, what?" I said. "What was something . . . ?"

"Well, um, how to say this," the flight attendant said. "It says on your tickets, 'Emotionally distressed passengers, please take care.' So, we are just wondering if it's something KLM did." She looked concerned and defensive in her caring, like a hospital billing manager. She didn't want to know the answer, but she had to ask.

I didn't want a stranger to try to comfort me, but I did feel the need to comfort her. So I said, "Oh no, definitely not. We were just kidnapped and we want to go home."

I couldn't believe how easily the sentence came out. *We were just kidnapped . . .* I'd never said it so plainly before.

The flight attendant exhaled all her breath at once, stunned and relieved. "Well, good," she said.

Well, good?

"KLM does our best. How about business-class seats for you two?" She printed our fresh, flat boarding passes. Tommy and I boarded the plane.

We ate every meal and every snack that was offered to us on the long ride home. My hunger was like a portal opened into a galaxy—infinite, absolute. When I was in middle school, I used to watch my older brother, David, eat, stunned by the mountain of food he could consume. Now, it felt strangely freeing to eat with that type of abandon. I hadn't done that since ninth grade, when I became obsessed with climbing.

I could eat, but I still couldn't sleep. My anxiety kept me wide awake, and my wakefulness in turn meant I had nothing but space and time for the anxiety to spin itself tighter in my body. I kept wondering if the plane would crash. That seemed possible, maybe even probable, given how the rest of our trip had gone. An appropriate ending, in a way. I wondered if I'd be scared. What would Tommy say to me before impact? Would it hurt? Our backpack, stuffed at our feet, was filled with souvenirs purchased in a blur during our strange interlude in Bishkek, between our flight with the president and our diplomatic drive across the border. I had stuffed the paltry remains of the airport chocolate into our bag alongside the rest of the things we'd acquired: a hand-carved wooden chess set, a wool hanging. Proof that we'd done something major and been somewhere cool. What were we thinking?

The backpack that sat at our feet had been lost in transit when we'd first landed in Kyrgyzstan, full of hope for our climbing adventure, and was waiting for us, perversely intact, at the hotel in Bishkek after our escape. We'd left San Francisco with twenty expedition duffels, and all I had left was this backpack filled with trinkets from a country to which I'd never return. Maybe that was why we'd bought them, with the money Tommy had wadded up in his sock just before we were marched away from our camp at gunpoint. Maybe it was some attempt to fabricate a decent memory of the place.

My hands trembled the whole twelve hours to San Francisco. I knew I needed sleep, but if the plane did crash, wasn't I supposed to be awake for that? I had no idea how to act, what to do or say or who to be when we saw our parents. I'd left as a twenty-year-old girl full of herself, ready for the world, sure I was doing something extraordinary. I was living out the dream I'd stared at in the posters I hung on my bedroom wall: climbing to incredible heights in far-off places. My mother had hardly traveled, certainly not by my age. I'd felt so awfully superior as I'd walked down the jetway when we left. I didn't even turn back to wave.

My parents had given me everything—pride, freedom, confidence. They trusted me. They trusted my decisions. They trusted the world.

Now I was returning home a broken mess. I'd spoken to them a few times from the embassy in Bishkek, the words mainly drowned in my tears. I wanted to be small again, so small I could crawl through the phone into their arms, where they'd hold me and shush me and stroke my head. I wanted my mother to say, *Mama's here, Mama's here,* just like she always did when I was a girl. I wanted to shrink back into that little-girl body and lay my head in her lap and cry.

Now—how to do this? How was I supposed to carry myself getting off the jetway? Was the idea to act strong, like I was fine? I was weirdly good at that. Or should I literally run into their arms, like I had been dreaming of doing for the past eight days? I'd never spoken easily with my parents about feelings. They were so kind, so present, and gently but firmly on my team. But inside, I always felt nervous, like there was a line I was afraid to cross, like I needed to be tougher, solid, unbreakable. And even if I could lay my head in my mother's lap and have her say, *Mama's here,* would that still work to soothe me? I was not the same person I had been when I left. My thoughts flapped like the loose end of a film in an old-fashioned movie projector, the front reel spinning empty.

I looked over at Tommy. Maybe he'd know what to do. His head was slumped at a 45-degree angle to his chest, his mouth dropped open, snoring. He was sick. His brain was more lucid and less spastic than mine, but his body was breaking down. He had a fever. I envied Tommy's oblivion. I felt so alone.

We landed. My palms were sweating, but Tommy's hands felt strong. That felt like a plan: I'd hold his strong hand and we'd present a united front, though I hadn't told him about my looping, flapping mind. I was trying to stay composed—for him, for me, maybe for my parents too. We collected our bag of souvenirs from under the airplane seats. The souvenirs promised our trip was normal. *We* were normal. I grabbed a free chocolate bar and a package of cookies from the plane's galley as we exited. I never did anything like that, but now instead of saying, *Don't eat that, Rodden,* I thought . . . *Just in case we don't have any other food.*

I didn't race off the plane like I had seen people do in movies, straight into their loved ones' arms. Instead I walked so slowly that other passengers started passing us. I was desperate to return home, to the narrow twin bed in my parents' house, on our quiet block filled with minivans and white Honda sedans, to replant myself in the flat farmland around Davis, California, to recommit to the safe wide sidewalks. I just didn't know how. I wondered if people could tell we'd changed: if we walked differently or stood slightly less straight, if we'd absorbed so much fear and terror that we now emitted it.

Our two sets of parents stood behind a blue roped barrier outside customs. My mom wore blue jeans and a canary-yellow T-shirt, its own simple sun, and she didn't cry. Tommy's father, Mike, waved frantically, as if we couldn't see him. My dad just smiled his warm, calm smile. We hugged. They acted normal and asked, "How was the flight? Did they serve you good food? Do you have more bags?" We told our parents about our upgrade to business class.

On the drive to Davis we stopped at Dos Coyotes, my favorite restaurant. I got the chicken Caesar salad with dressing on the side and extra "crouton chips," a Dos Coyotes specialty: fried tortilla chips, layered onto the salad in place of the usual cubed bread. I'd thought about this meal for hours straight, for days on end, while I was hiding under boulders, spooning with our photographer, John, shivering and clenching my teeth and wondering if I was going to die. The chips were crispy and double deep-fried.

◆　◆　◆

"So!" Mike said. We'd only been home for a few hours. I'd already learned that literally everything Mike said had an exclamation point at the end. *Hello! Good morning! So!* It was jarring and unsettling, especially because Mike was a big guy, a holdover from his bodybuilder days. He looked so impatient, like he'd come for a presentation that hadn't started on time. He continued, "When is a good time for you guys to tell us about the event?"

Tommy and I sat on the couch, beside the brick fireplace where I'd left cookies for Santa long after I knew Santa didn't exist. Our parents were coupled on the rest of the living-room furniture, exuding nervousness and earnest care. One of my grandmother's paintings, a watercolor of an old waterwheel, hung above the stereo and bookshelves. I tried to hang on to its familiarity, tried to ground myself in this safe place. I couldn't make eye contact with anyone, couldn't look anywhere on my parents' faces. I didn't want to see their hurt and worry. I knew if I did, I'd feel like I needed to console them, and I didn't have it in me. So I stared at the fireplace, at the painting, at the hardwood floor, a smile plastered to my face like a cheap disguise, mind spinning. What happened to the Berber rug our dog Steffi used to lie on? Didn't there used to be a Berber rug here?

The changes in our home—were they even changes?—added to my distorted sense of the time we'd been gone: a little under a month, but it seemed so much longer. My mind darted around the room, trying to avoid the flashbacks that kept rising: the man we'd been kidnapped with, his body limp after they shot him; John's body huddled against mine; the constant, sucking hunger; the grotesque smell of Abdul's beard. What did they want to know? What did everyone want to know?

"We were high on the wall trying to do this new free route," Tommy started out.

Mike interrupted to ask a question about the quality of the rock face. *Really?*

Tommy obliged. The cliff was coarse granite like in the Rocky Mountains, not Yosemite granite. It was pretty low-angle, not overly impressive. The hardest part was about to come, a roof right above where we'd set up our portaledges—the hanging tents where we'd sleep for the night. The next pitch was a 5.13 layback, he supposed. We were still asleep in those portaledges when we heard gunshots that, at first, we thought were rockfall.

11

Tommy spoke so calmly, with such competence and conviction. He started from the beginning and stuck to the facts: the abduction, the forced marches, the firefight. The days of hunger. The final, terrible hours after we got away. He never mentioned being scared. We hadn't really talked alone since our escape. We hadn't discussed how each of us was doing, but he sounded okay. That seemed so nice: to be okay.

I wanted my parents to think I wasn't crazy, even though I felt crazy, so I added concrete, preposterous details that Tommy missed: what I wore, the color of Turat's sleeping bag, the taste of the yogurt balls we'd eaten near the end. I felt like this was a test—a test to fool people into thinking I was still sane. I kept my eyes on the floor as much as possible. Nothing I contributed mattered, nothing I said alluded to the fear that was still with me. I was drowning.

I was twenty years old. I was a professional climber, a professional risk and emotion manager. I clenched my teeth. I pinched my arm like I did when I was getting blood drawn, or right before a big competition—anytime I needed to maintain discipline. I needed all my discipline not to cry.

"Wow, you kids sure went through a lot!" Mike said when Tommy finished. "We are so glad that you're so tough and back home!"

Tommy's mom's face was a watery mess. I still couldn't look at my own parents, so I looked at Terry and Mike. I didn't have so much invested in them. Were my own parents sad, or angry? Any response they might conceivably have, even affection and love, seemed impossible to deal with. In that moment, I wished I'd had even one hard conversation with them before. I wished we'd had a sex talk, or a drug talk. I wished I'd been in trouble, real trouble, at least once in my life.

I felt Mike give me a jolting hug. Tommy hugged my parents. *I guess we're done. Did we pass?*

CHAPTER TWO

Davis, California, August 2000

Our parents took care of us in all the ways they knew how. My dad bought four new tires for Tommy's van, which he'd parked in front of their house before our trip. Our moms went to the mall and bought us new underwear and socks. While we were away, my parents had hauled a double bed frame down from the attic to replace my old twin. My mom had bought a new mattress to go with it and spread a quilt that my great-grandmother made over the top. I felt a little embarrassed about that bed, or about the line of thought, kind as it was, that must have gone into it. I guessed she'd figured I wasn't a teenager anymore and I had my first real boyfriend, so it was time to upgrade. She'd had no way of knowing that Tommy and I would be settled in there, together, so soon, with Tommy's parents camped out in my brother's old room across the hall.

Tommy was still sick. The fever, chills, and body aches had set in when we reached the American embassy in Bishkek, and they still had ahold of him by the time we got home. We saw so many doctors. His blood tests showed an elevated white-blood-cell count, probably from drinking muddy black water. They said he'd be okay, though. Were they sure? It was impossible for me to believe we were safe, even though we were so many plane rides away from danger.

Tommy was the one with the persistent fever, but I saw half a dozen physicians too, hoping someone could tell me what was wrong with me—I knew that something had to be wrong with me—but each time I got a clean bill of health. I did have jet lag, though, so every morning at 4:00 a.m. I power walked in the dark with my mom to the twenty-four-hour supermarket. We used to do this in middle school: I'd wake up early, snuggle in her lap while she drank her coffee, and then tag along on her early-morning exercise walk. Now we skipped the snuggle and just walked. I cruised the supermarket aisles, fixated on food. Before Kyrgyzstan, my eating was a point of constant fixation: I restricted. I obsessed. I binged. Now I saw coming back after real deprivation as a second chance, a possible reset. I was skin and bones from the days in captivity when we'd gone without food. This time I would eat to be healthy, I told myself. Not just to control a number on a scale. *Don't mess this up, Beth. Just be normal.*

Once the sun rose, Tommy walked with his parents too. I'd stay in my room, lying on the strange new bed that meant I was an adult now. I didn't feel older, exactly. More like I had left my old self behind, somewhere in the rocky valley in southwestern Kyrgyzstan, and what I'd brought back was empty.

Each day, I grilled Tommy when he came home.

"What did you talk about?" I asked.

"I told them what happened," he said.

That was an obvious summary, which annoyed me, so I asked him what he'd really said.

"You know—I just told them."

It wasn't that Tommy couldn't talk about hard feelings or couldn't go deep into his emotions. Before Kyrgyzstan, we had just started dating, and he was always open and honest with me. He'd tell me that he was head over heels about me, about us, and there were ways in which I found I could be vulnerable in return: I could show him my dark side when we climbed, could scream and cry without shame. But since Kyrgyzstan, he seemed to have a buoyancy I lacked—an ability to just see the good in things and move forward, without being towed under by all the memories. All the fear.

Climbing culture had taught us both that doing hard things would only make us stronger, better. We trained hard, pushing our muscles to exhaustion, so we could pull ourselves higher. We pulled on holds until our hands bled, to grow the calluses we needed to succeed. We ignored fear and pain in order to send. And we were good at it. We were professionals. But this hard thing didn't make me feel stronger, and I had no language to tell Tommy or anyone else how very fragile I felt. I couldn't show him this darkness, could not tell him that I was still braced, every second, for the next threat. I could not imagine being able to "just tell" anybody anything. I couldn't think, let alone talk, in a coherent way about "what happened." I was trying to build a wall around Kyrgyzstan in my mind, seal the memories in, and walk away.

Did our parents and friends really want to know what happened? Did they really want to know that I heard, on repeat, the sound of our captor's spine cracking on a ledge?

I tried to hang on to Tommy's buoyancy, to let his confidence that we were safe now keep me from going under. My fear, my hypervigilance, felt shameful: Shouldn't I be tougher? In those first days back at home, if I tried to tell anyone that I didn't feel safe, I would be gently corrected: *You're safe now, Beth. You're okay.* So I stopped trying to explain and tried to shove the fear down inside me instead.

One morning, my dad opened the door to my bedroom and asked how I was doing.

I decided to try to say something true, but I didn't know where to start. "Mortars are really loud," I said. I wanted to add: *And they are scary. I'm so scared. How do I go back to normal? What is normal? What's the point of living?* But I just let that statement hang in the air.

My father had been in the army. He smiled, sadly. "Yes, they are, honey."

◆ ◆ ◆

After a few days, Mike and Terry returned to Estes Park, Colorado. A few days after that, my mom appeared in the doorway of my bedroom while she was getting ready for work. "You know, sweetie, if you want to go to a therapist, your dad and I could help you find one. I've been to a couple sessions now and it's really helped."

I stared at her. Why did she need to go to therapy? She was always here, in her scrubbed suburban bubble in Davis, where the bike lanes are wider than the car lanes and nothing bad ever happens. Suddenly I was angry. Who did she think she was?

"Why did you have to go to therapy?" I said. My tone was not nice. "You didn't go through anything."

My mom stood there, trying to keep it all together—dark-blond hair, like mine; blue-green eyes, like mine—hurt by my rudeness and my vortex of pain. Then her face softened. "Well," she said very tenderly, "when your child almost dies halfway across the world and you cannot be there or do anything for her, it's very, very hard."

I didn't get it. I said, "I'll let you know, but I don't think I want to right now." I closed the door.

◆ ◆ ◆

I can't remember who first told us that the authorities in Kyrgyzstan thought they'd found one of our captors, unexpectedly alive. We didn't really believe it. We'd heard the crunch of bone on rock—I was still hearing it, over and over, most days.

A day or two after we got that news, my dad walked toward me, down the hallway to the kitchen. "Is this Su, the guy that you pushed?" He held out a pixelated image, a photo he'd just printed out of a man who resembled Su. The man's face was pudgier, and his hair looked darker. But there was that mole on the side of his mouth, that exact same mole I'd stared at for six days.

My father was the steadiest force in my life, my fortress and my rock. But the photo he held made fear spew from my stomach. I didn't care why he had it, where it had come from. I felt like my teeth were on fire.

"Why would you show this to me?!" I screamed. "Why? Who are you?!" I felt so betrayed and confused. I ran to my parents' room, the farthest possible point in the house from where my father stood, slammed the door, and sat down on the floor, bawling.

Now, in my parents' house, in Davis, there was a picture of Su. He was alive. He'd found us. He'd come to take revenge. My father had invited him in. Had he also offered Su lunch?

"Sweetie," my father said through the door to his own room. "Sweetie, I'm so sorry I upset you." He repeated this over and over. My mother wasn't home. Where was Tommy? Had the two of them gone out shopping? Now that his own parents were back in Colorado, she was trying to take extra care of him.

My body felt like a meteorite, a hundred million pounds. I felt myself drag it to the door. My father was still standing there. I looked in his eyes—he always had such soft, kind brown eyes, framed by his black-rimmed glasses. He smiled awkwardly, not moving toward me but using those brown eyes that had made me feel safe for so much of my life to reach out from behind his glasses and give me a hug.

We were in uncharted territory. My father had never misstepped with me. All through my adolescence and high school, he always knew the right thing to say. He got out in front of my anxieties, catering to my superstitions—and there were many. He knew we had to fly Delta on our way to climbing competitions. He understood that we had to rent a Mercury Mystique from Hertz (it had to be from Hertz). That I needed one plain, one blueberry, and one cinnamon-raisin bagel from Safeway on the morning of a comp. But with this picture he'd made a mistake. He too was not equipped to handle this. Was I supposed to tell him it was okay? I did not feel okay.

"Maybe that's him," I finally said, shifting my eyes to the floor.

My father touched my shoulder. "I'm sorry," he said. His hand on my shoulder felt warm and huge. "I had no idea that would be so upsetting."

We stood there. I wanted normal. He wanted normal. Nothing was normal.

Finally we heard Tommy walk down the hallway. He saw the crappy printout in my father's hand, and he saw my face. Tommy's were the only eyes I felt safe looking into. He was the only person who understood what I could not explain.

"Oh, that's Su," Tommy said, so casually. "That's the picture they sent you? To make sure it was the right guy?"

My father seemed jolted by Tommy's ease. I was too.

CHAPTER THREE

Yosemite Valley, California, June 2000

By expedition standards, our trip to Kyrgyzstan had come together fast: it was weeks in the making, rather than being planned over many months. A last-minute adventure with an unlikely crew—me, Tommy, John, and Jason.

I had known John since my days at Mission Cliffs, the San Francisco climbing gym that I used to commute to, to train and compete. Back then I was fifteen and scrawny and still being chaperoned and chauffeured by my parents. John worked the desk and seemed so grown-up, living in San Francisco and having a real job. "Beth!" He'd greet me with his huge grin and warm laugh. He had dark-brown hair, always messy, like he didn't care about a comb or a brush or a barber—a quintessential climber. Later, over the years, I'd see him in the parking lot by Camp 4, in Yosemite. He'd walk from car to car, striking up a conversation with anyone about anything.

On my first serious climbing trip to Yosemite Valley, my backpack was stolen, and with it my climbing shoes and all my gear. The next day, John came up, excited and upbeat. "You should do the East Butt of Middle with us!" he'd exclaimed. "I've seen you do laps on 5.13s for hours, you could absolutely do it in your flip-flops!" He chuckled in a way that was complimentary and inviting. I laughed and declined and instead ate a pint of Ben & Jerry's by the river, sulking over my lost gear.

But John always felt like a friendly, protective older brother, the kind you'd see on TV. (That had never been the dynamic between my real older brother and me.) John felt like the closest thing we would have to a chaperone in Kyrgyzstan, like somehow he'd always know what to do.

My relationship with Jason was much newer and more complicated than my easy friendship with John. I'd met him during my first season in the Valley, the season I'd spent fawning over Leo, a well-known and accomplished British climber. I'd heard of this guy "Singer" who sewed his own clothes and lived out of his white windowless van. In our first encounter, he'd hopped out of the side door with black flip-flops, old North Face shorts, and light brown hair. "You must be Beth!" His smile was wide. I'd looked at my feet and then remembered what a mentor had told me at my first industry trade show: "Always look people in the eye; you could be working for them next week. Climbing is so incestuous; never make an enemy." So I looked up. Jason had a boyish face that hadn't been shaved in a few days. He had a youthful energy that was palpable. "I've heard so much about you! Let's rack up and climb!"

We'd climbed the Rostrum, a Yosemite classic. I was green and new and terrified. Jason had just soloed it the week before, a very rare feat, and he was happy to lead and guide me up it. The whole way, I followed and listened to his banter about which person was a fake, who was sleeping with who, what I should and shouldn't do to earn respect here in "the Ditch." Jason was the opinionated guy who was the ultimate Yosemite Valley climber. The one who could talk shit but then back it up, holding his own with the chest-thumping guys who spent their time stealing coffee and occasionally picking leftovers off tourists' abandoned plates in the park cafeteria. But he was also so inviting: taking me under his wing, showing me the ropes, asking me to climb when he certainly didn't have to. We'd road-trip together to North Face events, where we mingled with important buyers and dealers, taking them out on guided climbs to entice them into ordering more gear. And he was fun: hilarious and smart and witty.

Things had gotten awkward between Jason and me when Tommy entered the scene the next spring. I guess I was blind to it, but everyone said that Jason had a crush on me, and when I started dating Tommy it all went south. Not in an overt way, but in a very awkward *We're all still friends so let's go on an intimate six-week expedition with each other on the other side of the world* kind of way.

Tommy and his friend Topher had been planning a trip to Kyrgyzstan that summer, but Topher's wife got sick that spring, and it fell through. At the same time, one of The North Face's expeditions collapsed too, and Jason let me know that if we wanted to pitch something to our mutual sponsor, we had an open lane.

There are only so many places in the world where you can climb big walls on even bigger mountains. There's Patagonia, but their summer is our winter, so that was out. There's the Karakoram, in Kashmir, with all its geopolitical complications. There are some big objectives in the Alps, but those were already well known. Baffin Island, Greenland, Norway—those more northerly areas were already being covered by other teams. And there's Kyrgyzstan. The small, mountainous country tucked between China and the other "Stans" was just becoming a serious climber's destination. I knew Tommy had been excited about going there, and I knew Lynn Hill, my hero, had been there a few years earlier too.

Lynn's team had climbed in the Ak-Su Valley, and if we were going to get funding, we had to try something new. So we pitched a trip to the neighboring Kara-Su: a narrower valley, less known and traveled than the Ak-Su. It was lined with towering, dark granite walls, with a skyline of snowcaps behind them. It was perhaps not as starkly impressive as the Ak-Su, but I was drawn to its quiet, and to the fact that we were almost guaranteed to be the only team there. There were enough unclimbed walls in the Kyrgyzstan valley to give us endless possibilities.

The North Face signed off on sending me, Jason, and John as our photographer. Then, since the trip had been Tommy's idea in the first place, we asked if we could add him too. He was a Marmot athlete at the time, and ordinarily he wouldn't have been allowed on a different company's trip. But Jason and I pleaded, and John promised to take photos that wouldn't highlight Marmot's logo. The company agreed.

It's strange to look back now on those forks in the road—how things might have been different, if, well, if things had been different. If Tommy's original plan had panned out, or if he hadn't been allowed to join our team. If that one bag, one out of our twenty duffels, hadn't gotten lost on our way there. If John and Jason hadn't hiked down the valley to the nearest settlements, searching for that bag, and stumbled across a remote military outpost as they went. If we'd arrived one day sooner, or one day later. There were so many variables, so many tiny choices that aligned—or misaligned—to put us in the wrong place at the worst possible time.

CHAPTER FOUR

Davis, California, August 2000

The story broke before we had even made it home. After the four of us had each called our parents from the US embassy, Jason's mom sent an email about the kidnapping to friends and family, who forwarded it on to more people, who forwarded it on even further, and before long the media got involved. When the *Salt Lake Tribune* asked Jason's mom about the kidnapping, she told them as much of the story as she knew. It was like dropping a match onto a parched forest floor on a hot August day. Soon, all of our families were besieged by reporters. They begged for interviews, sending fruit baskets and flowers. On the day the newspaper in Davis ran my photo on the front page, I drove to the strip mall with my mom to pick up another chicken Caesar from Dos Coyotes. That had become our routine. While looking for parking, we saw two of my best friends from middle school, Kyle and Maria. We'd barely spoken since high school. They stared, open-mouthed, then smiled and waved. I didn't want to talk to them.

After that: NPR, all the magazines, the morning TV shows, the nightly news. Trucks with big antennae and satellites rolled into our perfectly suburban neighborhood—a neighborhood everybody here chose because it was boring, comfortable—dwarfing all the minivans and sensible sedans. Producers knocked on the front door of our house, confident and purposeful, like they had a right to enter our space. Like our story was at least partially theirs. Some brought gifts. One journalist brought balloons. What moron thought I wanted a balloon? When I closed my eyes, I saw myself shivering under a rock.

The most perverse part of all this media attention was that Tommy and I were *supposed* to be getting famous—but for our climbing achievements, not for being taken captive. Now, among the million other bad aftereffects, I'd have this asterisk next to my name, no matter how I proved myself: Beth, kind of a good climber, the one who was dumb and got kidnapped . . .

And none of that would matter anyway, a frantic voice in my mind whispered, because all these reporters shoving us into the spotlight could only lead to one thing. The rebels would find us. If Su was alive, he must have told them what we'd done—what Tommy had done, what we'd asked him to do. Their revenge would be awful.

Meanwhile, climbers kept congratulating us. *Dude, what an epic! So sick you survived! Seriously the coolest story I've heard!*

Climbing culture celebrated skirting death, or even dying, for a summit or an unclimbed peak. Surviving the unthinkable was almost more glorified than any athletic achievement. It felt like the whole climbing community kept repeating this back to me. *The best story of cheating death we've ever heard! Better than any mountaineer or alpinist, and you guys are just sport climbers!* Some climbers were even jealous, we heard secondhand. It all felt heartless and weird. We didn't send a route. We didn't conquer a mountain. We didn't do anything. We were kidnapped. We were the victims, not the victors. We triumphed over nothing.

"It's because you had a better epic," a friend tried to explain. "You were closer to death than all those hardcore, lifelong alpinists who made careers off of having the best, most harrowing tale."

I did not understand. Did people really think what had happened to us was the same as surviving some epic adventure? That we had fought gravity and nature, and won? Did they believe it was worth dying for a summit or a send? Did they know what death looked like—what it sounded like? I couldn't forget.

I felt ashamed and weak, not heroic, competent, and brave.

Before our trip, I lived that belief system, spoke that climber patois: the local dialect at every gym and crag. Coded into its syntax was a declaration that what we were doing, how we were living our lives, was better than how everybody else was living theirs. We existed more fully. We saw more clearly. We breathed better air and smelled better smells. All those poor stupid people sitting in cubicles with air-conditioning and fluorescent lights—they couldn't possibly understand. And even if they did understand, they couldn't hack it. They weren't tough enough to live out of their cars and sleep hanging off walls hundreds of feet in the air. They were too cowed by authority, even the modest authority that park rangers carried, to live without permits in the most beautiful places on earth. They clung to convention. We had freedom. We took risks. Risks were how you won. We told our own stories, and they were the best stories.

When I found the sport in my early teens, I remade my life and my ambitions around it, dedicating myself to gym climbing and competitions. The rewards had been almost immediate: in my first ever recreational competition, as a green fourteen-year-old, I beat almost every adult who'd signed up. A year after that, I went to France and competed in the junior worlds. I won the junior nationals four years in a row, and often placed higher than all the older athletes too. Comp after comp, I almost always landed on the podium—instead of crumbling, I climbed my best when the pressure was on.

By the time I was eighteen, I was sponsored: a professional climber, even if the money didn't resemble what most pro athletes earned. I moved away from the gym scene, started sending hard routes outdoors. Not long after, my hero, Lynn Hill, invited me on my first international expedition as part of an all-female team headed to Madagascar. I dropped out of college partway through my first year to focus on the career I knew I could seize if I worked hard enough, trained hard enough, and wanted it badly enough. My job was to travel, and climb, and literally live out my wildest dreams. It had seemed like everything. Now it all felt so pointless, so naive.

Even after Kyrgyzstan, Tommy still seemed to find comfort, maybe a kind of refuge, in that narrative. When we talked, he described it as "post-traumatic strength," the idea that adversity could propel us forward, stronger and better for it. He went back to the climbing gym almost as soon as we got home, and he seemed to leap right back into our old routine of training, dreaming, and planning for the next big climb. But I could not remember why I had ever thought it was heroic to spend a night on the side of a mountain in a storm. I regretted a lot of the times I'd made my family worry, all the nights I'd spent away from them in Yosemite Valley. I should have been with my parents and Granny at home.

I got only one email from a climber that brought me comfort. It was from Leo, the British climber I'd followed around Yosemite during my first trip to the Valley. *We're all thinking of you on this side of the pond,* he wrote from his home in the UK. He seemed to understand I'd be grieving, not celebrating. And just seeing his name in my inbox brought back all my girlish feelings, how much I'd hoped he liked me.

I was so happy to feel something other than fear, even for a minute. I deleted the message as soon as I heard Tommy helping my mother set the dinner table.

◆ ◆ ◆

I hadn't pooped in fifteen days. I had hardly eaten anything for the first six of those, but still, my abdomen was so distended that I looked pregnant. I tried Smooth Move tea, fiber drinks, mass consumption of legumes (black beans, refried beans, pinto beans), suppositories. Nothing worked. During that time, we decided to hold a press conference to try to appease the rabid journalists who would not quit camping on my parents' lawn, and I wore an adult diaper for it, just in case. I had so much food stopped up in me, and so many different laxatives on top of that, I was afraid I would burst in the middle of a question from NBC.

But that didn't happen. I was vaguely disappointed. I was so uncomfortable and so miserable. I could barely fit into my shorts.

The next morning, my mom took me to the emergency room. As we waited, I looked at the other people sitting there. Mostly old folks, a few middle-aged men and women limping or coughing. Were they ashamed of failing too? After a few minutes, my mom and I were called back into a small, sterile white room. She worked quietly on her needlepoint until a tall man came in.

"Elizabeth?" The doctor sat down on his stool.

I flushed with embarrassment before the doctor had said more than my name. "Says you are extremely constipated. Is that why you are in today?"

I nodded and looked down at my blue-and-black Sportiva approach shoes.

"Do you know why you are so plugged up?"

Oh, boy. Here we go. "Um, yeah, I was held captive for six days in Kyrgyzstan and only ate half of an energy bar per day and then have been eating a lot ever since and nothing has come out yet."

I spoke quickly, zero emotion. The doctor stared at me. Then he stared at my mom. I could tell he wanted to ask me questions. I just wanted him to give me a pill and get on with his day.

"Wow—well, um, are you okay?" he said, sensing my recalcitrance. "I mean, other than constipated?"

I thought about it. I couldn't answer. I was not okay. I was fat and bloated, I had nightmares, and even when I was awake I felt like I was in danger all of the time. But only the physical problems were things I thought he could fix.

"Yeah, I'm fine, thanks," I said. "My stomach just really hurts."

So we talked about constipation. I told him all the names of the laxatives that I had taken. He scratched out some words on the backside of a prescription pad.

"I've never had this thing fail," he said. "I call it dynamite in a bottle, and it's just an over-the-counter drink." He handed me his scribbled note, which I passed to my mom. I just wanted to be a kid. We stopped at the drugstore on the way home.

By the afternoon, I'd crapped out my entire digestive system. Each time I went to the bathroom I stared at each deposit. How many bars were in that poop? Had I gotten to the yogurt balls yet? The barley and warm buttered bread? I made a dozen trips to the bathroom that day, each time filling up the toilet, each time reliving the past two weeks, hoping that by ridding my body of any physical remnants, my mind would empty as well. By the end of the day my stomach was flat and my hip bones jutted out. I made a note to myself to remember the name of the "dynamite," in case I ever wanted to empty myself out like that again.

I liked this body. It was the biggest comfort I'd had in weeks.

CHAPTER FIVE

Sierra Nevada, California, September 2000

It was weird to head back to the cabin at Silver Lake. Its familiar musty smell greeted us when we walked into the dark, dusty old building. The same old refrigerator with the handle that pulled out when you opened it was tucked into the corner of the kitchen. And the same deck with a thousand splinters waiting to happen looked out onto the still surface of the lake. For a decade, our family had rented this cabin in the Sierras for two weeks every summer.

Since coming home from Kyrgyzstan, this was the first time I'd left Davis that wasn't for some television show or media frenzy. It was supposed to be relaxing, a "vacation," a time for me and Tommy and my family to get back to normal. I wondered if I would ever feel relaxed again. My jaw ached; it seemed as though I'd been clenching it ever since the first mortar flew.

Tommy and I took the bedroom with the two twin beds and dark-green quilts. My brother, who'd left his fraternity house to join us for the trip, slept in the living room on the couch. I watched him unpack on the floor. I felt bad for him. Did he feel like he was now the neglected younger child? I unpacked into the same old cedar chest I always did. It felt safe, almost.

I put a neatly folded pale-yellow running tank top into the top drawer. The color reminded me of a faded yellow-and-green A's shirt I wore when I was a kid. For a moment I unclenched my jaw and almost smiled.

My family always had traditions—not heavy rituals, but fun ones that became ingrained. Hiking during our cabin stays was a fixture, but I hated hiking when I was a kid. I would lie down in the middle of the dusty trail complaining that I couldn't go any farther, that my legs were incapable of any more exertion. My parents watched me, smiled, and kept hiking. Eventually I picked myself up and kept going too, nursing my rage. Back then, the most special day during our two weeks at the cabin was always the day my dad and brother went on a big hike and my mom and I went out to breakfast at the nearby lodge and sat by the lake and swam all day. I'd get waffles with whipped cream and hot chocolate and fruit and orange juice and play in the lake and look for fish and jump off rocks, free for once from the family death march.

My attitude had changed sometime in high school, when I realized that all the great climbers loved hard exercise. A big hike was often just the prelude to a great climb, so I had decided to embrace it. Soon, I'd learned to genuinely enjoy a death march (at least, I had before Kyrgyzstan). I loved the feeling of trying hard, of full exertion, of lactic acid filling my legs and the ability to keep going anyway. It made me feel I had something most people didn't, like I had grown up from that tantrum-throwing little kid, like I had it all figured out.

I hadn't done even mild exercise in the few weeks since Kyrgyzstan, nothing more strenuous than those early-morning walks with my mom. The last time my heart had pounded or my lungs burned was when we'd run to the military outpost, after we'd gotten free, after Su's body had sailed off the cliff into the night.

I'd tried to go to the climbing gym once, after Mike's *Get back on the horse* pep talk, but it felt so hollow and pointless. Every time I grabbed a climbing hold, I wondered why I was bothering. Tommy seemed to be able to climb his way back to himself, but I think I knew that if I kept grabbing the holds, if I felt that burning in my lungs, the pounding in my chest, it would remind me of something I didn't want to remember. So I stopped.

"Dave and I are going to do a twelve-miler tomorrow. Would you and Tommy like to join?" my dad asked as we were sitting on the deck looking out at the lake.

I stared at the big pine trees on the shore. I never would have even given this a thought when I was a kid—why would I give up waffles and whipped cream for twelve miles of boring pain? And then a few years later, my answer would have been just as obvious, as instant: bring it on. But now I didn't know who I was, didn't like who I was. Here was my chance to prove I was still an athlete, still the mountain person I had become, could still thrive on waking up early and working hard. I didn't need the safety of my parents' house and food on demand and locks on doors and a big fluffy bed.

"Yes," I said curtly. I didn't even ask Tommy if he wanted to join us. I just told him we were leaving at 5:30 a.m.

We pulled up in Tommy's van behind my parents' Honda Civic. As I opened the door the air had a bite to it, sharp cold with the sweet smell of the Sierras. The pine trees seemed to be amplified before dawn. Even the granite rocks seemed to have a fragrance that was unique. I knew it and I loved it. But I stopped with the door partway open, something inside of me buzzing, like an internal alarm.

Each mountain range I've been to, each climbing area, has its own unique smell, its own look and taste and feel. The Sierras are sweet and weighty, while the high Colorado Rockies are earthier, starker, with more bite. The forest of Fontainebleau, in France, feels so alive: the air still, and everything else in motion. And in the American South, the climbing areas feel damp, and a little more urban: the weight of nearby cities drowns out some of the aromatics. But still, all of them have some crossover. It's like the way you always know when you're near the ocean, with its hint of salt in the air, no matter which coast in the world you're on. That's what the smell of mountains is for me. There are things that are universal.

I shut the door to the van and sat still, staring at my pointy knees underneath my black softshell pants. I still hadn't gained back all my weight yet. I liked feeling a little skinny. My hands were trembling, and I looked out the window. In the predawn twilight, my dad, my brother, and Tommy were packing stuff into their backpacks. Tommy's was a yellow Marmot bag, sent by the company to replace an identical one that we had carried with us in Kyrgyzstan. Who thought it was a good idea to replicate that? I tried not to think about the last time I had smelled the mountains.

The car door jolted open.

"Honey, are you coming?" Tommy said. His nose was running a little from the cold air. His symptoms had cleared up a few days after we got home, but I still wondered if he was incubating some terrible disease from Kyrgyzstan.

"Huh? Yeah, sure, sorry—yeah, I just needed to get my ChapStick," I said.

We started up the trail. I tried to ignore the sirens going off in my head. Yes, I was in the mountains. Yes, it was cold—the first cold I'd experienced since Kyrgyzstan, and the first wild twilight I'd seen since then too, undiluted by the streetlights of Davis. Yes, it smelled wonderful and reminded me of many places, including Kyrgyzstan. But this was clearly not Kyrgyzstan; this was very clearly the Sierras. I could see my dad in front of me. I could see Tommy's van behind us. What the hell was wrong with me?

We walked for a few miles, and I hardly said a word. It was still early morning when something inside me switched. It was like my body could only take so many reminders or memories of Kyrgyzstan—so many triggers—before I overflowed. It was the cold, the alpenglow, the smell, the sound of crunching gravel under my feet, the wind, the sun; all of a sudden I couldn't go any farther. I stopped. Suddenly I remembered how vulnerable I had felt when the men had taken us, split us up. How keenly I'd regretted, then, that I had never slept with Tommy.

That I hadn't chosen, when I could have made a choice. I looked ahead at Tommy and realized I still had never made my choice.

I made some excuse about my stomach not feeling well, and Tommy and I turned around. It still hadn't been that long since my constipation cure, so the excuse seemed plausible. I wondered if my dad bought it, or if he saw how messed up my brain was even though I thought I was putting on a very good act.

Sex wasn't something Tommy and I had talked about a lot, before or after Kyrgyzstan. Tommy never pressured me, seemed content to let me set the pace. Back at the cabin, I told him I was ready. We drove out of the mountains, two and a half hours home to the empty house in Davis, to that double bed my mom had bought for us, and had sex for the first time. It wasn't earth-shaking or magical, but it wasn't awkward or scary either, like I'd worried it might be. Instead, I was weirdly detached from the experience, my body participating while my mind supervised from a distance, thinking: *So this is it?*

I felt virtuous, empowered, in making the decision, but disappointed in the aftermath. I didn't understand why my friends had whisper-talked so excitedly about it. Wasn't it supposed to feel good? I chalked it up to something wrong with me—one more area where I needed to try harder.

CHAPTER SIX

New York City, September 2000

Inundated with media requests, the four of us decided to pick one major appearance. We settled on the *Today Show*. I was actually excited about it. Katie Couric and Matt Lauer! Katie was so smiley and smart and at ease with everyone. I revered her. I had no idea how she did it, but I wanted her to interview us and give me some of what she had. Maybe I could be at ease if I was around her.

Before we flew to New York, my mom's old boss, Meryl, who worked in public communications for the University of California at Davis, came with a list of questions to prep us on what *Today* was likely to ask. That in itself felt disorienting. How could anybody know what to ask us when I didn't even really know what happened? It only came back to me out of order: the running, the push, the shots. Since we'd been home, I thought Tommy was going to die every time he sneezed.

"Why did you think it was safe to go there?" Meryl asked when she came to prep us. This was one of her rehearsal questions. I felt resentful, prickly with anger.

"There wasn't anything wrong with going there," I snapped. Meryl smiled—absorbing my anger, apparently used to this. My mom, who was also helping us prepare, sat behind her. I could tell she wanted to step in and give me a hug. But she wasn't going to be able to hug me when I was really on TV.

"I know that, Beth," Meryl said. "I know you didn't do anything wrong. But they are going to ask this one. We just need to come up with something to say, just what feels right to you."

"Well, it had the same level of warning as Northern Ireland, or that Australia had for the Olympics. Climbers go way worse places all the time," I said. I wanted to prove to her that climbers were better than normal people. We traveled to these places. People put up routes in Pakistan and India all the time, and no one had ever been kidnapped there. Why didn't *Today* go interview those people?

"Let's use that, then," Meryl said. "We'll use what the State Department had as a warning level. You did your research, but sometimes things go wrong—that's out of your control."

NBC flew the four of us out, put us up in a fancy hotel, then sent a black car early the next morning to take us to Rockefeller Center. In the greenroom, I could see that Ann Curry was hosting that day, and my heart sank. No Katie after all. Then I learned that Matt Lauer would be interviewing us. I was wearing a weird red J.Crew sweater and a collared shirt, both of which had been lurking in my closet since high school. I hated my clothes. Plus I wore my hair down, and I hated my hair down. I didn't know who I was with my hair down, but I'd done it that way because someone told me it made me look older.

I had practiced my answers so many times—in the shower, in bed, in my head during the car ride to the studio. I did not want to have to answer questions about why we'd gone there, but of course, seconds into the interview, Matt Lauer asked me.

"And, Beth . . . how aware were you of the situation there, and how afraid were you for your safety?"

I could feel sweat in my armpits. I didn't want to look like an idiot on national TV.

I tried to remember the words I had practiced. I opened my mouth, said something like: "We saw the consular advisory on the Web, but there was no heightened travel warning. We had spoken with friends who said it was safe, come on over." I knew I was talking, but I couldn't hear what I was saying.

I stared at Matt Lauer. He nodded and moved on to the next question: What did we do when we heard the gunshots? John answered that one, and I exhaled.

The rest of the segment was short, but it felt like years. I was still lost in the audio loop in my head, trying not to hear the sound of Su's body falling and his spine crushing over and over again, whoosh, crack, on repeat.

Back in the greenroom, one of the producers thanked us for coming to New York and telling our story, and then asked Tommy if he really meant it, if he really thought he'd be stronger from all this.

"Oh, for sure, we're already stronger for this. Just look at us, look at how resilient we are, look at what we've proven we can survive. Some people get weaker because of things like this, but we'll use it to become better."

I stared at a fixed point between Tommy's eyes, hoping he could make the loop in my head stop spinning. I did not understand Tommy's optimism, how he'd gotten to that place and how those words kept coming out of his mouth, but I was desperate to join him. I put on my training soundtrack in my mind, the only pep talk I had: *Get it together, Rodden. Suck it up. You are strong. You can overcome this. You will overcome this.*

On the plane ride home, I had a flashback: Su's body arcing through the moonlight, the crack of his spine on the ledge after he'd fallen out of view. I vowed to keep him down there, shoved off-screen.

CHAPTER SEVEN

Colorado, April 2000

In the aftermath of the kidnapping, Tommy and I were so inseparable, so bonded in our own eyes and in the glare of the media, that it was hard to remember how young our relationship really was. It was just a baby taking its first steps, tentative and uncertain. But in Kyrgyzstan it had been forced to grow up.

Back in the late winter and early spring of 2000, when I was nineteen, I'd spent a month training in Boulder with my friend Katie and one of our heroes, Robyn Erbesfield-Raboutou, who along with Lynn Hill was one of the best female climbers in the game. At that point, it had been a year since I'd walked away from UC Davis and become a full-time climber, and I was beginning to gain some real name recognition and credibility in the community. My first claim to fame: an iconic route called To Bolt or Not to Be, a smooth wall of strawberry-blond rock in central Oregon that requires precise footwork and minuscule crimps. My success there had made me the youngest female climber to send a route graded at a difficulty level of 5.14.

In the Yosemite Decimal System, which is North America's standard for grading difficulty in roped climbs, a 5.14 is right near the top. The higher the number after the decimal point, the more difficult the climb: from 5.5 at the easy end to 5.15 at the most challenging. Letters added after the numbers allow for further gradations of difficulty: a 5.12

is harder than a 5.11, a 5.12b is harder than a 5.12a, and so on. To Bolt or Not to Be was a 5.14a, and it was what we called stout—meaning its grade has held up over time. (The opposite of a stout route is a fluffy one, sometimes also known, derogatorily, as a "chick route.") I didn't like to choose my projects just to check a status box. To Bolt was and remains a beautiful line and a challenging climb, and I was proud to have sent it for more reasons than just its grade.

That spring, I was training to free climb the Nose—the most iconic line on El Cap, maybe the most iconic line in the world. Its hardest sections were as hard as or harder than anything else I'd ever climbed, and while To Bolt had been a single pitch (a section of a climb, like a chapter in a book, loosely equivalent to a rope length), the Nose had thirty-one pitches. It was an audacious goal, one that would put me in the history books forever if I could pull it off. But I knew I needed to build my base before I could make that kind of leap. I couldn't swim across the ocean before swimming across the pool.

At the time, Tommy was twenty-one and living an hour away from Boulder at his parents' house in Estes Park (when he wasn't living out of his van, near whatever climb he was working on), but he drove in each week to train at the city's world-class climbing gyms. He was like me in some ways: another very promising young climber who was turning heads and gaining sponsors. But while I had come of age in the gym and then moved outside, he'd been raised by his dad on big walls and sufferfests. A few months earlier, in late 1999, he'd made the first ascent of a climb he called Kryptonite, the first ever American route rated 5.14d. That same year, he had free climbed the Salathé Wall, a route up El Cap that was just very slightly more achievable than the Nose.

After a slideshow one night in the weight room of the Boulder Rock Club, he walked up to me and asked me to dinner. I stared at him. The competition scene was a tight circle, so we'd been crossing paths for a few years—sharing group meals at comps in Europe, training together at the crags, overlapping at trade shows. But now I looked him over more carefully than I had in the past. He was wearing a white tank top from the national sport-climbing competition we had all gone to a year earlier. He had a swimmer's body: broad, strong shoulders that tapered in a V down to his waist, above legs that were strong but not bulky. His fair skin was freckled, his dirty-blond hair perpetually rumpled. His ears stuck out a bit, and his eyes were soft and squinted a little when he smiled. Butterflies shot up in my stomach. I'd never been asked out to dinner before.

A few days later he picked me up in front of the Boulder Rock Club at 5:30 p.m. for an early dinner at the Cheesecake Factory. I was jittery and nervous, but luckily it was Tommy: everyone knew he was the gentlest person around. I wore my good Verve shorts that I had gotten for free and weren't covered in chalk, and I ordered the chicken Caesar salad, because I always ordered the chicken Caesar, plus a piece of chocolate cheesecake for dessert. I wanted to prove to Tommy and to anyone who might be watching that I could eat without worry, without obsessing over the consequences.

After dinner we drove in Tommy's full-size Chevy van into the foothills between Boulder and Coal Creek Canyon, where I was staying with Katie and her dad. The van was white with blue stripes, kitted out with a real futon mattress, a Coleman stove, and a plastic water jug held in place by bungee cords—a huge step up from my usual climbing bivvy: my two-door Honda Civic, which was just big enough for me to sleep stretched out, with the back seats folded down and my feet sticking into the trunk. (I loved my Civic, though—it was so covert. While my friends in pickups and vans got hassled by Yosemite rangers all the time, I made it through two full seasons under the radar, sleeping for free, living the classic dirtbag climbing life in stealth mode.)

We lay down on the bed in the back of his van, and Tommy cued up some climbing movies. My mind was a blender of emotions. This was my first ever date, and somehow I was already horizontal. Were we supposed to have sex? Did I want to have sex? I was nervous, but I didn't feel the desire to rip off his pants like I'd seen in every single romantic comedy. Maybe that stuff would come later?

We cuddled a little, just lying there with his arms around me staring at the television. I felt awkward. I'd had a few big crushes and kissed a couple of guys before, but I'd never had a boyfriend. I wasn't sure how I was supposed to feel.

After Tommy dropped me back at Katie's, she wasted no time.

"So, did you sleep with him?" she asked as soon as I kicked off my shoes. I loved Katie. She was a loose cannon in her tight religious family. After meeting at our first junior national competition in San Diego, we'd become inseparable, and five years later we were both sponsored, and still close. We'd blast Eminem and chatter about getting our periods late. We loved to talk about sex, which neither of us knew anything about.

"No!" I exclaimed.

"Well, will you!?" she said, laughing eagerly.

"I don't know! I mean, yeah, sure," I said. "I wonder what it feels like. But, I mean, it's Tommy . . ." She too had known Tommy through his dorkiest years.

Tommy and I went on a second date, also nice but with few of the sparks I had expected to feel. Then, a few weeks later, we both joined a bunch of climbers caravanning to Indian Creek, Utah. The uniquely parallel red sandstone cracks there were a perfect training ground for the upcoming Yosemite season. People assumed we were dating at that point; I wondered if we were. I rolled out my sleeping bag and pad on a flat area of sandstone. Tommy walked forty feet away and unrolled his; all the others did the same. Nights were spent around the stove cooking quesadillas and stuffing our swollen, cut-up hands into a communal bag of chips. Katie cuddled with a guy named Mike. I smiled and turned away when Tommy made eye contact. The entire landscape was scattered with tall maroon sandstone buttes. Days we'd hike up the steep red and brown hills to the base of the vertical walls to climb. Tommy and I often split off from the group to talk about all the Yosemite routes we each wanted to tick off—the Northwest Face of Half Dome, Astroman, the Nose, the Zodiac. And all the places we wanted to travel—Patagonia, Canada's Cirque of the Unclimbables, Australia, Norway.

After Indian Creek, I'd climbed into my Civic and headed to Yosemite. It was my second season in the Valley. Now I was a regular on the dirtbag circuit: cafeteria, deli, Mountain Room bar. A lot of the guys who hung around did more shit-talking than climbing, but I was earning my standing in the community and did my pull-ups in secret every morning on a low branch in the trees above Camp 4.

I remember when Tommy drove his van into the "Center of the Universe," the parking lot across from Camp 4 where we all loitered. "There's Tommy," some brown-toothed guy said, sitting on the back of his tailgate. "Wonder if he's driving through to rangerland. Such a douche." My skin crawled, and I felt ill.

Tommy had climbed the Salathé Wall the year prior with a new partner named Mikey—probably because Mikey actually wanted to go climbing, instead of sitting around and talking about it. But he also happened to be the stepson of everyone's least favorite ranger. Climbers and rangers were oil and water back then, playing a continual cat-and-mouse game: we dodged and evaded while they attempted to enforce fees and regulations. As climbers, we felt like we had a right to own Yosemite, to live how we wanted in the park. And at the time, many rangers seemed to take a specific joy in punishing any missteps on our parts. So when Tommy climbed with a ranger's kid and parked his van in a ranger's driveway, he was sleeping with the enemy.

Still, I hated that they shit-talked him. He was the nicest guy I'd ever met. I remembered his strong arms around me in the back of his van a few weeks earlier. We hadn't climbed together since Indian Creek. He parked next to my Civic, hopped out, and smiled a huge grin with his crooked teeth. I heard someone grumble, "No one is climbing with a ranger lover." My skin bristled, and I felt my eyes get hot. *Fuckers,* I thought to myself. It wasn't right. So I went over to talk to him. Soon, we decided to attempt Lurking Fear together.

There are a lot of different climbable routes up El Cap, the beautiful granite mass that dominates Yosemite Valley. But back then, only a handful of them had ever been free climbed—which means that you climb it, bottom to top, without falling and without pulling on any gear (known as aid climbing) to help you. Just rock and fingers and feet to propel you upward, with rope and gear used only to protect in case of a fall. Free climbing is prestigious because it's really hard to do—and for a certain type of climber, it's the only kind of climbing that really matters.

Lurking Fear was one that had never been freed. A local legend named Steve Schneider had come close, putting in a season or two of work and linking nearly all its toughest sections before falling short on the two hardest pitches, numbers three and seven. It was a big, tough objective.

El Cap was everything to me. Climbing it required skill, fear management, toughness, and the ability to suffer, all in the most glorious setting, the heart of Yosemite. I had gotten my first taste of it earlier that same spring, when Hans Florine, the Yosemite veteran who would eventually climb El Cap nearly two hundred times, had taken me on the Nose. I'd gone up with him and Jacki, his pregnant wife, and I was terrified. I hoped she would be my scapegoat, that she would say what I couldn't: let's bail. But she was even radder than Hans and just kept plugging away. I stayed up there for three days, leading things that scared me, vowing to become a boulderer when I finally touched safe ground again. But when we did come down, I only wanted more.

Lynn Hill had been the first person, man or woman, to free climb the Nose, which drove the guys insane. I'd spent so much time in high school staring at a poster of her that I had hung on my wall. She looked so fearless, so totally self-possessed: a badass in cutoff jean shorts two thousand feet off the ground. I wanted to be in that poster, wanted to feel my fingers in that sun-warmed granite. I wanted muscled arms and puffy blond hair and bronze skin, and the kind of brash confidence that marked Lynn's iconic line, delivered after her 1993 send on the Nose: "It goes, boys." I wanted to have that kind of swagger.

Lynn was not only better than all the women, she was better than all the men. But despite Lynn's dominance, and her stature in my personal world, not many girls were up on El Cap—and especially not to free climb, which made doing so even more appealing to me. I always wanted to outshine other women. There were plenty of men making big names for themselves, but I only saw a fraction as many women in the same spots. I didn't know if that was because there were fewer women in the sport, or if there was less appetite, less acceptance, for women at the top. Regardless, I wanted a seat at the table, and I thought that free climbing might be how I got there. Tommy had already freed the Salathé. In my world that was like quarterbacking the winning team in the Rose Bowl. And he was just so nice. I thought he would be a perfect partner for a big objective like Lurking Fear.

Dean Potter started out trying the route with us, probably because he and half the hardcore climbers in the Valley thought Tommy and I should just overcome our shyness and become a couple already. Dean was several years older than us, bold and wild, but good at putting people at ease. I liked having him there in the early going: a veteran climber, and a buffer for the tingling awkwardness between Tommy and me. But soon Dean left to work on the Triple Crown: climbing El Cap, Half Dome, and Mount Watkins in a day.

Tommy and I spent the next month trying to decode the ascent. This meant spending hours, days, hanging on a rope, staring at the granite face, searching for any crevice or bump that might help us lever ourselves up. Once those were found we dangled for hours more, searching for cracks and weaknesses in the surrounding rock in which we could place our gear.

Tommy was a master of finding tiny edges and choreographing moves. (Climbers talk about things in terms of moves, a hand move or a foot move, and a collection of these together is called a sequence. Link together enough sequences and you have a route.) But he was five foot ten with a wide wingspan, while I stand five foot one on a good day. He had a much longer reach, but his feet and hands were bigger than mine and less precise, less able to fit themselves into the subtlest indentations in the rock. The route was barely the same for the two of us. Yet we were all in, together, sunstruck, heat-struck, hands swollen. My fingers bled most of the time we spent working out the two cruxes. The crux pitches, the hardest moves on the route, were blank, discontinuous sheets of granite. The tiny granite features cut like blades. I didn't care.

"You must be really psyched," Tommy said, looking at my destroyed hands with clear approval.

I was. I was not the most gifted athlete, but I could work harder than anyone. I loved feeling my arms fill with lactic acid. I loved hearing the voice inside my head say, *You should stop now,* and then quieting that voice and pushing on. When the voice came back, I'd shush it again.

I loved pulling with arms that I could barely lift above my head. I loved feeling my grip open with exhaustion and forcing my hands to hold on, even still. I loved rising to a level that forced me to grovel. I never had or wanted a coach. I just had the clichéd soundtrack in my head. Over and over I'd play myself the theme to *Rocky*. Over and over I heard Yoda say, *There is no try, Rodden, only do.*

Tommy was basically the same. Mike had taught him his version of manliness: Pain is weakness leaving the body. Toughness is a skill. The fun we both understood was Type-2 fun—the kind that is only fun in hindsight, the kind you make for yourself through the work you put in and through your decision to see it, after it's over, as delicious and grand. El Cap was a Type-2 fun amusement park, the sufferer's Disneyland. When no one else was on the wall, it felt like the greatest playground in the world, and I was the happiest child.

This was a truly strange place to form a relationship: hanging off a sheer granite face, a thousand feet above the ground. Even just peeing on El Cap is difficult and embarrassing, as it requires you to lower your pants while still in your harness. The leg loops are connected to the waist belt in front of your crotch and over your butt cheeks. The back ones are just elastic straps, so if you transfer all your weight to the back you can stick your butt out and pull down your pants and leg loops, and voilà.

Once your pants are down you need to make sure that the rope is not below you, and people are not below you, and the wind is not going to fling your urine back in your face. Pooping is a whole other matter, and always a subject of much discussion among climbers—the best, most horrifying stories of being caught unprepared are almost a point of pride. It requires the same position, but instead of just letting the pee fly, you have to capture the actual poop. On each trip to the Village Store, I prayed to find the medium-size paper bags instead of the smallest ones, which left dangerous room for error.

After pooping into a paper bag, we'd stuff it into a gallon-sized ziplock bag and then into a three-foot-long, four-inch-wide PVC tube with screw caps on each end, appropriately named the Poop Tube. In the beginning I'd ask Tommy to climb a pitch ahead so I could have some privacy while taking a crap. He did, with great gallantry. But climbing big walls together leaves little room for physical mystery, and I got over my inhibitions pretty fast. I wasn't sure I wanted a romance anyway. Tommy was the greatest climbing partner I could have wished for, but I thought maybe I just wanted to be friends.

What took longer was letting Tommy see me cry. Crapping is not against the climber code. Weeping is. But after a few weeks, while leading a hard pitch that was flaring and slippery and full Yosemite funk, I cracked. I yelled, "Take!" down to Tommy, climber speak meaning he should reel in any slack on the rope and hold me up there firmly. Then I let go of the wall and wept.

"Is everything okay?" Tommy shouted up from the belay, twenty feet below. "It looks really hard right there."

I wondered what Tommy thought of me, hanging there, bawling. I wondered if he thought I was weak and I should just push through. He complimented me all the time—on my climbing, how pretty I was, how much he liked me. No one had ever complimented me like that before. It was nice, but awkward to be liked that much.

"Beth, are you okay?" he said after a few minutes. "Do you want me to lower you?"

"Yeah, you can lower me," I said, defeated.

Back on the belay ledge with Tommy, he asked what happened and I just told him the truth: I didn't have it in me to suck it up. I got petrified up here. I wanted to be a girl who continued up the pitch. But I wasn't, not yet at least. I was a gym rat leading a 5.13 a thousand feet off the ground. Who was I kidding? "The gear isn't good, and the cracks are flaring, and I didn't want to fall . . . ," I said all in one gasp.

I knew Tommy didn't share my fear. But his face softened with compassion. "Would you like me to go up and see if I can find a better way?"

I nodded.

On big, multi-pitch free climbs like Lurking Fear, it's typical to have a longer period of decoding, days or weeks or even months of figuring the route out move by move, before you go for the completed ascent—the push, in climber speak. During those first weeks we had freed all the pitches on the lower part of the route, and for our last push we spent two days on the wall, finishing the top half. We slept head to toe in our portaledge, Tommy snoring even before I could put my head on the makeshift pillow I'd built by stuffing my fleece inside my smelly cotton T-shirt.

In the cold, thin light of dawn on our second day, I led the last of the hardest pitches, a 5.12 known as the Grand Traverse. Despite the morning cold, my hands were sweaty as I started up. I knew that if I could do this pitch, I'd have a good chance at doing the entire route, and I surprised myself by doing it on my first try. As I belayed Tommy up, I was giddy with excitement. Everything I had been dreaming of was coming true. Dropping out of college was paying off. Pretty soon I'd be traveling the world, getting paid the medium bucks.

With the Grand Traverse behind us, we decided to take a gamble: we left our stuff hanging off the wall to the side of the route, a promise to ourselves that we wouldn't need to camp again that night, and pushed for the top. When we pulled onto the low-angle granite slabs that marked our finish line, I took a picture of us that still today is one of my favorites: just two kids, in front of a disposable Kodak camera, with Half Dome in the background, nothing but happiness on our faces. We had made the first ever free ascent of Lurking Fear. We were on the map now. So far, it has never been repeated.

Sometime during Lurking Fear, our understanding of our situation began to match what everyone else was already assuming: we were a couple. There was no big speech, no *What are we?* conversation. It felt simple in some ways, an easy extension of our partnership on the wall. I felt lucky to have found such a kind first boyfriend, and one who wanted to do exactly what I did: climb hard routes. But the physical side . . . I was no expert, but what I felt didn't seem to match what I'd been told I would feel. There was no wild attraction, no fireworks. By the time we left for Kyrgyzstan less than two months later, in late July, I had decided I didn't want to be his girlfriend anymore.

At The North Face headquarters in San Ramon, a couple of weeks before Tommy and I were due to fly across the world to be in remote mountains for six weeks with just two other people, I tried to break up with him. I gave him the old *It's not you, it's me. Let's just be friends.* It was awful.

Tommy slumped in the fluorescent-lit hallway. He never quite looked like himself indoors; he hated places like this even more than I did. Worse, Tommy was only in this concrete corporate cubicle hell because I had asked him to be. I wanted him to climb with me in Kyrgyzstan because I didn't want to climb with anybody else. I loved our dynamic and the way we worked together. We were such good partners—climbing partners. But I felt so guilty, knowing he wanted more. I really *wanted* to want him to be my boyfriend too, but if I was honest with myself, I didn't think the desire was really there. Was a desire for desire enough? Could it grow into the real thing? Now he was sitting on the floor, his head dropped in his arms.

After we'd finished packing up six weeks of freeze-dried food, we drove together to my parents' house in Davis. All of Tommy's stuff was there—we'd used it as a base during our Yosemite season. He asked me if we could take one more trip to the mountains. That was where we thrived together—maybe all this concrete was the problem? I hated conflict. I agreed. We drove up to Donner Summit, we climbed, we ran. I thought about Tommy, who was so kind and patient, and wondered: *What if I'm throwing away something precious here?* So I changed my mind, or at least deferred my decision until after Kyrgyzstan.

After the kidnapping, we never talked about our brief breakup again. It was part of a past that no longer seemed connected to our present—I was different, and so was Tommy. We were an inseparable "we" now.

A couple of weeks after we got back, I asked a jeweler to inscribe a silver pendant for Tommy that read: *T.C. MY HERO. MY LIFESAVER. MY LOVE.* He wore it on a leather cord around his neck. I didn't entirely know who I was anymore—but BethandTommy felt like a kind of anchor, something I could grab and hold.

CHAPTER EIGHT

Estes Park, Colorado, September 2000

About a month after we made it home to Davis from Kyrgyzstan, Tommy drove back to Estes to be with his parents, and I went with him. Mike believed that the best way to get over our trauma was to get back on the horse—to climb. He said it exactly like that: "You just need to get back on that horse!"

Mike had been a serious climber but also a competitive bodybuilder. (A strange combination, seeing as climbing culture prizes strength, but not bulk. We learned early not to do anything that might add more weight you'd then have to pull.) He had been crowned Mr. Colorado in the late 1970s and Mr. Mid-America in 1980, two years after Tommy was born. In the old pictures he looked bronzed, oiled, and sculpted, with a tight afro—Arnold Schwarzenegger of the Front Range. Then he tore his bicep while he was spotting someone, saving them from serious injury. That ended his bodybuilding career.

Now, all these years later, his garage was mostly dedicated to shaping Tommy into the best climber he could be. Mike had fabricated all the equipment himself with an arc welder that he taught himself to use. All the barbells, dumbbells, weight benches, and machines—Mike made them by hand. Tommy's mother sewed the cushions for the benches. All of it could make you tough and strong. None of it was pretty.

I'd had some small homemade walls—my dad built me two; I inherited another from a mentor—but never a full-blown home gym before. I always trained at bigger commercial places. This was so different: every piece of equipment coated in a paste of old climbing chalk and sweat. At first I did not understand why Tommy didn't want to strength train in Boulder at one of the sparkly world-class gyms there. We already drove into the city to climb inside; why not just finish our day there too? Only half of Mike's garage walls were insulated, which was pointless. The Estes wind was brutal and ripped right through.

To his quiver of regular weight-training gear, Mike had added a torture device of his own invention, built specially for Tommy. They called it the Finger Machine.

The Finger Machine was seven pieces of metal welded together in such a way that you could stack weight plates on it and then grip and squeeze—like a lat pull for your fist. It didn't look impressive, but it could add up to sixty pounds purely on your fingers. Mike had built it while Tommy was working Kryptonite, which had a notoriously difficult pinch hold. Now it lived on in the gym, but it was small enough for us to easily pack in the van, to keep our fingers strong on climbing trips too.

Behind the Finger Machine was a 43-degree, twelve-by-fourteen-foot bouldering wall. This was not gussied up either. No cheerful paint job. No colored tape marking routes. Over the years, Tommy had just scribbled jumbles of numbers and letters next to the holds. It looked like scratch paper from algebra class. The largest holds were barely big enough for half my tiny fingers.

I didn't even understand how to warm up in here.

◆ ◆ ◆

Katie called a week after we arrived back in Estes. "Can I come up and see you guys?" We hadn't really been in touch since Kyrgyzstan.

I put on my most cheerful voice. "Sure!" I said. "We're going on a snowshoe, then training in the garage, then we'll have some time around the afternoon. Does that work?"

"Whoa. Um, yeah," Katie said. Her dad's house was an hour's drive away. "I'll come up when you're done."

I pretended I was fine but I'd been having nightmares again. I'd see Abdul walking down Tommy's parents' hallway. When I shook Tommy awake at 2:00 a.m., my whole body clammy and convulsing, he didn't know what to do. "Oh, honey," he'd say, holding me until the worst had passed.

Tommy was searching for boulders in Rocky Mountain National Park, ski touring, laughing out loud, and making plans that he would stick to—all the normal stuff that felt so hard for me. The news that Su was alive seemed to have laid whatever lingering fears and doubts he'd had to rest. But, even though we never talked about it in the morning, I knew he must be worrying about me. I was twenty, he was twenty-two, and we were both in way over our heads.

"Hello!" Katie shouted when she closed the dark-wood front door and stood in the pale-blue-tiled entryway. I ran downstairs and we sat on the Caldwells' big blue suede couch, Fox News on the TV turned off for once.

I tried to make small talk, just like I had been doing with everyone since we returned. "What have you been up to? Have you climbed lately? I've hardly been climbing at all. How are things with Mike?" The guy from Indian Creek was her boyfriend now. "Do you want some Wheat Thins?"

Katie tried to stop the barrage. "How are you?" she asked. "How are you really doing?"

I watched her mouth move and heard sounds come out, but it was as if we were speaking underwater across a swimming pool. My mind had created for itself an intense distortion field, a thick gel-like bumper that damped and deflected all incoming assaults, both real and perceived.

Care was a threat; the suggestion that I wasn't okay was a threat. So, internally, I pushed the threat away. Katie was a good girl like me—the way I had been before, anyway. She couldn't understand. I had matured over these past two months; she had not. I knew what was important; she did not. I'd seen the world. I knew what life was really about; she was stuck back in childhood, discussing rap music and boys. I couldn't tell her about the nightmares. Nope, no way. If I told her about the nightmares then she might offer to help, or act like she understood, or suggest I get help. No one could help me; no one could understand. They would just want to hear the story. They just wanted to take something from me.

CHAPTER NINE

Kyrgyzstan, July 2000

It's not easy to get from California to the Kara-Su. We flew from San Francisco to London and then got diverted to Tbilisi, Georgia, for several days before finally landing in Bishkek, the capital of Kyrgyzstan. From there we chartered a huge Russian helicopter, a vehicle so massive you could drive a tank into it. Our sprawling pile of expedition duffels looked tiny inside. There were bench seats, and no seat belts, though I spent a few moments looking for them. A handful of locals boarded with us, catching a ride. We sat there in our bright, shiny technical clothes, and they sat in their layers, frayed patchworks of muted colors and fabrics. As they loaded up, a woman set a baby on my lap so that she could grab a rucksack. I stared. I wasn't her husband, I wasn't the aunt or even her friend. I hadn't held a baby in years. I looked down at her tiny face, dirty but beautiful, her squinty infant eyes staring back at me. I was mesmerized. But I felt an itch of worry. I should not be responsible for this baby. I was not ready to be responsible for a baby.

The rotors of the helicopter revved up with a jolt, and the baby, swaddled in her faded red blanket, started to shake off my lap. I caught her and looked over at the mother, now sitting on the edge of the bench seat across from me. She gestured that I could pass her baby back. We didn't even try to speak. There would have been no point. The helicopter was so loud.

After first delivering the locals to a small town in the foothills, the pilot flew on, into bigger mountains, and dropped us off in a bright-green grassy meadow. It was so beautiful, so austere, and so pristine—we decided to set up camp right there. This valley was narrower than the next one over, the more famous Ak-Su Valley, where most climbers went. We would only have limited hours of direct sunlight each day, before the shadows off the massive rock walls crept in. They would be our canvas to paint; we were here to create some new climbs.

The grass was so soft that we almost didn't need our fancy sleeping pads and camp chairs. The grass was browner in the Ak-Su, more traveled. But we had these steep glorious hillsides of green. It was as bright as the wheatgrass shots I used to get at Jamba Juice on my way to the gym. We set up our tents—one huge, two-meter dome for cooking and playing cards, then two smaller sleeping tents, one for John and Jason, the other for Tommy and me. There was a boulder on one side of the camp with bolt holes drilled in it by previous climbers.

I was so happy to unpack our duffels and nest. I remembered hearing that the alpinist Alex Lowe always brought an ice ax on expeditions so that he could hang it with slings off a tree or boulder and do pull-ups in camp. I thought we should do that too—stay fit, do everything just right. The boys were less concerned. I took a Polaroid of Tommy and me and hung it above my sleeping bag in our tent. We filtered water from a nearby glacial river that swelled and subsided with the sun each day. It was majestic in its rhythm and power; it made us seem trivial, flown in from across the world with our travel CD cases, our Koosh ball sets, our clean underwear and socks.

On our first morning, a young father from a tiny cluster of homes down the valley walked up with yak milk and butter. Shorter and younger than Tommy, he wore military fatigues and had dark skin, black hair, and missing teeth. We poured the milk, still warm, on our granola. The milk was so white, the creamiest white I'd ever seen, and the butter was so yellow, so deep and pure.

After breakfast, John started organizing his camera gear. Jason rummaged in the gear bags for a CD. He loved Metallica, had all their albums memorized and had brought them on the trip.

As we settled in, I was relieved that no one was upset yet. Tommy's and Jason's energies were . . . not well matched. Tommy was understated, loved climbing for climbing, never had to talk about his achievements. Jason was very loud in every sense of the word and not shy or coy about anything. Looking back, I'm surprised everyone held it together as well as they did.

We were all so eager to climb. My hands were soft from the days at The North Face headquarters, and the rock chewed them up. But it felt good to move over the granite. It was coarse—much coarser than in Yosemite, and covered with lichen: green, red, and yellow. But the wind was calmer on the wall. Not like the gusts on El Cap. The grass on the hills wasn't as fluorescent as the grass down at camp, but it was still bright. Along with the tumble of the rushing water, you could hear the dinging of yak bells drifting up the valley. They grazed all day long, up on those steep hillsides. We ran into one yak, high on the slope, while doing some recon up one side of the valley. We didn't blend in at all, with our gear, ropes, and clothes, but I felt like the yak belonged there.

For the first few days we hiked around, but soon we started climbing. We'd selected a granite wall covered with lime-green lichen that offered the promise of brand-new routes. Tommy and I spent hours and hours up on that face, just like the hours and hours we spent on El Cap, feeling around for footholds and handholds and cracks where we could place gear. The Kara-Su made my ego settle a little. I felt less invincible, calmer, small in the way I wanted to feel small—awed but not afraid. This was an actual wilderness, not the family circus of Yosemite National Park, with its traffic jams, tour buses, and gift shops selling souvenir mugs that said *STEVE* and *LISA*. I felt more. I noticed more: the exact humidity, the precise moment when the temperature started to invert. It made me happy.

We'd lost a few bags somewhere on our journey, the ones with fuel and some important climbing gear—at least it seemed important at the time. John and Jason volunteered to hike down out of the mountains, to the nearest real settlement, to see if they could find a phone. They would make some calls, try to figure out where those bags were and get them delivered. But their errand was no small feat; it involved days of grueling logistics, thousands of feet of elevation gained and lost, and figuring out where the closest significant village actually was. Tommy and I kept climbing, picking away at a new route on the face known as the Yellow Wall, falling into the easy rhythm we'd established on Lurking Fear that spring.

When John and Jason returned, having found no word of our missing gear, we prepared for our push. We thought it would take three or four days to send the whole route. I was the designated packer—all the food, clothes, filtered water, first-aid kit, climbing shoes for slabs, climbing shoes for cracks. The control of loading up the haul bags worked for me. The day we left was Tommy's twenty-second birthday. I snuck a red emergency camp candle and some freeze-dried chocolate pudding into our gear.

We climbed that day to the base of a large roof and the start of the hard climbing. In the evening, I sat in the portaledge next to Tommy in my blue-and-white beanie, my brand-new blue jacket, snuggled in my sleeping bag. I felt so proud. I was wearing clothes I had gotten for free, covered in a sleeping bag I had gotten for free, hanging in a portaledge that we had gotten for free. I was a sponsored athlete on a far-flung expedition, just like the climbers I'd most admired in my teens. Below us I could see the raging river. I could tell where it narrowed and we'd crossed it with all of our stuff. I looked even farther down the valley and saw the mouth where the Ak-Su met the Kara-Su. Take that, high school. Take that, Davis. This was winning. I took out the freeze-dried chocolate pudding and the camp candle and fumbled around for the lighter.

John and Jason were only a few feet away. We all sang "Happy Birthday," and then they pulled out a small boom box, took out an Ozzy Osbourne CD, and started playing "Crazy Train." We could still hear the yak bells dinging. Lying head to toe in our tiny portaledge, we said what we'd always said to each other before we closed our eyes: "See you in the morning, see you all night long."

That night I dreamed I heard gunshots. But when I woke up, the guns kept firing.

CHAPTER TEN

Yosemite Valley, California, October 2000

Tommy had always kept a list of his goals: the El Cap routes, the Half Dome routes, the desert routes, the Europe routes. It was long, heavy, and ambitious. After Kyrgyzstan, he went right back to chasing the next climb on the list.

He'd tried to do the first free ascent of the Muir Wall on El Cap the previous spring, before our ascent of Lurking Fear. Now, just over a month after we'd made it home, he wanted to try the Muir again with me. Like we could pick up where we'd left off in Yosemite. Like life would just go on.

Up on the wall I felt empty. I wanted to love being there, wanted so badly for it to feel like my everything again. I'd try to smile, try to remember to say things like "We are so lucky, look at this view!" But even the fresh October air, the smell and feel of Yosemite, couldn't help me. I associated climbing with death. I didn't even try to climb the pitches; I just belayed. I felt like we were cursed, as though the executions we had dodged in Kyrgyzstan would find us here.

On our first day, five hundred feet off the deck, the sheath of our rope was cut by a sharp rock edge, exposing its dense nylon core. Cutting a rope to the core is like an airbag deploying—no one ever really wants to get to that point. Tommy hung twenty feet below me with the bright-white innards of the rope showing. It looked like he was hanging on dental floss. I wanted to lose it, to freak out, to tell him that this was proof of our curse. Instead, I stared down at Tommy and said, "That's not good. Do you think you can hand-over-hand back up here? Or should I throw you down a loop?"

Two weeks later, we got caught in a bad rainstorm in the middle of a 5.12 traverse, half a mile up in the air. A friend called and asked if we needed a rescue, but I forced a smile and laughed the idea away. My pride still outweighed my terror, though not by much. I felt scared on every pitch, sure that the rope would break for real. Or the bolts would pull out. Or loose flakes would dislodge from the granite face and tumble down, killing people below. Or Tommy would die, by some turn of events I hadn't yet imagined, and I wouldn't even know what to do. Could I get him down? Would I leave him dangling there? How would I tell everyone? It would be easier, I thought, if I died up there too.

The joy I'd found on Lurking Fear the previous spring was long gone. Every single thing was exhausting, and not in that wonderful, bone-tired, well-earned way. Just something like getting soup from the bottom of the haul bag took ten minutes. And then, once I'd repacked the bag and realized I'd forgotten the can opener, I had to unpack and repack it all over again.

When the rain subsided briefly to snow, we accepted defeat, and Tommy led us back to the top. We had to hike down the long way, eight miles. I cried the whole way. We retreated to Davis, soggy and dejected. But Tommy went back in November, with his best friend, Nick, and sent it.

◆ ◆ ◆

That winter, The North Face asked me to fly to Thailand for a photo shoot. In January, I flew to Bangkok with Katie. I had a fever and chills—I had hoped I would be sick enough that I could be justified in staying home, but Tommy offered me an Advil and dropped me at the airport with an encouraging kiss goodbye. When I started crying on the plane, I told Katie it was because I felt so sick, and I did feel sick. But mostly I was terrified.

The humidity in Bangkok felt like an assault. The air was a thick paste, and the heat sapped all my energy. I wanted to warn everyone else in the group that we weren't safe, that someone would be coming to kill us. I wanted to use my hard-earned knowledge to protect us, this time. But I knew that I couldn't.

In Railay Bay I shared a bungalow with Katie. My weeks of stasis were starting to catch up with me, and I obsessed over whether anyone would notice that I was wearing a size small harness now, instead of an extra small. I worried that I would be too heavy to climb anything, that the photographer would avoid shooting me, that Katie would get all the photos and the resulting raises from sponsors.

While all the other sponsored climbers spent their days dangling off the cliffs above the beach and flirting, I lay in bed: sick with a fever, terrified of the locals, and ashamed. It's mortifying to admit this now, more than twenty years later, but it is the horrible truth. It didn't matter that Thailand is largely Buddhist. It didn't matter that my feelings would have been irrational and wrong even if I had been climbing just over the border in Muslim Malaysia. The particulars of the group that had taken us hostage—the Islamic Movement of Uzbekistan, based in Tajikistan, on a bloody incursion through Kyrgyzstan—didn't change anything either.

My terror could not be confined to a specific geography, a single geopolitical event. Kyrgyzstan was a world away: dry alpine meadows and dark cliffs, versus the white-and-blue of the tropical seaside limestone here. The people there had worn muted hues, while the clothing here was eye-catching, bright. The food, the smells, the damp ocean air and searing turquoise water, the quality of the light—it was all so different from that mountain valley. Somewhere inside me, I knew it wasn't right to let my fear refract out from the prism of what a small group of men had put me through and paint whole swaths of humanity in an ugly light. But when I looked around me, I saw my kidnappers.

Despite the differences I could see and smell and hear and taste, some part of me latched on to a superficial sameness: skin color, hair color, eye color. All I felt was foreignness and threat.

I know now that trauma is both rational and irrational. It is the body's response to danger, a deeply rooted instinct to protect itself. But it can manifest in unhelpful, unreasonable, and deeply unpleasant ways. For days, my body screamed at me to escape before I could be taken again. I felt the flicker of Abdul's beard on the back of my neck. I smelled it. I cried to Katie each night about how much I wanted to go home.

"I thought you sounded crazy when I saw you in Estes," she said bluntly.

I didn't know why I'd come to Thailand, except that I was a good girl who did what I was told, and this trip meant I still had my seat at the table. If I wasn't there to be paired up with Katie, two young female climbers together on a sunny coast, someone else would get slotted in. Being dropped by a sponsor always seemed imminent if a sponsored athlete didn't say yes, especially as a woman.

But each day after climbing, everyone else would laugh and smile and eat curry and pad thai and talk about what climbs looked fun, and I'd just stare at my feet. I scoffed and silently cried when everyone else extended their trips to ride elephants and swim in the warm ocean. I left Railay by myself and arrived in Bangkok alone. I hired a private driver: thirty dollars got me two days of sightseeing. I bought silk scarves and bright, elaborate wall hangings to give to my family, souvenirs to match the ones we had toted home from Kyrgyzstan. I bought another one of those yellow disposable Kodak cameras and took pictures of myself in front of temples and Buddha statues. I tried to smile in every one, but I knew when the photos were developed I'd see that I was in pain.

I had a long layover in San Francisco on my way back to Colorado. My parents drove into the city and met me at the gate so we could spend a couple of hours together. I so desperately wanted to just go back home with them, to crawl back in time to when they were all I needed to feel safe in the world, but instead I ate three bagels with cream cheese, hating myself for each bite, and waited until I boarded my connecting flight to Denver to break down and cry. When I arrived in Colorado, Tommy was waiting for me at the airport, looking like a chipmunk. He had just had his wisdom teeth removed. He took me to a fancy dinner, an Italian place on Pearl Street in Boulder—a big step up from our debut at the Cheesecake Factory. But he couldn't eat solid food, so he just watched me consume my pasta and brownie dessert.

My mind kept darting around, wondering why Tommy hadn't brought me flowers, whether his mouth would be healed enough for us to train at the gym the next day. But he tried so hard. While I was gone, he'd built me a system wall in the garage to help me train my fingers on specific types of holds. It was modeled on the one my dad had built for me—he knew how much I missed it.

◆ ◆ ◆

Nothing got better after Thailand. I decided I couldn't hack it at Mike and Terry's anymore. So much pressure to be happy, so much pressure to climb. So many nightmares. I'd become scared to fall asleep at night.

In February I flew home alone to my parents' house and reluctantly started therapy. Each Wednesday at noon I drove to downtown Davis, to an office above the Baskin-Robbins. I hated it. Therapy felt like swimming through hot lava.

Meanwhile Tommy drove to Indian Creek to go climbing with Nick. I wallowed in self-pity and resented him. He was moving on, enjoying life, not protecting me from my worst self. I spent all my time moving between the couch and the living-room floor, watching day-time reruns of *NYPD Blue*, *Law & Order*, and *JAG*. The major event of my day was my dad returning from his sixth-grade teaching job with a pint of ice cream. Then I'd sit around some more, watch more TV, and eat ice cream with my parents. Those three fixtures—house, TV, food—formed the triangle of my safety. I tried to stay in the middle of it, where it was easier to stay numb.

Every evening I talked to Tommy, and every evening he gave me the same advice, the best advice he had to give: "Maybe you'll be able to sleep through the night if you climbed more?" I resented him for this too. I didn't want to take off my sweatpants, which were all that fit anymore. I didn't want to face my deterioration, which was exactly what would happen if I went to the gym. I hated climbing. I hated my body. I hated that I even had a body. I hated my brain and its horrid, glitching thoughts. By the time I'd grudgingly finished my six sessions of therapy—all the insurance would pay for, which was frankly a relief, in the way that skipping school is a relief, even knowing that education is important—I was fat. And not what I'd once thought of as fat, in my obsessive competition days, back when I'd first absorbed the mantra that "nothing tastes as good as skinny feels." I had gained twenty-five extra pounds—weight that would almost disappear on someone taller or larger, but it was more than a quarter of what my total body weight had been before Kyrgyzstan.

"BB, looks like you've put on a little weight," one of the owners of the climbing gym said when I finally followed Tommy's advice and walked in.

I had a fake smile stuck like a clown nose on my face. I fooled no one. I put on my shoes, traversed the vertical kids' wall, and walked out after five minutes. I came home and called Tommy.

"I'm not going to eat for six days," I said. "I'm going to get skinny again." After all, I had already gone six days with hardly a bite of food. And I'd done it while hiking for hours, sleeping on the cold ground, freezing and wondering when I might be executed. How much easier would it be with a warm bed to sleep in? This would be my path back to climbing, to my career.

But that night when my dad got home from work, I ate my pint of ice cream.

The next day I returned to the climbing gym, but with little intention of working out. I just went out to lunch with Marko, my first mentor and the other owner of the gym, and I ate a huge burrito.

Soon the burrito too became an anchor in my day. I could stick with the game shows in the morning and the drama reruns later in the day. But the afternoon was soap-opera time, and that was too much wallowing even for me. Disengaged, I wandered from room to room in my parents' house, checking in each corner, worried that Abdul might be walking down the hall. I spoke a lot with my parents' cats.

"BB, where should we go today?" Marko said gamely each day when I showed up at the gym. I appreciated that he never shamed me—not like when I was younger, and someone I'd looked up to watched me eat two bagels with cream cheese before a competition and then said, "You'll never get up anything today." Every day I gave Marko the same answer: to Chipotle for a burrito with beans, guacamole, and cheese.

I thought, magically, that the pounds might protect me from bad people and bad thoughts. But they just filled me with neurotic self-loathing. I hated my hips. I hated the rolls of fat on my belly.

I'd found a way to bury the thin girl who'd been kidnapped. But I only knew how to love that now-distant version of myself.

CHAPTER ELEVEN

Kyrgyzstan, August 2000

When the shooting started, I jolted awake. Tommy did too. Without talking we both put our backs to the wall—a reflex, really. We assumed the loud cracking was rockfall, and that was what climbers did when we heard rockfall: we put our backs to the wall so we didn't get hit and killed. But this wasn't rockfall. Some part of my brain knew that. There were men down on the valley floor, shooting at us. But rockfall was on the list of bad things I imagined could happen in my life. Shooting was not.

We could hear rustling from the other portaledge, just five feet over. This was so far outside anything we'd trained for or understood. John volunteered to rappel down to talk to the shooters. At twenty-five, he was the oldest of us. He brought them cigarettes.

While he was gone I started to curl up inside myself. I felt so much regret: Why had I left Davis? If we'd never left, this wouldn't be happening. If I'd never learned to climb, this wouldn't be happening. Tommy and I were so naive. Why did we think we could do this? I wished we had convinced The North Face to spring for a satellite phone.

The guys on the ground did not want to make peace, despite the cigarettes. John radioed up to us without any of his normal jovial tone: "You need to come down."

Two men. Black hair, black beards, grenades, rifles, their belts studded with bullets and knives. One was tall with short hair, a round face, and a large mole on his mouth. The other was short with long hair. A lifetime of watching violence-drenched movies and video games could not even begin to prepare me for the terror of seeing men laden with weapons like these in real life.

I tried to hold on to the hope that they just wanted our money and our gear. They motioned with their guns for us to walk back to our base camp. But when we got there, it was a crime scene. Our tents were slashed open. Our gear was strewn across the wheatgrass-green hill. Two more strangers with weapons were there, and a fifth man with blood on his pants sat slumped against the boulder with the bolts in it. He looked despairing. He had a flannel sleeping bag under his arm.

The tears didn't start right away. I was so very good at control. We sat against the boulder next to the bloodied man. He looked at us and ran three fingers across his throat. Then he did it again. And again. Until we understood. What he was saying was: He'd been captured with three other men. Those men had been killed. The blood that was on his pants belonged to them.

I wanted to go home. I wanted to die. I had a thousand desires at once. I wanted it all to stop. I wanted to have spent more time with my granny in Davis. And—my mind kept looping on this—I wanted to have had sex with Tommy. If I'd had sex with Tommy then I could have chosen when. I could have chosen where. I'd been so profoundly stupid—so many girlish ideas. I'd thought I should wait so it could be special. I'd thought I should wait until the moment was just right. I'd thought I should wait to feel that wild attraction people felt in the movies, the kind I'd heard friends talk about, like you can't wait to get your clothes off.

Now we were here, and the threat of rape draped over my mind, heavy and oily, staining everything. I tried to shrink myself, scrunch down inside my chest, create an air gap, some kind of space between my thoughts, me, whoever that was, and the tiny girl body that could be tossed about and used.

My teeth felt hot. My breath had curdled. We'd made so many mistakes. We weren't actual adults, not like Lynn Hill or the other big-name climbers who'd been here before us. We shouldn't have come. But I needed not to break down. I needed not to call attention to the fact that I was a child. I needed not to scream, not to draw anyone's eyes to me. I was desperate to disappear.

Our captors barked and gestured for us to get our passports. We crawled into our ruined tents to find them, grabbed whatever jackets or long-sleeved shirts we could find too, and stuffed the pockets with PowerBars.

Tommy hid some money in his socks. John found the Polaroid of Tommy and me and showed it to our captors. He wanted to try to convince them Tommy and I were married.

Then we marched—four of them, the four of us, and our fellow hostage, the man with blood on his pants. He managed to tell us his name: Turat. He still carried the flannel sleeping bag. The hills were still beautiful, which was confusing.

They marched us down to the mouth of the valley, past a cluster of huts that had been full of smiling, waving locals when we'd last hiked by. The buildings were ominously empty now, and I wondered if they'd all been killed, or allowed to flee. Where the surging Ak-Su and Kara-Su Rivers met, frothing with glacial silt, we crossed a rickety wooden bridge, and I looked around, wondering if someone would see us. If anyone would save us. We climbed a steep grassy hillside, and then our captors gestured for us to settle in and wait. They put John, Jason, and Turat behind one tree, and Tommy and me behind another. Across the valley, I thought I saw movement, and then the gunshots began. Someone was shooting at us, and our captors fired back. Tommy and I tried to squeeze as much of ourselves behind the bulk of our tree's trunk as we could, tried to stay still, tried to keep breathing.

I had never seen, or heard, a battle. The waves of mortars and gunfire came and went like stomach cramps. I'd feel one starting, close my eyes, want it to stop, but then the pain and intensity would just build until the world was all noise. I had no idea if the noise would ever end, and I sat there pressing my eyes shut, like I was five years old and hiding it from sight might make it all go away. I clenched my teeth so hard I thought they'd crack. I tried, and failed, to take my mind to a happier place. I didn't know what was real and what was fake; everything horrible felt real.

In a brief lull in the noise, two of our captors yanked Turat out from behind his tree and walked him behind a large boulder.

The next gunshots we heard were shorter, more final, less dramatic. We didn't hear a thud. Turat must have been kneeling. We knew.

When the mortars paused again I opened my eyes and stared at the brown grass in front of my feet and at the big pine trees along the hillside above us. Then our captors grabbed me and Tommy and made us run in behind the boulder too. John and Jason were already there, along with Turat's body. Jason told me not to look at it. I knew he was right. Some part of me understood that if I looked, it would ruin me, and if I was ruined, our captors would think I wasn't worth saving.

When the light softened and the shadows disappeared from the trees, the shooting finally stopped. One of our captors, the one who called himself Abdul, motioned for us to run from behind the boulder. Jason went first, sprinting hard up the grassy hillside to a tree. He stopped, caught his breath, and then repeated to another tree. As I waited, I kept thinking that I should look back at Turat's body, that we shouldn't just leave him there, alone. I started to glance back. My eyes landed on his boots. They were dusty and gray. I thought I really should continue to look, up along the length of his body, at least to his back. But I couldn't. My mind just stopped. I couldn't let it in that they'd killed him. Executed him at point-blank range. I felt selfish and timid, too selfish to do him the honor of bearing witness. But I was afraid of the guilt and grief. I stared at his boots. I knew he was dead. We were abandoning him.

CHAPTER TWELVE

Estes Park, Colorado, May 2001

In the spring, the renters moved out of the old cabin Tommy had purchased just before Kyrgyzstan. There wasn't really a discussion, just an assumed next step: we moved into it together. We'd been kidnapped together, he'd saved our lives, and now we were here, in a six-hundred-square-foot fixer-upper across the street from the Estes Park town dump. In June 2000, Tommy had paid $70,000, with 10 percent down and an interest-only loan. I made less than $10,000 a year. I thought Tommy's homeownership was so grown-up.

I started packing up my room in Davis: all my competition T-shirts in one box, all my climbing medals and trophies in another, both destined for my parents' garage. I left my climbing posters on the bedroom wall—Lynn Hill on the Nose, Ron Kauk on Peace, Peter Croft on the Rostrum. Hanging those up in our new place felt childish now that I was featured in my own posters too. But I packed my framed pictures of my parents and Granny, my childhood dog, Steffi, our cat Sammy. And I packed the tan-and-brown felt wall hanging I'd brought back from Kyrgyzstan, because I wanted my house to seem worldly—even though looking at it made me feel nauseous, and I never wanted to travel again.

Tommy drove his van to Davis to help ferry stuff to Estes. I sent my bookshelves and a small collection of wooden masks, also from my travels, with him. The last thing I packed was my huge purple iMac computer, which looked like a gumdrop. Then I walked back inside to check my room one more time. My mom followed me back out to the driveway, trying to be supportive, to get on board with my move. But she knew I was still too fragile for this. She handed me a loaf of nut bread for the drive. I could barely look at her. I summoned the same fake perma-smile that had been on my face for too much of the past nine months, gave her a hug, and drove off.

On the way, Tommy and I chatted between our two cars on the walkie-talkies we used for big walls. I blasted Jennifer Lopez and wondered what he was listening to. I ate Raspberry Crunch granola and apple slices. I hoped the change in our surroundings might be good for me—might let me reassert some control. Between Winnemucca and Elko I radioed Tommy to see if we could pull over and go for a quick run.

"Of course, honey. Anything you want," he said, and then gamely ran with me on a frontage road along the side of I-80 until my watch read exactly twenty-two minutes and thirty seconds, at which point I said we should turn around to complete a forty-five-minute run. Tommy always let me set the pace.

When we got back to the cars, I fixed Tommy a peanut-butter-and-jelly sandwich with half the jar of peanut butter piled on. It almost filled my empty stomach to see others eat. Or, if I had eaten too much, it made me feel less alone. Tommy obliged. "Yum, thank you so much," he said, flashing his crooked smile.

We arrived in Estes after midnight. I made Tommy carry me over the threshold. Somehow he had never heard of this tradition, but I wanted to do all the things I thought you were supposed to do when you moved in with your boyfriend for the first time. He picked me up, cradled me like he had in his van hardly more than a year ago. Inside, we collapsed on the futon Tommy's parents had brought over from his old bedroom.

The cabin needed work, serious work, and we didn't wait around. The next morning we ripped out the bathroom and started using the toilet in the gas station across the street. I felt like I was winning. Like I was proving everybody wrong. You didn't need to hire a fancy contractor; you didn't need to go to college; you could just do it all yourself. Take that, Davis.

Tommy's parents were do-it-yourselfers. They had bought their house and remodeled it into two units and rented out the downstairs for income. Then one day Terry made an offer on a house across town. They moved into it, rented both units at their old house, remodeled the new house, sold it for a profit, and moved back upstairs to their old house. They built the garage that Tommy and I trained in from the ground up, with help from Tommy and their friends. They were the ones who showed Tommy the cabin to buy, and even bought the cabin next to it, remodeled it, rented it, and then sold it.

This was the opposite of how I was raised. My dad built the back deck and a set of shelves, but both my parents had steady jobs with pensions and benefits, and they hired out big remodels. The Caldwells felt their way was more virtuous in their self-reliance, and I loved their attitude of sticking it to the man (or at least I loved it in a nice-girl-from-Davis way). Construction wasn't astrophysics. I just had to try hard and have an end goal in mind.

You also didn't have to be a man. When we were reroofing our cabin, Mike and Terry came over to help. The day was horrible—hot Estes summer, blinding sun, ninety degrees. The old roofing shingles were stuck together from twenty years in the elements, melted into each other and the house itself. I felt awful up there, even in my hat and slathered in a tube of sunscreen. Terry climbed up the rickety old metal ladder that we had pilfered from their garage and joined me. She grabbed one of the crowbars we had rented, got down on her knees, and started peeling off the weathered green shingles one piece at a time.

After about an hour, Terry said, "Michael, I don't feel well. I need to head down for a minute."

Tommy's dad said, "Okey dokey. Could you grab us some Diet Pepsi before you come back up?"

Terry climbed down the ladder, walked over to the trash full of old tar paper, threw up, and walked inside. A minute later she returned with Mike's soda. I stared at her. I was so impressed but also felt guilty and alarmed. She didn't need to be up here, doing this for us. This was terrible work, but it was our house and we were kids, and maybe she should just lie down on our couch with an ice pack on her head and relax? Tommy and his dad didn't even flinch. This was just the deal. Everyone contributed. It didn't matter who we were or how we felt. We just put our heads down and kept grinding out the work until we reached our end goal.

I placed my family pictures on the wooden bookshelf I'd brought from home. I printed and framed new photos of me and Tommy. I nested and organized meticulously, color coordinating our clothes on shelves and arranging our books from smallest to biggest. Tommy deferred to me on mealtimes, training times, the endless loop of Vivaldi in the CD player. I baked cookies and muffins that I never let myself eat. I put them in his backpack with notes that said, *I love you, can't wait to see you, be safe.*

Since Kyrgyzstan, the months of staying with one set of our parents or the other had sometimes felt like a long ellipsis. But now we had a clean page: our own home, a new story. Our cabin was a supersized dollhouse that I arranged and rearranged until I started to feel safe.

CHAPTER THIRTEEN

Kyrgyzstan, August 2000

I ran until I thought I'd arrived at the top of the hill—but it wasn't the top of the hill. It was just a boulder. We had run so far upward, and now it was getting dark and the sounds of the firefight below had finally stopped. Maybe whoever was shooting at us had run out of ammo. Maybe they just stopped because they couldn't see. Abdul got out his rug and prayed. He made Su pray too. They started talking among themselves. For a moment, I could breathe.

"Jesus, that was intense," someone, Jason or John, said. I couldn't tell, and it didn't matter. I was happy to be in a pack. The captors gave us Turat's sleeping bag. It was flannel on one side and green nylon on the other, and it smelled like him. Musty, unshowered, comforting. We lay directly on the ground, the flannel side against our bodies and the nylon facing the elements. Between the boys, under our flimsy cover, my body started to relax slightly. But then, as my nose rubbed against the flannel, I started to cry. I wanted to tell Turat that it was all going to be okay.

At some point during the night, two of our captors split off from our little group. I remember, when they left, thinking we would see them again. But we never did. In the morning, when it was almost light, the remaining two men jolted us awake. The stars had just started to soften. This used to be my favorite time of day.

We ran across the hillside and slightly down-canyon. When we reached the river, we stopped. They split us up: me with John, Tommy with Jason. I gathered that we had to hide from whoever had been shooting at us yesterday, and two small groups would make that easier. Before we split I took off the small Timex Ironman watch that my dad got me for Christmas and gave it to Tommy. It wasn't a gift. I just wanted to be less seen. I didn't want Abdul to notice my watch and then think he should brutalize me.

Tommy bit his lip as he walked off with Jason. It was what he always did when he was worried but thought he should be strong.

Abdul pointed for John and me to squeeze our bodies under a boulder right at the river's edge. I hoped the loud rush of the water would drown out the thoughts in my head, so I crawled to the very back of the narrow space, nearest to the river, and lay down. My head on a few small rocks and my nose mere inches from the bottom of the boulder. It was a coffin. I had no idea where Tommy and Jason had been taken, but John lay next to me. I was grateful.

The water smelled fresh and new and clean, and we just lay there for one hour, two, six, twelve? Time lost its meaning. When the sun got high the water level rose, our clothes got soaked and freezing, and my jaw ached from clenching my teeth. Right next to us, Abdul masturbated with a reed.

My mind fled. Food. Tommy. My parents. Warmth. I was so exhausted. I shivered up next to John, trying to get warm, to absorb his strength. My eyes burned from all the crying. I was scared to sleep and desperate not to be awake. I needed to be both alert and inured. What if another firefight broke out? What if they killed the boys and I woke up alone? I didn't even know where I was. I could never get home. When sleep became preferable to the swirling terror in my head, I willed myself to drift away, clutching John's arm.

At dusk we were allowed to climb out and stand up, and I saw that Tommy and Jason had been nearby all along. When the four of us gathered together I recoiled from Tommy's embrace. I could not look at his face. I felt too responsible for him. Each of us ate one half of a PowerBar—two bites and it was gone. We gave a PowerBar each to our captors too.

I smiled at them. I wanted them to like me.

CHAPTER FOURTEEN

Estes Park, Colorado, May 2001

In Estes, our days soon developed a pattern. We'd wake up and go for a walk: up past the dump, past the dozens of vacation homes, up to the glorious national park skyline, down to High Drive on the other side. Then we'd reverse the route home.

It was our time. We (I) liked routine. Life felt so organized and steady with Tommy. So safe. Every day he was his same stable, accepting self, his mood as constant as his long, straight nose. I brought the chaos, my emotions ricocheting like power-launched squash balls. If I'd binged on Wheat Thins and Oreos the night before, I'd be a mess, thrashing and kicking myself and Tommy in our bed, under the red flannel comforter that my mom had bought us. If I hadn't, I'd be sweet—grab Tommy's thick, strong hand and talk about our sunny future together: climbing plans, house plans, getting old.

For my first three weeks in Estes, we alternated each day between renovation work and climbing. On our climbing days, all I wanted to do at first was hike two miles to do the 5.7 route on Hallett Peak. It was high above the tree line, smelled like the crisp alpine tundra, and, best of all, there was no one around. I still hated climbing in the gym. I felt so heavy on the holds, felt people watching me. I hated myself and my body when I was there. But moving all day in the mountains both cleared my head and suppressed my hunger, and my number one goal was to shed all my ice-cream-and-burrito weight.

I wanted to fit back into my old life, the climber's life, and that meant fitting back into my old body. But some nights, back at the cabin, I couldn't handle my own hunger—it reminded me too much of Kyrgyzstan.

◆ ◆ ◆

After a few more weeks, I was a few pounds lighter. I decided that meant I had myself together enough to drive down to Boulder and train, though I still insisted that we go in the middle of the day, when the gym was empty. I was embarrassed to climb in front of other people, especially at the Boulder Rock Club, where sponsors were always lurking and almost everybody was an industry somebody.

There, we did lap after lap, up and down, up and down, until we were both destroyed. We'd do our final reps to failure, until our fingers hurt so much we could barely tie our shoes.

When we got back to Estes, I always wanted to drive straight to Mike's garage—I knew if we stopped at home first we might not make it back out of the house, and I'd hate myself for that. In the sweat-and-granite-dust paste we'd first waste ourselves on the bouldering wall—making up problems for each other, listening to rap music at full volume, bouncing down onto the old mattresses we used for crash pads.

"Come on, honey!" Tommy yelled when my fingers started to open up. I loved it when he did this. It motivated me to tense my whole body and latch on to the next hold. As soon as I crashed onto the mattresses, exhausted, I could not wait to go again.

After bouldering, we worked on our fingers. For me this meant system training, focused on specific types of handholds and body positions, on the smaller wall Tommy had made just for me. Using it was a little like learning to type (F-F-F-F, F-D-F-D), or like practicing a tennis forehand over and over again in front of a ball machine: you might never have that exact angle in a match, but the repetitive training would prepare you. I'd practice on tiny crimp holds, wrapping my thumb over the tip of my index finger on one hand, and then the other, holding on one-handed for three sets of ten seconds on each side. Then I'd move on to the next type of hold, and the next.

Meanwhile, Tommy campused, which is like doing an inverted stair workout only using arms and hands. Using a wooden ladder-type contraption hanging from the ceiling, we'd climb from rung to rung, using only our upper bodies, feet dangling. Even in my fittest days I could never campus. Tommy was like a freight train when he did it, shaking the entire board and breathing so loudly it sounded like he was hyperventilating. We talked while we hung there. Should we run tomorrow? Should we tear down a wall? What color tiles should we use for the backsplash? Did he like those muffins I baked for him? Tommy always said yes.

Next, pull-ups. My goal was to do fifty in at most five sets. Tommy cranked out over a hundred, his breath loud at both the top and bottom of each. He could do twenty, easily, in a row.

Then, to finish, weights: triceps, chest, biceps, abs, and fingers on Mike's beastly Finger Machine. We'd made up this train-to-obliteration routine on our own, with no science or rationale to back it beyond the fact that it made us happy and produced fairly good results. Back then, climbers didn't have access to cutting-edge research to help us perform, and now, I look back and cringe at how we punished our bodies. By dinnertime we'd have trained for seven hours. After pasta or burritos, we'd cue up a movie and lie down on our slanted floor. Usually we'd fall asleep in each other's arms and at some point wake up and stumble to our futon.

I only knew one path to success as a female climber: smile for the camera, always say yes and be grateful—for the opportunity, for the photo shoot, for the free gear—and work harder than anyone else. I had all the incentives I needed to get back there, back to where I'd been before Kyrgyzstan. So the additional pressure we received from Mike was unwanted, unnecessary. The inevitable criticisms would arrive each month, as regular as the climbing magazines in the mailbox. If neither Tommy nor I was prominently featured, his father expressed his concerns. "What's this route that Dave did? Is it harder than Kryptonite?" he'd ask. "What's he doing that you're not?"

It sometimes seemed like Mike was trying to live out all his own dreams of athletic stardom, of climbing greatness, through Tommy—through us. And at the same time, living vicariously frustrated him: he'd been Tommy's climbing partner, once. I knew it had to be hard for Mike to watch Tommy leave him behind—not in terms of envying his talent; he was always genuinely thrilled by Tommy's achievements. But Tommy reaching that level meant finding new climbing partners, and once I came along, Mike had been truly, fully displaced. That chafed, and he let us know that he felt like he wasn't enough of a priority. He wanted Tommy to climb hard, but he also wanted Tommy to climb with him. It felt like we couldn't win.

Being laid into for not doing enough made me angry. Tommy's acceptance of it, his refusal to defend us, or me, made me angrier. That was just how Mike showed his love, Tommy would explain. This was his dad's way of trying to help us. Then he would smile and nod, letting the criticisms and the demands wash over him. And the next day he'd train harder. We'd learned we could endure more than we thought possible, endure more than we ever had on our hardest climbs, and his upbringing had primed him to embrace the trauma-as-strength narrative. And so now he knew what to do. He'd pour himself into climbing. We'd be a team, stronger together.

I had no vision of what my life should be, not anymore. So I went with his.

◆ ◆ ◆

All that summer, we trained hard. Sometimes I binged, sometimes I fasted, and some of the ice-cream-and-burrito weight came off. But I didn't have it in me yet to start chasing any notable ascents—to get my career back on track. Tommy sent a route called the Honeymoon Is Over, a 5.13c that sits at fourteen thousand feet in the Colorado alpine, with me supporting him on belay. That was a good day: twenty-two hours from leaving the car to returning again, and although the route was Tommy's, I had my own small victory: I ate only one perfectly quartered apple all day.

In early September 2001, we were hired to chaperone two kids on the Nose—a ten- and a thirteen-year-old, at the time the youngest people ever to climb El Cap. Our job was to keep them safe while the filmmakers shot some footage. That trip was one of my least favorite times on El Cap—it just felt so forced. After three days on the wall, we drove back to my parents' house for a few nights. My quads almost gave out when I climbed out of bed on our first morning in Davis. The first hike off El Cap each season always destroyed my legs.

I made myself a cup of tea and went to sit with my parents while they got ready for work. I always loved watching my dad tie his tie and my mom blow-dry her hair. As usual their room smelled like a mix of shampoo and mocha coffee. I should have noticed, even before I entered, that both my parents kept walking to the back of the bedroom to look at the television, which was not part of their routine. Their faces tensed when they saw me approach. I was doing okay lately, sort of. Tommy and I had installed new windows and new doors in the cabin.

My parents said nothing. They just kept looking at the screen. Then I saw it too: the building engulfed in black smoke and flames, the inset pictures of a field and the Pentagon.

"Sweetie," my dad started. The announcers were talking about terrorists; there were words on the screen, names I recognized from an attack on a US navy ship a year before. Osama bin Laden. Al Qaeda.

After we made it home, we had learned a little about the group that had captured us. The Islamic Movement of Uzbekistan hadn't cared about Kyrgyzstan at all: when we crossed their path, they'd been cutting across from their bases in Tajikistan to mount an invasion of

Uzbekistan, intending to overthrow the president there. They hadn't gotten far in their attempt; they were a small group, but, I'd learned, they had some powerful allies. Osama bin Laden. Al Qaeda. And now those allies were here.

I should have stayed on El Cap, I thought as my heart rate accelerated. I tried to hang on to the memory: the birds, the frogs, the walls, the cracks, the rock, the sounds . . . But the images on the screen cut through. A sour, curdling fear burned in my chest and in my teeth. The saliva in my mouth overflowed.

"They don't really know what it is—it's an attack of some sort. They aren't sure who caused it, but they think they know . . ."

I tried to listen, but—Tommy. I needed to go make sure Tommy was safe. *What if they're coming to get him next? What if they've gotten to him already? Did I lock the window? Did my parents lock the front door? Is he still in bed? Could they have dragged him out through the bathroom window?*

I ran out of my parents' room and into my own. I burst through the door, my palms sweating and my face covered in tears. I expected to see an empty bed, signs of struggle. But there Tommy was, lit up by the sunlight streaming through the window, mouth open, snoring loudly, still asleep.

I ran over and shook him awake, shouting, "There's been an attack! I'm sure they are coming for us next—they have to be. We have to hide! We have to do something!"

He blinked and stared at me, half-awake, confused, clueless. I ran back into my parents' room and told my mother she could not go to work at the university today.

"Bethy," she said, "I think my work would be a very unlikely target."

CHAPTER FIFTEEN

Kyrgyzstan, August 2000

On the second night, or maybe the third, they took us to a natural rock amphitheater. We sat on a log and some smaller boulders, and I wondered who had dragged the seats together. Happiness seemed like such a distant idea. I held my half of a PowerBar in my hand. It was too cold for the chocolate to melt, but I was still careful that no precious calories got lost. It felt so naive and hopeful to me that, just yesterday, I'd eaten my bar quickly. I thought I'd have more food. Already I could feel my ribs through my shirt. I held the brick of mashed-up powders and chalky chocolate and slowly ate away at it, like I used to watch my pet hamster do.

The air felt heavy, the humidity soaked into all the cracks and crevices of our clothes, the openings and weaknesses that I wanted to fill with warmth. I wished I had my blue-and-black down jacket. Why hadn't I grabbed that one? I stared at the moon, so bright it cast shadows from the trees, and I tried to focus on the smell of pine trees to get over the stench of Abdul. He was fifteen feet away but I could smell him still. I ran my cold fingers over my hip bones through the mesh inside pocket of my pants. My clothes felt heavier in the evenings.

Abdul and Su gestured to us that one of them would try to find a sheep and kill it for food. I couldn't fathom another death. I felt in my pocket. We still had a few more bars, enough to last another day or two.

Surely, I imagined, the marines would save us by then. That was what happened, right? How these predicaments were resolved? A whispered command, night-vision goggles, shots, and a dramatic rescue. But what if the marines didn't come? It had become obvious that our captors had no real plan. We were like strange jewels they had stumbled upon: they didn't quite know what to do with us, but they knew we were valuable, so they wouldn't let us go. What if this was going to be our lives for whatever was left of them? What would we do when winter came? What would we do when our energy bars ran out?

I looked at John and Jason and Tommy. John had become my warmth and strength the past few days. I had so much appreciation for him. For the distracting conversations, for making me feel an ounce of safety in a dire situation. Then I remembered climbing the Rostrum with Jason, how easygoing he was, how he always made a joke whenever he could. I wondered how he would look, frozen in the snow. Would I be scared to look up past his boots too? I glanced at Tommy, then away. I didn't want to picture him frozen in snow, hear his teeth chattering. I was the reason he was here, the reason he was suffering. How would I tell his parents?

Maybe eating a slaughtered sheep wouldn't be so bad. The sour and startling smell of a butcher shop I'd once visited in Austria came back to me, all that raw meat just hanging there. And then the scream of the zebu we'd seen killed in Madagascar, sacrificed in our honor. The sound had only lasted for a second or two, until its blood started pouring out of its neck. Would the sheep scream, if Abdul found it? Would he try and skin its wool coat? Would it be warm? Would he share it with us? My mind churned, all questions and no good answers.

In the end, he came back empty-handed.

CHAPTER SIXTEEN

Estes Park, Colorado, October 2001

I missed being in control. I missed feeling like my body, my life, my decisions were mine. I didn't have the language for it then, but on some level I could feel that, too often, I was still reacting to the trauma of Kyrgyzstan. I wanted to act, not react. I wanted to truly be as *fine* as I always claimed to be.

Tommy and I never talked about it. We would talk about the business side of things: the book money, the interview we had to do with another TV show, the movie rights, the new script that had come in. (We called it the *Hey, baby* script because every time my character addressed Tommy, she started with "Hey, baby.") But the actual Kyrgyzstan trip? The nightmares, the flashbacks, the paranoia I still struggled to contain? Maybe we were scared to talk about it, or embarrassed. Maybe Tommy was over it. He seemed like he was okay, he always said he was okay—but then again, so did I. These were intimate details that maybe a couple could—should—talk about, but we didn't.

By late October I knew I needed some semblance of normal. My collapse on 9/11 showed how far I still was from getting there. My six insurance-approved therapy sessions earlier in the year had gotten rid of the regular nightmares, but they didn't even begin to scratch the surface of everything else that was going on. My eating was out of control. I'd binge for days in a row, until I felt so distended I would burp sulfur burps because I was literally making myself sick. I knew I was going to hate myself, hate how I felt, hate Tommy, hate the world, but I couldn't stop. I hated that feeling too.

We never really talked about the problem, but we'd talk about the solution: the exercise. That became a love language for us. Tommy hated seeing me so unhappy, I hated being so unhappy; the fix was clearly to exercise myself into oblivion so that I'd feel better.

Tommy had goals, I had goals, but they all seemed so far off right now, so out of reach. I needed a bridge, so I decided to try the Sphinx Crack in the South Platte of Colorado. The South Platte has a much starker kind of beauty than Yosemite. There are no big trees or shade. The rocks are all rounded and yellow-white-gold. It looks almost like another planet, remote and vast and strange.

The Sphinx Crack is a completely manufactured route. A long, pretty splitter crack that runs diagonally through a huge, yellowish boulder, it looks like a Hollywood ideal of a rock climb. It was created when the Colorado School of Mines blew it up back in the 1970s, which should probably have put a stain to its name, but oddly enough the explosives created an amazing climb that seems quite natural. It was doable as a day trip from our cabin in Estes, it was only one pitch with a short approach, easy to set a toprope on, and I was almost guaranteed no one else would be on it to see me trying. I hoped the project would feel like someone was holding my hand: a gentle on-ramp back into climbing hard.

My body felt foreign as I started up, like I was wearing a weight vest when I pulled on the rock. My hands felt tender and tore instantly. Rolls of stomach skin spilled over the top of my harness; I hated myself, tucked them back in, hoping they would disappear if I couldn't see them. Each time I pulled on a hold it was shocking, like picking up a huge cardboard box I'd thought was full of pillows but instead was full of books. My brain remembered what had been forged into it for the past seven years: light, snappy, strong muscle and arm responses. If I had to get used to this box full of books I might quit.

After a few attempts, I slumped back into the passenger seat of the van. The backsides of both my hands were bleeding from being jammed into the crack. Normally after a Valley season my skin would have been hardened, resilient. My feet hurt too, my toes no longer used to being cramped inside of tight climbing shoes and shoved into vertical crevices in granite. But the pain felt like I was actually doing something with my life again, instead of floating, wallowing, like I had for the past fifteen months. I felt like I had a purpose.

The next morning I woke up feeling like my body had been through a blender and then through a pasta-making machine, like it was torn up and flattened all at once. I smiled, soaking in the pain. This was what I remembered; this feeling was as close to heaven as I could be. Sure, I couldn't do half the moves on the route, and it would take at least a week for the scabs on the back of my hands to heal, but maybe, maybe, I could start to feel like a climber again.

A week later, when my skin was healed, we drove back to the Sphinx. This time I was prepared and taped my hands. I had an elaborate taping routine that I had perfected in Yosemite. First, I'd coat my hands with Mueller Pre-Tape Spray (like a mild liquid glue, in an aerosol can). Then I took various lengths of athletic tape and placed them in a specific pattern: three full-width pieces on the back of each hand, one around the meat of my thumb, and three tiny strips around the base of my fingers, overlapping the strips on the back of my hand. Finally I'd carefully wrap tape around my entire hand, trying not to get too much on my palm where I needed contact to climb. By the end I resembled a boxer about to enter the ring.

My next attempt on the route was so different, so much better, than my first. I began to remember how to decode a route, how I thought of it as an entire puzzle instead of just small pieces to conquer. My mom loves jigsaw puzzles, and the first thing she always does is lay out all the pieces and find the corners and edges; then she slowly works through the colors and shapes. I love a good puzzle too.

I reminded myself that each piece was instrumental to the send, to try and take the victories when I had them, to remember that even figuring out to turn my big toe another 15 degrees upward was a success. My fingers started to remember how to jam in the crack of the rock. My skin started to get tougher, able to squish and squeeze and hold my body weight without ripping. By the end of the second day I had done all the moves. I felt lighter than I had in months.

Slowly my mind filled up with the puzzle of the Sphinx Crack, forcing out the wandering thoughts that would bring me to the edge of nightmares. It was always the puzzle I had loved best, the thing that set climbing apart from every other sport I'd tried. On my third day, I led the route with two falls, which meant I placed all the gear in the crack and I only fell twice before reaching the top. I needed to climb it all in one go, with no falls, to be able to claim a free ascent—the first female ascent. I dangled on the rope at the end of the climb and noticed my stomach rolls weren't folding over my harness anymore. The past two weeks of climbing and focus had actually worked. I liked how I felt: it was familiar and sane and controlled and known. I wanted more of this. My breath came fast and my arms were tired, but I felt at home.

A few more rest days, another training session in the garage, and I was ready to send. We pulled up in the van. I cinched down my harness, at least an inch tighter than on my first day on the route—a victory in itself, I thought. I tied into the end of the rope and felt the familiar butterflies in my stomach. My tape job was perfect: not too tight, not too loose. Besides, I knew the jams well enough that I might not even need the tape, my hands nestling into their places like pulling on a favorite pair of jeans.

I started climbing. It felt like running downhill with a wind at my back. My mind was quiet, and my body felt like it had a choreographed dance to follow, seamless and without friction. What a treat. I was wedging my fingers in tight, sharp constrictions, and it put a smile on my face. Compared to the dark pathways where my mind had lingered over the past year and a half, bleeding fingers and the crisp, dry Colorado wind seemed like a vacation.

Partway up, I could feel the lactic acid starting to burn, and I paused. There's a point that I think of as the normal-person stopping point, when I am short of breath, when my lungs are on fire, when my arms ache and my fingers start opening, when any sane person stops running, stops climbing, knowing they pushed hard, they got a good workout in, they made improvements. But I could go further, sometimes. When it was time to send, I could access another well of energy, my reserve. It was probably what propelled me in those last hours of captivity, when I didn't want to go any farther, when I just wanted to give up, but then found I could run for hours, run literally on empty.

I tried not to let my mind wander to Kyrgyzstan. I shook my hands behind my back, stretched my fingers on my legs, and got some recovery. I started climbing again, breathing methodically. My hands wanted to open, wanted to fail, and if I had been on a normal climb without a crack I would have fallen: my fingers wouldn't have been able to stay closed and grip the holds. But there's a special type of pain, a special type of fatigue, with crack climbing, because your hand is literally wedged in the rock: no place to go. It doesn't matter that your hands are failing you, because they are stuck until you pull them out and place them higher. It results in an even higher level of fatigue and more massive pump (as we climbers call forearm fatigue) that burns and stings and aches all at the same time. That pain was my specialty.

The last thirty feet of the climb, I felt like each move was my last. By the time I pulled over the top, all I could do was lie on the golden slab, panting and moaning and groaning. My fingers were so tired, my forearms so full of acid, I couldn't even untie my rope. I was destroyed but so happy. I had forgotten how much of a sweet escape a hundred feet of rock could be. My waist was tiny, my mind was full of climbing. Tommy was right. The more I could do this, the happier and saner I would feel.

The climb gave me a professional boost too. My picture landed in the magazines, alongside the first articles about one of my climbing accomplishments since Kyrgyzstan. For several months, around this time, I had been asking one of my sponsors for a raise: from $200 to $500 a month. They had always evaded the question, found some subtle way to dodge or say no without outright shutting me down. Shortly after I sent the Sphinx, we were on a road trip near their offices and stopped in. I figured, why not ask one more time? Tommy came along with me. And this time, as he sat in the room, watching while I made my request, they said yes.

I'd known since Lurking Fear that being partnered with Tommy could bring advantages, privileges that other female climbers didn't have. But I also knew he couldn't prop me up indefinitely. I had done the Sphinx for me, to get my career and my dreams back on track. I hoped that this ascent would start to drown out the media coverage of Kyrgyzstan. I wasn't proud of Kyrgyzstan, didn't want to be known for Kyrgyzstan. I wanted to be known for my climbing. Maybe if I just kept piling on hard ascents, they would bury all the news about the kidnapping. Would people lift up a dozen, a hundred, a thousand blankets to see what color the bottom one was? Probably not. This was the first blanket I'd put over Kyrgyzstan.

CHAPTER SEVENTEEN

Estes Park, Colorado, November 2001

Just a few weeks later, I was on the phone with my mom when I heard Tommy scream. I'd heard that scream exactly once before. It began after he pushed Su and stopped when we engulfed his trembling body.

I dropped the phone and heard it crash on the newly tiled kitchen floor. I had only been gone a minute. When I left, Tommy had been ripping wood with his parents' table saw to build a platform for our new washer and dryer—we were getting our own, finally adults. I'd just ducked inside to get us some chips and salsa. Now I sprinted back.

"My finger, my finger!" Tommy was yelling, full throttle, holding his hand, which was covered in blood. "I fucking cut off my finger!"

The table saw was still running, the blade hissing away. I unplugged the machine. "It's going to be okay, it's going to be okay," I yelled, trying to drown out Tommy. I spotted the finger in a pile of sawdust, just resting there, like it was its own autonomous being. It was his left index finger. I picked it up. It was warm. It felt like Tommy's hand.

Inside, the phone I'd dropped beeped incessantly. I grabbed a clean cloth so Tommy could compress the wound, found the phone, hung it up, then dialed 911. It seemed to take forever for the dispatcher to answer, and then he kept asking questions like "Is he breathing? Is he lucid?" We were having two wildly different conversations. I asked if I should put Tommy's finger on ice, if I should put any water in the bag with it. The dispatcher asked me, "Can he stand on his own?" I dropped the finger in a ziplock baggie with water and ice, told the dispatcher we were leaving for the hospital, and hung up on him. Then I shoved Tommy in the Civic, a towel on his hand, the finger in the center console.

As I sped to the Estes Park hospital I kept telling Tommy to compress the stump. The towel was bright red after sixty seconds. I felt like he'd cut off his leg. Climbing was Tommy's life, his happiness. If he lost climbing, what would he have? What would we have together? I stroked his hair as I sped through town. "You are going to be fine. It's going to be okay. They can do amazing things now, honey. They are amazing at what they do." I was babbling, totally unsure what I was talking about, but Tommy had stopped speaking, his terror now internal. It had been an exhausting year.

The doctors in Estes Park bandaged Tommy up to stop the bleeding and immediately sent us on to Fort Collins. No offer of an ambulance ride, no helicopter, no police escort. Just: "Here's the address of the hospital—they'll have your referral in their system." Didn't they know how dire this was? It took an hour to get there. We drove in silence, Tommy's finger still between us, my mind racing. What would the doctors be able to do? Oh my God, what if Tommy couldn't climb anymore? What would he do? What would *I* do?

Tommy happened to be on the cover of *Rock and Ice* magazine that month. I always hated Mike's boasting, but now I thought the magazine cover might help. The doctors needed to know how important Tommy's finger was.

That afternoon a hand surgeon tried to reattach the finger by pinning the bones. Four days later, after the first surgery didn't work, a plastic surgeon performed another surgery. Tommy's artery reattached just fine, but his veins were overwhelmed. Blood just pooled in his finger but couldn't flow out. I spiraled: blaming myself, one minute, for adding water to the baggie, and blaming that 911 operator the next. Nurses removed his nail to give the blood more room. They placed leeches, real live leeches, on the tip of his finger. The plastic surgeon did a vein graft. Nothing worked.

Tommy had lost so much blood he needed two transfusions. I knew a climber whose dad had died of AIDS from a tainted blood transfusion. I felt like I was back in the Amsterdam airport again, scanning for threats—and here was one, barreling toward us.

"Um, well, what's the, um, chances of, you know . . ." I paused, hoping the nurse would fill in the embarrassing blank for me. She didn't. "You know, the chance of disease spreading, like AIDS or something?"

I felt so ashamed and paranoid. I knew my thinking was wrong—and bad. But I needed to know; I needed to keep Tommy safe.

"Well," she said, "it's extremely unlikely, very, very unlikely. Let's just say it's as rare as getting struck by lightning."

My breath caught in my lungs. Our friend Topher's dad had been struck by lightning. Another friend had been struck too. Odds were no comfort to me, not when we seemed to be so cursed. Could I give blood to Tommy? Or his parents? We ran the tests. None of us had the right type.

To regain control, I made up the pullout sofa chair next to Tommy's hospital bed. I only left to eat one meal per day, always at the Olive Garden. I told myself that if I organized his room very neatly, just like I organized our home, Tommy would heal faster. His finger would stay on.

My mom cashed in her sick leave, flew to Colorado, and got us a hotel room near the hospital so I could sleep in a bed and still be near Tommy. She was a pro at hospitals and doctors after seeing my dad through a near-fatal cancer early in their marriage, navigating the system under life-and-death circumstances. The stakes were much lower for Tommy's finger—but to us, it felt nearly as critical. The problem, the surgeons explained, was that Tommy had such incredible circulation in his hands. He'd always had a sort of superpower when he climbed in the cold: his blood would stay in his hands, keeping them warm and functional. But now that same blood was pooling in his injured finger. After the leeches failed, nurses attached a catheter and let blood drip out for a week.

I read Tommy the first Harry Potter book as he passed in and out of consciousness from the morphine. I wished we'd gone to the gym that day instead of working on the house. This was all my fault: if I had taken my training more seriously, if I hadn't flaked on going to the gym, Tommy wouldn't have been anywhere near that saw. I tried to pray. I prayed to God, any god. *Please listen to how much Tommy needs his finger to reattach. Please listen to how much we need to go back to normal. Please don't throw any more disasters in our path.* The last time I'd prayed was in Kyrgyzstan, to save our lives.

I felt selfish, only praying when I needed something. I felt like a bad Christian. I berated myself for quitting Sunday school. If I'd stayed, I thought, I'd know how to pray. I'd have faith. I should have convinced Tommy to attend church in Davis or to find a church in Estes. I'd asked about it, over and over since Kyrgyzstan, and we'd gone once, but he'd found it far too judgmental. And now look where we were. If we were church people, I thought, clutching for a reason, this would not have happened.

After a couple weeks we left the hospital, Tommy without an index finger on his left hand. But he had not forgotten the lesson he'd applied again and again after Kyrgyzstan: trauma could propel a person to bigger and better things. He became a rehab maniac, and even before his stitches came out, he started climbing again. Six weeks later, he was doing boulder problems.

My success on the Sphinx Crack had convinced me to get on board with his approach. No more wallowing: climbing was the way forward. Excelling, together, was the way forward.

Normally I like to take my time with a new project. Some climbers specialize in onsighting, meaning free climbing a route all in one go, with no falls and no resting on the rope, without any information or practice ahead of time. That hadn't been my style since I was young and on the competition scene: I wanted to hang on the rope, stick my nose up against the rock, examine the holds, and find my way slowly before I went for the real send. But after Tommy's accident, after everything that had happened, I was in a hurry. Later that winter, I did the first female ascent of Grand Illusion, a dark granite crack near Sugarloaf that was rated 5.13c—it was famous for being the first 5.13c in the country. And in the spring, I climbed the Phoenix, rated 5.13a, a proud, gorgeous line that splits a headwall above Yosemite's Upper Cascade Falls. It was the first—and, so far, still the only—female onsight ascent. I was back on track, and so was Tommy. The doctors had told him his climbing career was over, but that same spring, six months after the accident, he free climbed El Cap in a day.

CHAPTER EIGHTEEN

Kyrgyzstan, August 2000

Another dawn meant another hiding place. Abdul found a big rock and shoved John and me under there and put pine needles on top of us to hide us more. I spooned with John. He felt warm and safe. Like an adult. I could feel my ribs starting to jut out more, and I thought it would be good for my climbing: I'd be light, I could send hard routes. I found something like comfort, some measure of control, in my hunger. And then I hated myself for thinking that. I asked John if he thought they were going to kill us. I asked him to analyze the situation. He was so good at redirecting my thoughts, answering quickly and then moving on. He asked me to talk about my favorite meals, my childhood home. I told him about the Caesar salad from Dos Coyotes. I told him about my brother, who'd gotten nearly perfect scores on the SAT and had started taking math classes at UC Davis while he was still in high school.

This time at dusk everyone's cheekbones were more pronounced. I tried to remember how to move. It felt foreign. Walking at night felt wrong. We were just blindly following our captors, vaguely traversing down-valley. I thought I saw more armed men hiding behind the trees in the moonlight. The grass was getting more brittle, less lush. I tried to appreciate my feet beneath me. I wanted to stretch my arms as wide as they could, but I didn't want to be seen. I tried to listen for other animals that were out—the crickets, the rustling. If we'd been there alone, just the four of us, it would have almost been magical. I could not get Cat Stevens's "Moonshadow" out of my head. When that faded for a moment I tried to replace it with Bob Marley's "No Woman, No Cry" and "Three Little Birds." I wished I'd memorized more songs.

Before we'd left our camp, on that first day of captivity, we had all submerged our faces in the river and opened our mouths and guzzled as much water as we could hold. It was funny to think that even hours earlier, we would have painstakingly filtered that water before taking a sip. Now, every night as we walked, we drank from any stream or puddle that we crossed, no matter how black and muddy, how crusted its surface was with dead bugs. Jason told me that when I cried, I was just wasting water.

During the days, hiding with John, I was profoundly, shamefully relieved not to be with Tommy. If I were with Tommy, I thought, I would have to take care of him, and I could not even handle myself. I kept seeing Tommy's mother. I kept seeing his dad's bravado. I had begged The North Face to let him come on this trip. Now we were here. Abdul packed us in, covering the opening between the rock and the ground with pine boughs. He stood outside sometimes and other times masturbated without leaving our hiding spot, and then he got cold and spooned with us. When he was especially tired and lazy he just masturbated in place. I tried to focus on John, tried to focus on John's warmth.

I thought about my dog, Steffi. Was she scared when she died? Did Su, Tommy and Jason's captor, spoon with them? Did he masturbate? Did he stink? Did the hairs on the backs of their necks stand up when he put his arms around them?

I only ever slept for an hour or two at a time. At least, that was how it felt. I had no true concept of time since I had given Tommy my watch. Each time I drifted away, it could have been for five minutes or seven hours. But when I woke I always had the false sense that this had all been a dream and that I was really in the lumpy bed of Tommy's van or on my thin Therm-A-Rest in my Civic. It would be safe there, and warm.

John answered my questions about what would happen to us with questions of his own, usually about home, my family. *What are their names again? Your parents? Tell me about your grandparents, what is their story?* I remembered Granny's smell. It was sweet, but with sophistication to it, like she knew what was right and proper. Always dressed well, always the host if needed. My mind went to her house, in South Carolina. Her black leather dining chairs with the backs that swiveled. I'd get in trouble for spinning them over and over again. It was warm in South Carolina; I wanted to be warm. He asked me about my brother and any pets I had. I thought about Steffi, about her soft fur. I wanted to nuzzle my head into that fur instead of these fist-sized rocks that were poking into my skull and felt like they would break through my skin at any moment. John moved closer to me. I was so thankful. My body was quivering uncontrollably. The water that seeped out of the damp ground where we lay had started to soak my back. I tried to remember if my T-shirt was cotton. "Cotton kills" kept looping in my head, that familiar saying about why you should never wear cotton in the mountains—once wet, it's freezing. I knew my outer layers were synthetic, but was my T-shirt? What was I even wearing?

John told me about his family too. I asked about the color of their hair, how tall they were, how old. I wanted to feel like I was standing right next to them in Texas, feel the warmth of the sun, taste a burrito. In between all these conversations we'd catch a nap here and there. Like I was rushed to sleep, like I knew I needed it. But lying there awake, minutes felt like days, just waiting for something to change. We still had no idea who our captors were or what their goal or mission might be. We were just waiting for them to kill us or free us or bring us food or give us a blanket or rape me, or for another firefight to break out.

In the nights, as we walked, Jason and John had started talking quietly about how they were going to kill our captors. The idea seemed unreal, impossible. I knew I could keep suffering, keep shivering and hiking and starving, almost indefinitely. But attacking armed men? Suffering seemed safer. So I didn't engage with the conversation, just let their talk slide off me. Instead, my mind looped on every way I'd ever been awful. Why was I so competitive? Why did I have some urge to one-up my mom? Why had I felt so smug when I turned my back on her to board the plane? Right now she was probably at work, in one of her green suits, beneath a poster I'd given her that read *To the greatest mom in the world.* Granny was probably playing bridge, with Peter Jennings on in the background.

I felt myself sinking. I just let go. I stood on the steep grassy hillside and couldn't walk anymore. I told the boys to leave me behind. I was done—destroyed, consumed by fear and hunger and fatigue. It wasn't a bad place to die, I supposed. Some might even think it was idyllic and beautiful. And it was a relief for it to be over. Jason had said we needed to seem strong, and like we were on their side, so they would trust us. But it was okay to cry now. I wanted the tears to come. This was an appropriate time to weep—the end of my life.

But nothing came out. I thought I would just sink into the hillside. The boys tried to get me to come back, to keep going. Tommy said he couldn't live without me. He said I was the strongest woman he knew, which I knew was bullshit. I was not a woman, I was a girl, and I was not strong. They carried me, physically, down the hillside for a while, and then they put me down. I smiled and said, "Just go on without me."

John said there was food at the hut down the hill. Just make it five more steps. I made it five more steps. Then he said it again. And again. When I got down I felt like I'd made it to the other side, gone through the worst. But there was no food.

CHAPTER NINETEEN

Estes Park, Colorado, February 2002

"Hey, which CD has that song you really like by Eric somebody?" Tommy never put on music. We had just driven home to the cabin after a Valentine's dinner in Boulder.

A minute later he was down on one knee, biting his lip, while we listened to Eric Clapton's "Wonderful Tonight." I acted surprised. I wanted to be surprised. But we had looked at rings in my parents' favorite jewelry store over Christmas, and I'd seen the UPS envelope from my parents to Tommy earlier that week. My parents never mailed anything to Tommy. Plus, it was Valentine's Day.

"You're the best thing that ever happened to me," he said. He always said the sweetest, corniest things to me, and meant them. "Will you marry me?" It had been a year and a half since the kidnapping. We were twenty-one and twenty-three years old—still just skinny, calloused, earnest, wounded kids.

I tousled Tommy's hair and asked him to stand up. It just felt too weird to get down on the floor too. We celebrated our engagement by watching HGTV, eating organic Honey Nut O's, and snuggling on the couch. Then we fell asleep in our bed instead of passing out on the floor like we did at the end of so many training days. There was no sex. We barely ever had sex, and that was another thing we never talked about.

That next morning I looked at my ring and felt embarrassed: real climbers didn't bother with normal things like marriage, mostly. I was glad to have an excuse to take it off when we drove down to Boulder to climb at the gym.

But if I was going to get married, I was going to do it right. I would make it perfect, and then we would be perfect. So now, every night, I looked at bridal magazines. I'd only ever put on dresses rarely, spitefully, and under pressure. Now I obsessed over gowns. I studied and categorized dresses I liked by fabric, neckline, and cut. I thought if I could find the perfect dress it would release a cache of perfect feelings, the missing pieces of my life suddenly materializing after my achievement, like a reward for completing a level in a video game.

The first place I called for an appointment was one of those bridal superstores. Saturday at 10:00 a.m. in Sacramento. I wore my baggy Verve climbing shorts and oversized white Sportiva T-shirt. A receptionist checked me, Mom, and Granny in, like I'd arrived for a medical procedure.

"Rodden in room four for a flower-girl dress," the attendant said as she showed us to a dressing room. My face flushed red. I knew I looked young, like a teenager at best, but couldn't she at least give me bridesmaid?

I could hear, in the nine other dressing rooms, the nine other wives-to-be gabbing with their girlfriends about their fiancés. I felt like I was back in high school, eavesdropping on the popular girls. I hunched low in my chair.

When the attendant reappeared, I said, "Actually, I'm here for a wedding dress." She stared at me, then at my mom, then at Granny, like we should all be ashamed because clearly I was a child bride.

"I'm afraid we don't have anything that would fit," she said. I wasn't quite back down to my fighting weight of ninety-five pounds, but I had lost most of the post-Kyrgyzstan pudge. "Most of the sample dresses are size eight." For my senior prom, my last major dress-buying occasion, I had worn a 000. To cover up my mortification I pulled out my organized folder of clippings, with sticky notes attached to them. I felt very mature about my clippings until I noticed they were all wrinkled and covered in chalk.

The attendant flipped through them professionally. A few minutes later she returned with a few samples she'd managed to find that might come close. My mom helped me into one of them, gathering up all the extra fabric and pinning it back with clothespins. I still looked like I was wearing a sleeping bag.

I asked to try a few more. "This is the one that Monica wears in *Friends*," the attendant said when she returned. "It's one of our most popular styles."

I saw another bride-to-be trying it on. She looked so confident and grown-up with makeup on. I'd literally never looked in the mirror and seen a woman. I shook my head to my mom, and we walked out of the store.

Getting engaged formalized our personal partnership, but our professional one had already leaped forward. We were BethandTommy now. We were welded at the hip. We did everything together, and not just in the sense that we were a couple; we were each other's best friends, climbing partners, business partners. We had a film made about us called *The First Couple of Rock*—a label that was both embarrassing and validating. (That was the dream, after all, being recognized for our climbing exploits instead of the worst thing that ever happened to us.) Any hint of the separate lives we'd led before had vanished. I only climbed with Tommy, Tommy only climbed with me. We'd see our parents and people at the gym, but always as one unit. We had one email address and one phone number for us both.

We had a slideshow we presented at climbing events. In a way, we had embraced the narrative that I had found so alienating, so meaningless, when we first made it home: *Dude, what an epic!* Now we shared our achievements and a positive message: *We got kidnapped, it was terrifying, we escaped. And we're now better, tougher climbers because of it.*

CHAPTER TWENTY

Kyrgyzstan, August 2000

It was our sixth day of captivity. We were in a cave beneath a truck-sized boulder next to the raging Kara-Su River, only a short distance from our original camp. Our captors had driven us in a giant circle, running and hiding and running again. John and I tried to sleep huddled together. Abdul, as always, joined us.

Near dusk, Abdul got up. His beard peeled away from my skin. When John and I came out from under the boulder, the air was cold. Jason was talking frantically to Tommy about his escape plans.

I went over to a tree, pulled down my pants to pee, and saw a deep-maroon stain in my underwear. It wasn't too large of an area yet, but I was totally confused. I had just had my period at the beginning of the trip, so why was I bleeding now? What was wrong with my body? Was it cancer? A tumor? Was I dying? I started crying. I walked out from behind the tree, and Jason said, "Are you wasting water again?" with a smile. He was always trying to lighten the situation. I tried to smile; I was terrified but embarrassed. I coughed out a little laugh. Should I tell them? *No, that's inappropriate, and it's gross—and what am I going to do?*

But then I reminded myself of my situation. That I had been spooning with John for six days straight, talking about simple things in the most vulnerable setting. Abdul had put his arms around me for warmth shortly after he'd masturbated beside me, and what could be more inappropriate and disgusting than that? I tried to whisper, like I needed to be careful no one else heard, because I was too ashamed and ill prepared for what I was about to tell them.

"So, um, I just had my period, less than a full cycle ago, and I think I started bleeding again and I don't know why. I'm worried I'm probably really sick and there's something wrong with me, and I'm scared and I have no idea what to do."

I stared at the ground. I was twenty years old and had had my period a total of seven times in my entire life, all in the last seven months. Being late to get started had always felt like an advantage: a sign that I was disciplined, I was controlling my eating, staying skinny enough to climb hard. I'd felt proud not to have it, and when it finally started, I had felt like I'd failed, somehow. But its absence had also been an uncomfortable marker of my difference. I'd missed out on the chance to learn about these things with all the other girls, in a normal place and time. And now this. My stupid, faulty body.

But Jason and John smiled. "Oh, that's just because you are stressed. Liz had that happen all the time, Cedar told me," Jason said. "And one of my exes had really random infrequent periods too."

John nodded and said, "Yeah, my girlfriend isn't very regular either, and stress has a huge factor in it."

I stared at them. They weren't freaking out or making fun of me; in fact they were giving me a comforting lesson on my own female body and how it worked. I felt a wave of relief run over me. But then we had to start moving. Su was motioning for us to head up the ridge. I couldn't dwell on the blood starting to pool in my underwear.

The conversation turned back to how to kill our captors. Each day we gave them new nicknames so we could talk about them without their knowing: Big Dog and Little Dog, or Number One and Number Two. We could push them into the river, or drop a boulder on them. Tommy was quiet during these conversations, detached from the other guys as they hyped themselves up.

A storm was coming. We could feel it in the wet, heavy air. Abdul and Su stepped away to chat.

"We're fucked unless we do something," Jason said.

Tommy wrapped his arms around me. I stiffened and immediately felt guilty for stiffening, but I didn't want to be touched after all those hours with Abdul. Tommy's body was a furnace. He so clearly needed love. I kept my arms tucked close to my body as he engulfed me.

A few moments later, Jason muttered, "Heads up, Big Dog is coming over."

Abdul, pointing his finger up-valley, explained through hand gestures that he was going back to our original base camp to resupply. Our food, warm clothes, batteries for his radio. We tried to ask him for Tommy's extra contact lenses and saline solution. We'd climb a ridge with Su and meet up with Abdul again on top.

He set off. I smiled and waved. Then our sad, tired group, plus Su, started up the ridge. Jason kept saying, "We're not going to get a better chance than this, you guys. There's four of us and one of him."

The ground here was brown, as we were close to the base of the Kara-Su Valley. The drier grass reminded me of the Sierra foothills, that long, straw-like grass that Hollywood cowboys always put in their teeth. We could grab it by the handful and use it as a makeshift hold while climbing up. I was so tired, but as soon as we gained some altitude and got out of the trees, my body knew what to do. The moon lit up the ridge like it was almost daylight. I looked up at the sky. It was so dark, like really dark, the kind of blackness you never experience in civilization, but with that bright moon.

After almost a week of only moving at night, our eyes were sharp and our footwork delicate and refined. We'd all learned to chart the topography of the ground by feel before weighting our feet. This ridge we were on was tall and would have definitely been intimidating to someone who didn't climb professionally: five hundred feet of rock outcroppings and loose scree. To us it felt like walking along a sidewalk—our hands and feet didn't even pause between moves. But Su, wherever he'd come from, was far outside his comfort zone. He walked tentatively, like a puppy on freshly polished floors. Large granite cliff walls flanked the valley. Behind them rose massive snowy peaks. Every time the terrain got steep, Jason muttered, "Come on, you guys. This is it."

I wanted him to stop talking. He'd been hissing directions for days, with no follow-through. We reached a long steep section, almost fifty feet. It felt calming to be climbing again. Climbing meant control. My hands and feet fitted themselves into holds like they belonged there. Moon shadows stretched across patches of grass far below us. John and Jason were in front. Then Tommy, then Su, then me.

Su's body was tense, stiff, and ungraceful on the sheer terrain. His feet skidded off the rock. He grunted, loudly, to get Tommy's attention. Tommy just barely raised his head. His eyes were dull. Su held out his hand for help—it was so vulnerable, it was almost sweet. Tommy grabbed Su and pulled him up onto a ledge.

Jason and John smiled at Su, patted him on the back. "Good job!" they said, though he did not understand. John flexed his biceps, to tell Su he was strong.

"Right now," Jason said. "We have to do it right now. Somebody's gotta just push him off."

I looked down. Jason meant shoving Su off the cliff, killing him.

"We totally should," Jason said again.

Tommy and I were silent. "I guess we should," John said.

"Nobody is coming to help us," Jason said.

The idea terrified me. My entire sense of self was wrapped up in the protective value of being good. I had survived tough climbs by being good. Arguing with my brother produced nothing. Breaking up with Tommy produced nothing.

Su scrambled ahead of us, tired and uncomfortable, with the summit in sight. Jason walked next to me, muttering about all the opportunities we were wasting. I felt so exhausted. Jason's talk was endless. We scrambled onto a big grassy ledge, near the top of the ridge. Tommy stepped close to me, with the same look I'd seen when he'd hung his head between his knees, sitting in the beige hallway of The North Face's office. His eyes, closed halfway, were empty and lost. He bit his lower lip.

"Should I push Su off?" Tommy said. "Jason's not going to do it."

I froze. He was so kind, so patient. I stared at my feet. I always stared at my feet.

"Beth?" He was collapsing and did not want to be alone in this decision, but I did not want to decide. What if Tommy missed and Su grabbed him and pushed Tommy off? What if Su saw Tommy coming and shot Tommy and killed him, or maimed him? What if Tommy wasn't strong enough? It sounded so nice to not starve anymore. I so desperately wanted to be done.

Tommy needed a lifeline. He needed an answer. He stared at me, and I said nothing, my mind ping-ponging between every scenario. Finally I looked up from the ground and into his eyes without saying anything, which we both knew meant yes. I saw the moment when he decided, when he saw the decision in my eyes. He moved quickly up the slope toward Su, and all I felt was nausea. John and Jason walked over to me on the ledge. Above us, Tommy was so fast, his body confident, his shoulders broad and strong.

I thought I saw relief and excitement in Su's movements—he was so close to the summit. Tommy grabbed Su's gun strap and pulled. Then Tommy let go.

Su's body arced through the night sky and hit the earth with an awful thud, a crunch, and an exhale. A skull? Or a spine snapping?

That sound echoed. The moon was really bright. Su's body bounced off a ledge below us, out of sight.

John called for me to run toward him. My feet felt frozen. But then I was climbing—my hands grabbing edges, my feet bounding up tiny steps. At the top of the ridge, Tommy was screaming, yelling, "I just killed someone, I fucking just killed someone!" A cold wind slapped my face. Tommy was curled up in a ball, tufts of sandy hair poking out from under his crossed arms. I wrapped myself around him.

"I can't believe I did that. I just killed someone, I fucking killed someone!" Snot ran from his nose. I laid myself on top of him. I wanted my small arms and skinny body to overpower his shaking.

"I just killed him. I just killed him." He was sobbing, his shirt soaked.

I told myself right then that I could never leave Tommy. He had done it for me, for all of us. I couldn't contradict him or let him believe he'd done wrong. I had to take care of him.

John thanked Tommy, over and over. It did not soothe Tommy a bit. He was still shaking and crying uncontrollably.

"How can you ever love me now? How can anyone ever love me now?" he kept saying. Over the howling wind, I whispered, "I could never love you more." I was filled with a sudden, decisive clarity: I needed to remember this, etch it in sharp lines into my mind. I could never forget what he had done for me—this terrible, heroic thing. *I can never leave Tommy now.*

"You just saved my life," I said. "You just saved our lives. I love you so much."

I felt panicked, rushed, both by what was happening and what I was telling Tommy. Tommy's face began to rearrange itself. I had to keep saying those words: *I could never love you more. I love you so much.*

Tommy wiped his eyes with a filthy hand and sucked the snot into his nose.

"I love you, thank you," I said again.

He smiled faintly. "Okay, okay, okay, okay," he said.

CHAPTER
TWENTY-ONE

Davis, California, May 2003

On the afternoon of our wedding, I lay on the floor of my childhood bedroom in jean shorts and a T-shirt, eating a pint of Ben & Jerry's Mint Chocolate Cookie. My uncle vacuumed around me, like my mother had asked him to. I'd never been able to settle on a wedding venue. Napa felt too fancy. Tahoe felt too trendy. The Ahwahnee hotel in Yosemite Valley would have been perfect, except we'd have all the dirtbags crashing the wedding. So we were getting married here, in my parents' backyard. My mother, who always kept her house tidy, was stressed at the prospect of fifty guests, plus a photographer. Our friend Corey had often handled our sponsor photo shoots. He had memorialized our sends, and now he would capture our wedding too.

I called Tommy. I felt like I didn't have anyone else to talk to, even though Katie, my maid of honor, was staying right there in my parents' house. After our move to Estes, we had grown close again—she was the best friend I had. But part of me worried that if I talked to her, that might open up questions and feelings I'd been deliberately putting away. Like: Was this wedding what I really wanted?

Tommy didn't answer. I called back two minutes later. "Where were you?" I asked curtly.

"Oh, sorry, I was swimming with Nick in the pool. Corey thought it would make cool pictures, plus now I don't need to shower." So Tommy wasn't going to shower before our wedding. Maybe I hadn't needed to worry so much about the dirtbags at the Ahwahnee.

At some point I picked myself up off the floor. My mom and Katie and Granny helped me get ready in my parents' room. I adored my dress, which was a weird feeling—I had identified as a girl who hated dresses for so long. But it was lovely and understated and just what I wanted. I put on some makeup that I had bought for prom. I decided, at the last moment, to go barefoot—I loved the dress, but I hated the shoes. Then, somehow, it was time.

I felt like I did right before a hard climb or a competition. I wanted to pee once more, even though I had peed five times in the past hour. My manicured hand looked strange to me, carrying my bouquet of flowers: light purple, yellow, and white, just like the wildflowers on the backside of Lumpy Ridge in Estes.

My father had replaced the crooked brick path in our garden. The plan was for me to meet him by the garage before walking outside. On the way, I passed Tommy's mother in the kitchen.

"Oh, hi, Beth! You look amazing!" she said.

I was furious, my maniacal bridezilla screaming at her in my head: *Bad luck! Bad luck! Go to your seat! No one is supposed to see me beforehand.*

I should have noticed I was out of control.

"Here, stop for a second, I want to get a picture!" she said, her hand disappearing into her giant purse to fish out her camera. I put on a smile.

When I finally reached the garage and my steady rock of a father, I was ready to crumble. I didn't want this. Why had I put everybody through so much stress? Couldn't we do it another way, where I wouldn't have to be the center of attention and nobody had to conform to the preposterous script I'd downloaded into my brain from *The Knot*? I just wanted to put on my shorts and a T-shirt and be invisible. I couldn't believe I'd let the manicurist scrape the hard-earned calluses off my hands and feet.

"You ready?" my dad said when we heard Mozart start to play in the garden. That was our cue. I'd tried so hard to fill in all the blank spaces for this paint-by-numbers wedding, but none of it was right, because that perfect, dolled-up, blissed-out bride—that wasn't me. Tommy stood there in his suit, clean but unshowered with chlorine-filled hair, looking so young, so innocent, so in love, and so proud. I wanted to feel that calmness I saw in his face, the sense that everything was right in the world. I just could not get comfortable. This was my house, but this wasn't our space. Our space was covered with dirt and sunscreen.

I wondered if he would remember how we were supposed to kiss. I'd made him practice that too.

◆ ◆ ◆

After the wedding, we arrived at a fancy downtown Sacramento hotel around midnight. Someone had tied strings of tin cans to Tommy's van, and I knew I'd need to clean them off the next morning or they would attract bears when we got to the Valley. My parents had booked us a night at the hotel as a gift. To check in we had to wait in line behind another just-married couple, clearly desperate to get to their bed.

When we got to our room, I put on my cotton Lycra shorts and my baggy Sportiva sweatshirt. I felt as if I could breathe again. Then I started thinking about all the things we could do instead of having sex. I wanted to watch *House Hunters*—that sounded relaxing. Intimacy with Tommy was so hard for me. My vow to try harder, after that first time, had mostly turned out to mean trying to avoid it. The perfect wedding, all of our friends dressed up, the perfect slideshow with the perfect music, my dad's speech—it was all supposed to make it feel right. But I was so walled off from my body, from my feelings. We tried having sex in the bathtub, which was a bad idea. I lay back, dissociating, trying to think about the good times we had together, like when we shined on El

Cap. We were both still so young, but even then, I think Tommy knew that our sex life wasn't normal. He seemed to take it for what it was, love me for how I was. His attitude seemed to be: nothing is perfect, but the good and great parts make it worthwhile.

I was just guessing, though, about what he thought, since he always went along with our silent pact to leave this undiscussed.

I showered off all the hairspray and makeup. In bed, Tommy put his heavily muscled arms around me and immediately passed out. I felt trapped. How had I gotten here? I was barely old enough to drink legally—not that I ever did, anyway. It had not even been three years since I had tried to break up with Tommy in The North Face headquarters, not quite three years since everything changed. Kyrgyzstan had welded us together in ways that felt deep, permanent. I told myself that meant our marriage was right. As I faded into sleep, I wondered what an orgasm would feel like.

The next day we went back to Yosemite. We were working on the first free ascent of the West Buttress, another route up El Cap, and we'd left our bags hanging off the wall while we ducked out to Davis for the wedding. Our honeymoon would be spent on the wall, eating cold canned soup and Tasty Bites. That seemed right, to me.

In Kyrgyzstan, I had promised myself that I would never leave Tommy. Now that promise was official.

CHAPTER TWENTY-TWO

Kyrgyzstan, August 2000

We needed to move. Abdul might come back. Su might have survived. Jason and John had seen a military base down the valley when they went to look for our luggage. So we decided to run—scrambling fast down the ridge, sliding over fifteen-foot drops, mindful not to dislodge any loose gravel that would make our location known. I watched Tommy the whole time. Was he still in front of me? Was he crying?

At the bottom of the cliff we reached the trail. John led, followed by me and then Tommy and then Jason. I didn't want Tommy in the front or in back. I didn't want him to get shot. Tommy could keep his eyes on me; I'd pull him along, and if he stumbled, Jason, behind him, would make Tommy keep up. If Abdul shot at us from behind, Jason could be the human shield. I knew I was a monster for thinking that. But Tommy was my responsibility now.

We must have run for miles that night, singing Cat Stevens's "Moonshadow" as we moved in and out of the moonlight. Our flight seemed strangely effortless, even though none of us had eaten more than six hundred calories over the past six days. Adrenaline flowed through my muscles, my heart and lungs, and I felt like an Olympic marathoner.

When the canyon walls started to pinch together, John and Jason let us know the base was somewhere just ahead. We ran on, and suddenly we were under fire again. I'd gone days without hearing gunshots, but I knew exactly what to do.

My body and face hit the dirt. It was sandy, with pebbles and rock chunks, and it filled my hands as I skidded to a halt. I felt a bullet whizzing by me, the air pushed aside, dirt clots hitting my body from the bullets landing in the earth near me. My first thought was: *Is Tommy okay?* I could feel my own body. I was okay. But I didn't know about him. I had started to think of him as a small helpless child after that moment on the cliff, one who wasn't capable of making decisions. Could he even think to dive out of the way in his state? Was he just standing there, ready to accept his fate? I understood if he was—part of me felt like doing that too. It seemed easier in some ways. John and Jason shouted, "Americans! Americans!" Tommy and I started shouting too, hoping to God that the bullets were coming from Kyrgyz military and not more rebels.

The shooting stopped. With gestures, the soldiers got us back on our feet. We were marched inside the stone wall of their ramshackle base and then ordered to lie down on the ground again.

I desperately wanted to look at their faces to glean any information I could. Were they bearded, like Su and Abdul? Whose side were they on? Was there anyone we could trust? Everything was happening too quickly, and it was so dark. They already had us on our stomachs, hands clasped to our heads, guns pointed at our backs. I hadn't checked in with Tommy. I should have checked in. Was he hurt? Was he scared?

I felt the weight of the guns being aimed at us. I was so tired. I wanted the tart taste of fear to leave my body. I started drifting away, waiting for the shot to come. Then my mind flashed to Tommy. I was sorry, sorry that I was giving up for him. I knew that being shot would be quick. I was ready. I wanted my family to know that I was okay, that I wasn't scared anymore. That they did a good job with me. That I loved them. *I had a good life, don't worry, don't cry for me.* But the shot never came.

My body and mind came back around with euphoric feelings about finally being safe. One of the soldiers spoke a bit of German, and I knew how to count to five in German. I kept saying *"Vier, vier"*—*There are four of us.* They gave us a few sardines and some water. They passed around a cigarette. I had never smoked anything in my life. Jason insisted I take a drag, and I did, even though I didn't really know how. Tommy passed, saying it was the last thing he wanted at that moment. I felt dirty, like I had betrayed him.

After dawn broke the next morning, a Kyrgyz military helicopter flew out to retrieve us. The walk from the base to the helicopter was terrifying. It was through a narrow canyon with a tiny path on the right side, squeezed between huge cliffs of reddish rock. On the path we saw bloody jackets and the other scattered remnants of a tragic battle. The Kyrgyz soldiers escorting us were constantly looking up, pointing their guns at the skyline to see if we were going to get shot at again. I thought: *Even though I'm safe, I'm never really safe.*

The helicopter deposited us at the next base. It was in the middle of a desolate brown plain. It had a temporary feeling to it: the buildings reminded me of the portable classrooms at my elementary school. The floors flexed a little when I walked on them, and the doors seemed only half as thick as they should be. This was where they fed us the barley and warm bread, butter melting into its grains. I ate plates and plates of it—no amount of food could keep me full.

We debriefed with a translator and an army official. It was mainly him telling us things, and us smiling and nodding. He told us he was so glad that the Kyrgyzstan military saved us, and that we should tell our government that the captors got their weapons from Afghanistan and the United States. He could have told me that my name was Betty and that I lived in France and I would have smiled and nodded and said *Yes* and *Thank you* and *Sorry* and *Thank you*. I was just so happy to be warm and full. I didn't want to burst this bubble. We were safe, but we weren't really safe. We weren't home; we were surrounded by men with machine guns and had zero idea where we were going or what we were doing next.

The third base was more like what I thought of as a military base. It was a small town, a really small town. But there was a normal dining hall with long tables, bathrooms, bunks. This was where we got to take our first showers. My first shower since I'd left the hotel in Tbilisi, so long ago I was literally a different person. This was also the first time I was separated from the boys. We walked to a huge tent where they had shower stalls set up. The boys went to the right, and I went to the left. Armed guards came with me but stood on the other side of a curtain. I felt that same sense of dread and panic that I'd felt when I sat behind the boulder at our camp when we were first captured. Like here I was, this tiny girl about to strip down and be naked.

The tent was partially open on one wall, where the fabric ended about six feet up. Visible through the gap was another vast brown plain, nothing in sight for miles. I could feel the warmth of the sun slightly. I turned on the showerhead and started to take off my clothes, still deeply aware that the boys were not near me and there were two armed men standing a few feet away, separated from me by a thin piece of woven cotton. I took off my tan synthetic softshell pants and saw a huge bloodstain in the crotch.

As I stared at my pants around my ankles I could feel the steam of the shower near me. I had forgotten, almost. I did have that sense of wet underwear at the first military base, but there was nothing I could really do about it.

I took off my blue stretchy long-sleeved shirt and my rank T-shirt underneath. My ribs were poking through, and my hip bones were prominent. I recognized this body. I hadn't seen it in a few years, not since I'd been an eighty-five-pound teenager at the San Diego X Games. I tried to take off my underwear, but it was glued to me. The blood had dried and it was stuck to my pubic hair. Again, I felt like a child in my body, thinking there was something I should have known or done differently. If I had been normal and started my period in middle school, could I have figured this out with all my friends? Instead, I was standing on one side of a dark-green cloth divider in the middle of a military base thinking I was going to have to employ the rip-off-the-Band-Aid strategy because I couldn't bear the thought of slowly peeling away each inch. My underwear was a stiff board. I shut my eyes, grabbed the front. Holy hell, did it hurt. I threw the bloody, hairy, stiff underwear in a trash can in the corner of the room.

The shower felt weird and amazing and sad and wonderful. The hot water relaxed all my muscles, tensed for a week now. I was so dirty. I stood under the hot water, and my mind just let go. I wanted to remain there and cry until someone picked me up and put me on a plane home. But then I heard one of the guards cough, probably on purpose, and it reminded me that I wasn't safe, and I wasn't home, and I needed to get it together. I tried to wash all the blood off my legs and out of my crotch and get the stench out of my armpits. I washed my hair, and I finally toweled off, but had no comb or brush, just this wet, cold rat's nest on my head. I tried to run my fingers through to untangle it, but it was hopeless. I stepped into some fatigues that the army had given me. I knew my period would soil them, but I had no idea what else to do.

I walked out of the shower, holding my dirty clothes in one hand, my hair jumbled on my head. I could feel blood running down my legs; I tried to keep them crossed as much as possible. They took us to a place with a room and four beds. A woman came in who spoke English, dressed in fatigues with a few patches on her shoulder. I gathered up some courage and asked her if she had any underwear and a brush. I was too embarrassed to ask for a tampon or a pad. She smiled and came back a couple minutes later with mom underwear and a comb. I put on the underwear and wadded up a bunch of toilet paper to make a makeshift pad.

An officer came in and asked us to write out our accounts on a piece of white paper attached to a clipboard. We weren't allowed to talk to each other. I started writing. It felt like I was in school, and I wondered if I was doing it properly. Should I make it fit just on the front side? Both sides? How did you summarize? I wanted to see what the boys were writing. I wondered what stuck out for them. I scribbled down a terse blow-by-blow. We had agreed in advance that we wouldn't single out Tommy, that we would say "we" had pushed Su. We handed in our papers and never talked about it again. Then we went to sleep on small, rickety twin beds with metal springs holding up thin mattresses that squeaked when we shifted.

I remember lying down. I woke up fourteen hours later in the exact same position. I was in so much pain. Every muscle hurt. This was something close to safety, I supposed: the crisis passing, the agony of the afterward setting in.

PART TWO

CHAPTER
TWENTY-THREE

Yosemite Valley, Late Summer 2005

There are all kinds of climbers with all sorts of dreams. But I would bet that most climbers, at one time or another, have dreamed of climbing the Nose. It is almost certainly the most famous route in the world. It splits El Cap in half, directly up the center: the most obvious line, the first line that was climbed on the wall, the first thing anyone sees driving into Yosemite Valley.

Each time something happens on the Nose, it's a big deal. For climbing, it's like Wimbledon, or the Tour de France, or the Olympics. The first time it was ever climbed successfully, by three men who spent many weeks working on the wall over many months in the late 1950s, it was news. The first time it was done in a day it was news. The first time it was free climbed, by Lynn Hill in 1993, it was news. The first time it was freed in a day (Lynn, again, the next year) it was news.

Two years after the wedding, in 2005, Tommy and I spent the summer in Estes training to free the Nose. I'd been dreaming of this attempt since I first started climbing, in 1994. Plenty of the world's best climbers had tried since Lynn's two legendary ascents, but even today, freeing the Nose remains a very rare accomplishment. There is some esoteric debate about which sends "count" and which include an asterisk for one reason or another. Back then, depending on who you asked, we were hoping to become the third ever to do it.

But we wouldn't actually head to Yosemite until the fall. For now, Colorado would be our training ground. Each day we put water and lunch in the Civic and drove forty-five minutes to the Monastery climbing area, in between Fort Collins and Estes. Tommy and Mike had discovered it when they were flying over the canyon in a friend's plane; they built a trail to the area and established almost all of the climbs. Now it was one of the best areas on the Front Range, but the road was a washboard and the hike in was an hour long. So we usually had the place to ourselves—heaven. All morning we ran laps on climbs that Tommy had established, honing our finger strength and stamina, wearing down our skin, creating the calluses we knew we needed for Yosemite. On our way home we always bought ice-cold Diet Pepsis at the gas station. Then we drove straight to the garage to train. We'd climb until our fingers opened up and our muscles burned with exhaustion, encouraging each other, laughing, hugging. In between laps, we'd snuggle on the mattresses that cushioned the floor below the wall.

After a few hours of that, we drove to the weight gym in Estes. It was a hilarious mix of retirees pulling their oxygen tanks around, doing printed-out workouts from their physical therapists, and meatheads who never wore shirts and had biceps bigger than my waist. We worked out in the gym for another hour or so, completely obliterating ourselves: pull-ups, bench press, military press, shoulders, abs, abs, and more abs. We didn't have a plan. I just went around and lifted until my muscles trembled and I felt nauseous. Then I knew I could finally go home.

Home didn't mean a nap. Home meant stumbling into our cabin with our empty lunch bags and gym clothes—and then changing to go biking. Tommy had a green Schwinn road bike that I'd bought for his birthday three years earlier. I had a black Trek road bike that he'd bought me for Christmas the year before. They were both on sale, frugality being a core tenet of climbing culture. Together we pedaled up Trail Ridge Road, the road that winds up from Estes into Rocky Mountain

National Park. It was a demanding but beautiful ride, the air thin and the mountains of the Continental Divide filling the skyline. I usually turned back after an hour; Tommy kept going. He wasn't just training to free the Nose with me. If all went well, after we sent the Nose together, he would try to free the Nose plus Freerider (a different, much easier route up El Cap), one after another in a single day. I didn't feel competitive or resentful that he was training for a second objective that would trump my achievement. Sometimes his accomplishments made me harder on myself—*Do more, Beth. Work harder.* But that didn't translate into envy or resentment. We were BethandTommy: his accomplishment was my accomplishment. His Double, as we called it, would accrue praise and respect to me too. When I turned my bike around, I'd tell Tommy that I loved him and coast back down to the house, flying by the tourists in their rental cars as they puttered slowly out of the park. I always had burritos or pasta with Newman's Own red sauce ready when he got home.

We ate, staggered to the couch, watched TV for ten minutes, and fell asleep.

◆ ◆ ◆

It's hard to explain the heightened anxiety that I feel the first time I rap over the edge of El Cap at the start of a new climbing season. It never changes, no matter how many times I've done it. The top of the wall is a mixture of granite slabs scattered with gravel and a few gnarled trees and stubborn manzanita bushes . . . And then you're over the brink and it's like falling down into the depths of the ocean. There's nothing to catch you for three thousand feet.

Back then, unless injuries kept us away, Tommy and I were in Yosemite every spring and fall. We'd drive from Estes, across mountains and desert and more mountains on I-80, to the Valley to work on one route or another. I always hoped I could hide how much the wall terrified me. Pro climbers were supposed to revere El Cap, not fear it.

I wanted to feel the way I assumed Tommy or Lynn felt up there: like the wall was my natural element, a second home where I could be my best self. Instead, my dread made me feel like an impostor just waiting to be found out. But finding the strength to push through that terror and onto the famous granite made me feel like a superhero. Somehow that endless wall undermined and emboldened me at the same time.

After the summer of hard training, I felt those same familiar nerves as I clipped my rappel device into a brand-new rope and started walking slowly down to the edge.

We'd hiked up the day before and camped on top of El Cap for our first night that season. It might seem counterintuitive, but when the harder sections of a long route are near the end of a climb, it's common to start working from the top. We'd rappel down to the sections we wanted to try. We used tools called ascenders, which attach directly to a climbing rope, to let us move back up the wall as needed (a technique called jumaring, or jugging) until we had all the pieces in place for a continuous ascent.

I never sleep well at first. The air was sharp, the ground hard. My pillow—a pair of pants and socks stuffed inside a sweaty T-shirt—did nothing for my head.

After I'd given up on sleep, I made Tommy's oatmeal and poured my cup of Yogi green tea. We were supposed to be equals, but I was nagged by the feeling that this time I was just tagging along. The previous year, I'd fractured some bones in my foot. A doctor had put me in a boot instead of a cast, so that I could shower, but I had taken that as permission to climb. I didn't want to stop; I couldn't stop. I needed to keep moving forward, keep sending. So I'd gotten one of my sponsors to glue the rubber that would normally go on a climbing shoe onto my boot. That was the kind of extreme commitment that climbers celebrated (*So rad, climbing in a boot!*), but I had done enough damage to turn what should have been a three-month recovery into twelve months of pain and setbacks. While I'd been in and out of commission, Tommy had freed two more El Cap routes.

It was hard not to worry that Tommy's career was rocketing away from mine. I kept a stupid tally in my head. Tommy carried a heavier pack and would rap first. Although we mostly climbed together and mostly had the same sponsors, he was consistently paid about a third more than I was. He was the current king of El Cap, but I was the current queen. What did that even mean? He had climbed 5.15 and I had only climbed 5.14. I had only freed one El Cap route, Lurking Fear, and he had freed five. On my side of the ledger: Tommy had tried the Optimist, my signature 5.14b first ascent, and couldn't do it. I'd onsighted the Phoenix, and it took him several attempts. I was fitter— or at least, I could go farther on less food . . .

Shit. I'd burned his oatmeal. I scraped off the bottom of our dented Teflon camp pan.

◆ ◆ ◆

Our plan was to work on the route for two months, and I was terrified. Like certified one hundred percent panicked. Like every minute I was not athletically exerting myself, a cold sweat drenched my armpits and my lower back. Were there sharp edges that I couldn't see on the way down? What if I placed the rope over a huge rock and dislodged it onto my head? What if the carabiner I was clipped into was defective? Would I scream if I fell? Would Tommy cry? Wasn't I supposed to be less fucking afraid? I looked down at the trees in the valley; from up there they looked like tiny pale-green pieces of broccoli. I wondered if most professional athletes thought constantly about imminent death.

Tommy never seemed scared, but I tried to hide my fear from him. Did he hide his from me? I had no idea.

The objective was to stand on the summit having climbed the entire route, bottom to top, without falling. If I let myself think of the entire route, each move, each foothold, learning each gear placement, how fit I needed to be on each pitch, which hold I needed to train for, how I had to get stronger for this part or that part, I would have given up, overwhelmed. But I was good—we were good—at breaking things down, understanding the intricacies of a ten-foot section of glassy granite. Hanging on a rope two thousand feet off the ground, literally running my hand over the wall trying to find weaknesses and edges to hold on to and stand on.

The hardest pitches were the Great Roof and the Changing Corners. If we could do those two, then we had a very good chance at doing the route. It's like knowing the Alpe d'Huez is the hardest stage of the Tour de France: obviously there is a lot of cycling before and after that, but if you win there, you are in good shape. We rappelled down and stood on the rank, sticky ledge known as Camp 6. Each ledge on the Nose has a name: Sickle Ledge, Dolt Tower, El Cap Tower, Camp 4, Camp 5, Camp 6. Camp 6 was truly disgusting. Decades of human waste lay trapped in the large gap between the ledge and the wall. You'd think the air would be fresh up there. My God, it smelled.

Tommy took his turn. He climbed like a tactician—not beautiful but with cold-blooded confidence, and he always got the job done. I felt a weight watching him. This was the first El Cap route we were trying together since the West Buttress, the one that had been interrupted by our wedding. The one where I gave up because I knew free climbing that route would take me a lot longer than it would take him. If I'd continued, my slowness could have jeopardized his chances of success. Now here we were, same cliff, different route. Should I just give up and belay?

When it was my turn to climb, I felt like a baby deer walking on ice. I hung on the rope, my back slumped slightly in my harness, my mind bouncing between *This is so cool! I can't wait to see if it comes together* and *You can't do this, Beth. No way. Just belay Tommy, you do better as his wall mule.*

We tried the Changing Corners three times each, and the feel of Yosemite climbing slowly came back to me. I knew more of the holds, understood the friction required. I remembered the delicate yet intense way to try hard on granite. My mind was stimulated and excited, even as my body grew tired.

A lot of people have said *I've freed the Nose minus ten feet*. Meaning they could fathom or do all of the moves, all three thousand feet of them, except for a notorious ten-foot section on the Changing Corners. So far, I'd only done a tenth of the moves on the Changing Corners, but I felt cautiously hopeful. I remembered the progression that can happen on projects—I reminded myself, loudly, in my head, about my process on the Optimist, Lurking Fear, To Bolt or Not to Be. I remembered the exhilaration of making progress each day, feeling good about a new foot move or a new handhold.

"Good job, honey!" Tommy yelled up from below as I got to the anchors on a 5.11 pitch. I hung in my harness and looked down. I watched him ascend the pitch with ease. He wasn't a baby deer, or even an adult deer. He was a goddamn lizard. I waited for him to start doing push-ups midpitch, like the little Sierra fence lizards that were always skittering across the granite, just to show me how easy it was for him. But as frustrating as it was to contrast his ease with my uncertainty, it was also a privilege to watch someone in their element, in their flow state. I had learned and would still learn so much from him. *There's no fear in his foot movements, there's no questioning,* I thought. *He is a child on the monkey bars, happy and content. I love him so much.*

CHAPTER
TWENTY-FOUR

October 2005

A couple of weeks into the climb I'd pushed through the worst of my fear and become a lizard too. I rapped over the edge without question. I didn't even blink or look at the trees. The fear, the wind, the racing thoughts of imminent death had been defeated by my focus.

We had settled into our training rhythm, a six-day cycle. Day one: we'd focus on the Changing Corners and the pitches surrounding it. Day two: we rapped farther down, twelve hundred feet to the Great Roof, the second-hardest pitch. We spent our bodies and minds when they were freshest, trying individual moves, sequences. Asking each other: Which hold felt better to you? Did you like the higher slippery foot? Or the lower sharp-edge foot? What about gear? Do you think we should use the blue Metolius there? Did you finish the dried peaches? Can I have some of the cashews? I loved the built-in restrictions that hauling all our food up the wall entailed: there was none to spare. Then we'd take a rest day on the summit, walking miles to fetch and filter water and doing camp chores. Another day on the Changing Corners, two days' rest on the Valley floor, rinse, repeat.

I've always loved collaboration. I was that kid who desperately wanted my older brother to play with me, or at least acknowledge my existence. Instead, he'd berate me or physically throw me out of his room. So working on a route with Tommy, breaking down and decoding pitch after pitch, was heaven to me. We were perfect partners up there. The usual stressors in our marriage—my frustrations with his family, our stagnant sex life, the things we never talked about—were left at ground level. On the wall, everything worked between us.

On the fifth day, we'd descend, physically destroyed, and stop at the filthy Curry Village showers before driving back to an empty lot we'd purchased nearby. On day six, we'd train on the climbing wall that was, so far, the only thing we'd built on our parcel of land. Six pieces of plywood strung between two massive Douglas fir trees. We cranked it up and down with an old blue climbing rope and a come-along. Tommy would eat Trader Joe's Joe-Joe's as I did pull-ups on rings hung from a branch.

After two or three of those cycles, or a couple of weeks, we had both figured out the Great Roof, all the 5.12 pitches, and the route. Tommy even felt confident on the Changing Corners. But after all our work, it still hung over me: that stretch where I couldn't move through the way Tommy or Lynn had. My stick arms were too short: I just couldn't reach. Tommy was ready, but I still needed another week of decoding and preparation. We only had so many days left, maybe three or four weeks at best, until the snow was likely to fly, ending the season.

I hated feeling like I was the slow one. I was terrified that I might hold Tommy back. More terrified of that than failing. And then there were other thoughts, weird competitive thoughts with Lynn, who had literally already done the route ten years earlier. But I wanted to be known and seen and acknowledged as much as she was. Sending was my path to that. Inside, I ricocheted between ego and brutal self-criticism: feeling like I deserved that renown and acknowledgment one moment and then telling myself how weak and pathetic I was the next. I thanked Tommy continuously for being my partner up there. I thanked him for making this climb possible for us, I thanked him for waiting as I struggled on the Changing Corners. He never showed any sign that he thought I was baggage. He always thanked me too.

I liked the narrative I told the dozens of parties we passed each day on the route. *Isn't this amazing?! Isn't this the best place ever? What about those poor souls stuck in traffic down on the Valley floor . . . They have no idea what Yosemite really looks like! Yes, we are making good progress! Tommy has everything dialed, and I'm not far behind! If one of us can't do it, then the other's success is our success!* Everything with an exclamation point, as if I needed to really prove I meant it. It felt like bingeing on food: in the moment, it felt good to be so positive and enthusiastic, but that night or the next day hints of doubt and self-loathing would creep in.

Finally, hanging on the rope one day, my forehead resting against the cool granite, I found my fix. The crack extended below where we were trying to come in, and I wondered for the first time if it might be possible for me to approach it from farther down. I lowered down. My fingers fit. I tried a few moves—they were hard but doable. It was counterintuitive, but coming in lower, adding in another ten feet or so of hard climbing below the infamous ten feet, just might work.

It wouldn't be easy. Contorting my body into that shallow corner, I had to expand each appendage outward and create enough friction on the correct bumps and edges to not fall. Then I would hold my breath, say a small prayer, move one hand or foot up the wall three to six inches, reset my entire contorted body, expand, and repeat. I was like an inchworm that needed to clench its body with each movement, hoping that I wouldn't slip, that the rubber on my shoe was placed exactly right on the small bump, that my finger was flexed at the correct angle in the crack. I knew that my success came down to these twenty feet. I knew my mind had to be silent yet active, my body fatigued but fresh enough. The wind had to be blowing hard enough to keep the rock cool for good friction but still calm enough for me to focus. It was a constant battle of opposites.

"I can't believe you found a way to go into the Changing Corners even lower," said Tommy as he grinned with his big crooked teeth and rubbed my back vigorously with his calloused hand. I smiled and nuzzled into his chest. I knew this was one of my strengths: my ability to not be funneled into the known or the common path. Or maybe it was just my stubbornness, my iron refusal to be defeated by a couple of stupid moves.

My solution was so tenuous. I didn't know if it would be enough.

CHAPTER TWENTY-FIVE

Yosemite Valley, October 2005

By early October we had figured out all the pitches. Four weeks of going up and down. My mind felt sharp and my body tuned. I just wanted one last day on the Changing Corners before going for a ground-up ascent. It was weird to feel so close to a lifelong goal, but it also felt dangerous to treat it as a momentous occasion: I didn't want to get ahead of myself. So I tried to approach that final day of preparation like any other climbing day. I tied into the rope and laced up my good Miura climbing shoes. I had other Miuras for the easier pitches, but I kept my good ones for this. They were firmer, less worn out, stiff enough to support the expansion and contortion I would need to do. "Thank God we're sponsored," I said to Tommy, forcing a laugh and trying to distract myself from the pitch looming above me. "We'd never be able to afford to free this route with all the shoes we need." He laughed and squeezed my shoulders. I chalked up my hands, dusted my shoes off on my calves, glanced quickly over at Tommy, and started climbing.

My hands had become so familiar with the slippery yet chafing granite. Somehow it managed to tear my skin and spit me off at the same time. I heard the swallows dive-bombing somewhere behind me, a sharper melody weaving through the background music of birdsong and traffic from the Valley far below. When I'm feeling good, those sounds surround me without distracting me. They become part of the sensory experience of the climb.

"I bet the rock feels sticky!" Tommy shouted up to me. It was colder than last week, colder than yesterday. In normal life, the weather is a mundane topic, but in climbing it holds power over everything, right down to the pads of our fingers. I laughed quietly. "Yeah, I can't blame the weather if I don't send now."

I felt good. I took a deep breath and almost allowed myself to stop and soak that in, but this was my last practice session. For a few moments I started to hear my doubts: *Tommy could have been done by now. If you can't do it, that's okay, just support him.* They were comforting, in a way. Familiar. I could retreat from my own ambitions and we would still be BethandTommy. But as I climbed higher on the large flake and approached the start of the corner, I could feel something else bubble up: my ownership of my desire for this climb. My hands gripped tighter and my mind zeroed in on the feel and texture of the jams I was grabbing. I felt my arms tense and strengthen, I felt my abs tighten and my mind sharpen. I liked the feeling of mastery. I didn't want to bury it below a supporting role. I didn't hate that role, but now that I knew I was ready, it felt like a cop-out.

I looked up and saw two Spaniards watching me from the 5.10 pitch above. I usually hated having an audience, but this time I wanted them to watch me send this pitch. I wanted them to see how good I was. I'd felt that same desire when I climbed in competitions: the drive not just to be great but for that greatness to be seen. This wasn't just a "girlfriend" lap; this was my lap. I climbed with authority. I felt strong and confident. But as I inched up the corner I could feel that I wasn't focused enough. I was too greedy; I wanted it too bad.

And just like that, I botched my right-hand placement. My body started to wobble. I was like the race-car driver who looks at the wall: pretty soon I was hanging on the end of the rope. I screamed and kicked the granite face. I forgot about the Spaniards, and I even forgot about

Tommy. I hung there on the rope yelling profanities. I threw up my hands and actually slapped the wall. It stung, and I immediately felt ashamed. I looked down at Tommy. He couldn't make eye contact. I didn't want to hear anything from Tommy. I didn't want to hear *Good job* or *Nice try* or *You have this next time.*

I knew what I needed to do.

Hanging on the rope, I tied my shoes extra tight, taking out my aggression on my feet. I wanted to look up at the Spaniards again, but I forced myself to look at my shoes and focus. I tried to get back into equilibrium, the wind and the birdsong and the drone of traffic in perfect balance with the narrator in my head. I could feel my mind settling into partnership with my body: I knew where to put my foot, my hand. *Gaston, not sidepull. Tighten your abs. Breathe.* I just needed to finish this section. I wanted to feel confident walking down the East Ledges to the Valley floor tonight, wanted to earn my two organic Oreos at the car. The other voices fell away: the cocky ones, the self-loathing ones, the spiteful ones. *Focus, Beth.*

To be at my best, I need to be the quiet force, not the loud one. That's when I shine; that's when I succeed. It's as though I open up a door in my mind and walk down a hallway with authority, good authority. Understanding the rock but also listening to my body, knowing exactly how hard I need to try while still saving some for the top. It feels like the pendulum of my grandfather's clock in my parents' house. Steady. Calm. Back and forth, back and forth. Push hard, pull back. Balance.

My arms started to fill with lactic acid, my feet started to cramp. I knew this feeling. I'd trained for it over the last month. I didn't run away from it.

I knew what I needed to do.

I closed my eyes and took a deep breath. This was my quiet superpower. Somehow, I didn't remember I was twenty-five hundred feet in the air. I was just at some obscure crag with no one around but Tommy. My favorite place to be with my favorite person. I started shimmying up the climb. *I'm just gathering data; this isn't the performance, just gathering data.* That softened the edge on the need to perform. I was able to focus harder and more closely. After twenty more feet I reached the anchors and breathed a sigh of relief. Sure, I had fallen once, but I knew that my solution could work if I kept my head together. I let myself feel this win for a moment. I smiled, put my hands on the rope, and rested my forehead against it.

A week later we had our last rest day in Davis. I wanted to rest there, away from the wall. I didn't want to stare up at El Cap each day or deal with the droves of climbers asking us what we were doing and when we were doing it. I wanted to lose myself in afternoon sitcom reruns and Trader Joe's trips. But even there, my mind was flooded with strategy and planning. I always said that we had a long time to figure it out, but I knew we really only had this one attempt before our window closed. The weather didn't care about my goals.

I ate another three squares of a one-pound chocolate bar. Back then, free climbing season on El Cap was over by late October or early November. We had three weeks to get everything done: our joint free ascent, and after that the two rehearsals for the Double (when I'd belay Tommy up both routes, jumaring while he freed each of them separately), and then his final, combined send of the Double. I wanted to talk to Tommy about the pressure I felt, but I didn't. I wanted him to reassure me that it would be fine, but in reality I knew that I was responsible for my send. If I wanted to free the Nose, I had to pull my weight. All of it. It felt scary and weird and hard to own that with him as a partner.

I don't really know how to explain it. It's like if you have Michael Jordan on your team: it's easy to always pass to him, but sometimes he's being double-teamed or he's on the bench or it's just not his shot and you have to rise to the occasion. That's where I was. I was getting ready to take the court with Tommy, and I knew I needed to hold my own. We'd be there for each other, but I had to connect everything for myself.

◆ ◆ ◆

We camped on our lot the night before our push began, slept for a few hours, and rose before midnight. By 1:00 a.m. we were on the Nose. El Cap was so peaceful in the middle of the night, and I much preferred climbing in darkness that gave way to dawn than climbing in daylight that disappeared. Still, climbing at night exposed a raw edge deep inside me. As we took turns leading each pitch, searching out the holds by feel and by headlamp, I had to work to shove it down.

Team freeing means you each have to free climb each pitch. Often that means you swap leads: one person leads the pitch clean and then the other follows it clean. So by the time you get to the top, you've each led half the route and followed the other half. "It's way harder than individually freeing a route," Tommy would always tell me. "You don't get caddied up the wall." He meant that in an individual ascent, the supporting partner would generally handle the belaying, the gear, the food and drink, leaving the one who was trying to free the route to concentrate only on climbing. But we were freeing the route *and* supporting each other. I always liked it when he made what we were doing sound more rad than other ascents.

All our rehearsals, all our grueling training sessions, were paying off for the performance. We ended our first day just below the Great Roof, the first of our two biggest challenges. In the morning, I felt like I'd been run over by a truck. I couldn't raise my arms above my head without gasping in pain. I'd been so psyched the day before that I hadn't even realized how much the effort was draining me. So my hopes weren't high for the Great Roof, but I surprised myself. I sent it on my second try. Despite the exhaustion and the soreness, I felt so good, better than I ever had on El Cap before.

We got to Camp 6 on the Nose after another hard day. I was ruined from the effort it took to get there. My feet were swollen, bulging even further out of my tiny climbing shoes; my tape gloves were shredded, exposing bloody skin underneath; and my level of full-body fatigue was overwhelming. I felt like a swimming pool full of petrified playdough instead of clean chlorinated water. Everything felt slower to move, heavier, like it was an almost insurmountable feat even to pull down my pants and pee. We set up camp and agreed to take a rest day. My body and mind desperately needed it. After dinner—Annie's black-bean-and-vegetable soup and a bagel for me, and Tasty Bite Madras Lentils and a bagel for Tommy—Tommy casually said, "I'm thinking of just taking a burn on the Changing Corners. Is that okay with you?"

Was it okay? I had to say yes. Camp 6 is just below the Changing Corners, so after we ate, I sat on the reeking ledge and belayed him. Tommy sent the pitch. I felt a rush of weight and pressure. Now we were just waiting to see if I could free the Changing Corners too. And if I couldn't, then what? Tommy would free the Nose without me?

I was like a needy puppy. I made him promise that if I failed he would come back with me so I could try again. We could complete this life goal together. He said yes, again and again, and reassured me that we had a ton of food and water. We could take two rest days now if I needed them. He would go back up and brush the holds and prep the pitch. We could even both descend and try the whole thing together another time. Everything I needed to hear, Tommy said, always.

Throughout our rest day, I tried to keep my head together. First thing the next morning, I free climbed the Changing Corners. It felt good, surreal, but I couldn't let myself feel my full elation yet: I knew the hardest part was over, but I still had to keep my mind sharp, focused on the few remaining pitches. I had just won the Alpe d'Huez stage; I couldn't botch it on the descent. There was a jittering throughout my body as I tried to contain my excitement. I dampened those feelings down as we climbed on.

On the last pitch, I led through the overhanging 5.12 section featured in that famous poster of Lynn on the Nose, the one I'd had on my wall for years. It was unreal: here I was, heel-hooking above my head, three thousand feet off the ground, and I thought to myself: *I can't believe I'm doing this. I can't believe I ever actually got this good.* I topped out first, scrambling up the last few feet to the famous tree on the top of the Nose. I'd been thinking about this moment since I first learned Lynn's name. Now my name, and Tommy's, would forever be linked with hers: Hill, Rodden, Caldwell. I couldn't believe it. I wanted to scream, a giddy, delicious scream—proud and thrilled and tinged with relief. But I didn't. Tommy wasn't there yet. Always superstitious, I couldn't celebrate until we were actually and truly done.

I took off my shoes. My feet were swollen from four days on the wall. Swollen from the past month of working the route to death. Swollen from the past decade of climbing in general. The Sierra granite under my bare soles was comforting. It felt like a warm soft towel, a signal that I could finally relax. I didn't need to go back on that cliff today. Maybe not ever. I set up the belay and worked the rope through my palms until Tommy topped out. I looked out at the view over to Middle Cathedral, the blue California sky. As Tommy drew closer I felt satisfaction, joy, so much relief. I was never one to whoop or yell out loud when I sent. It felt too boastful, like I ought to stay quiet and let my accomplishments speak for themselves. But this time, sitting on the top of El Cap, I let out a yell.

Tommy topped out, whooped, and gave me a huge hug. "We did it, honey!" This was huge for him too, even though he still had his Double coming up. His season goal was still ahead of him; I was so relieved that mine was done.

There was a rescue going on nearby: YOSAR was on top, setting up to rappel in and pull someone out who had fallen. Mary Braun, a longtime Valley local and YOSAR member, came running over, thinking we'd just topped out the Nose after a normal four-day ascent. Greg, a young, handsome hotshot who'd heard about our attempt, corrected her: we had freed it.

"Holy shit," she said.

Greg smiled and said, "So psyched for you guys. Pack up your haul bags. The helicopter can take them down for you—just put my name on them." That was VIP treatment for climbers—better than spraying a bottle of champagne. We hiked down with just a small pack and a bottle of water.

Two days later, fingers still bruised and sore, we started all over: an 11:00 p.m. wake-up and an all-night climb. I jugged and belayed Tommy as he freed the Nose again in twelve hours flat. A couple of days after that, I played the same supporting role as he freed Freerider, the second planned route in the Double. And then, after another several days' rest, we went back one more time, with our friend Chris to handle the support on the second route, and Tommy freed both the Nose *and* Freerider in twenty-three hours and twenty-three minutes. It was a stunning accomplishment, a feat that has yet to be even close to repeated two decades later.

But in those minutes after Greg offered to fly our haul bags down, after our team free ascent, I wasn't thinking about the Double's logistics and demands. Instead, I was daydreaming about the brownie fudge sundae I would order from the Mountain Room to celebrate. I had skipped my lunch, a protein bar, just in case.

CHAPTER
TWENTY-SIX

Yosemite Valley, California, August 2006

It was never a question if we were going to build the house ourselves. We had freed the Nose. We were BethandTommy. We could do anything.

We had the lot near Yosemite, a quarter acre scruffy with overgrown manzanita and whitethorn bushes, treed with cedar and fir. I wanted the quintessential mountain home: vaulted ceiling, big open living space, three bedrooms, two bathrooms. I bought a book of house plans, and we cleared our schedule of any serious sponsor commitments or projects. We started working in May 2006. Our friend Lance framed houses when he wasn't climbing, so we hired him to help out. We got professionals to pour the foundation because even Tommy's parents told us we shouldn't try to DIY that. Then it was framing and sheathing and on from there: pre-staining the deck posts, hammering in strapping and brackets to meet code, carrying sheets of plywood . . . The job seemed endless, but our path was clear. At first, the work felt clean and virtuous, one task after the next. No soul-searching or daydreaming, no aimlessness or boredom. No time to think about all the things I still tried not to think about.

One warm summer morning I was sweeping up the jobsite, preparing for the day ahead, when I heard a whistle—a snarky *Hey, lady* whistle. I stopped sweeping, looked up at the parking pad, and saw a full-size white truck with a lumber rack. Out of the driver's side stepped one of the crane operators coming to check out the jobsite for the roof beam we'd hired him to hoist the next week. He had a patchy beard, a black baseball cap, four teeth. He whistled again, and not with a friendly lilt. It was menacing and gross.

I took a big breath and yelled, "Are you Jim? From the Fresno crane company?"

"Yes, ma'am," he said, the *ma'am* jarring after his wolf whistle. "I'm not used to seeing a lady on the jobsite. You sure you know how to use all those powerful tools?"

My face flushed with a hot mixture of outrage and humiliation. But we really needed this crane to install our massive roof beam, so I did what I always did. I shoved my feelings away, laughed, and smiled. "Yeah, I've figured them out," I said. "You can come down and take some measurements if you like."

He walked down the path and climbed the ladder into the roughly framed house, looking around like he was an inspector instead of just a guy we'd hired to do a job. "Wow," he said. "This will be a nice house when it's done. Who's been doing all the work?"

One of the perks of being at the top of my male-dominated sport: I wasn't used to being talked down to. I knew other young women climbers would get patronized or condescended to at the crags, sometimes, but I was almost never treated like a second-class citizen. I tried to shove my disgust down. "It's just me, my husband, and our friend," I said. "We hired out the foundation, but we're doing everything ourselves from here."

"Such a pretty little thing out here doing all this hard work? Wow, I need to find me a wife like you."

He walked around a little more and then said, "When is your husband getting back here? I need to schedule the exact time and collect my deposit."

I felt diminished, by both his words and my apparent inability to stand up for myself. Tommy didn't know what day it was, or when the next lumber delivery was coming, let alone what time we'd be ready for the roof beam next Wednesday. I dealt with our finances and our calendar. I knew how much we'd been quoted and how much we had in our account.

"I have no idea," I said. "But I've got the checkbook, and we need you here no later than ten a.m. next Wednesday."

He uncorked a disgusting grin. "Oh, sweetheart, I'll just wait for your husband to get here. I think that's best."

I couldn't take his *ma'ams* and his four-toothed grins and his belittling questions anymore. I left him to his measurements and waited up on the parking pad for Tommy to get back from his errand. When he arrived, the story poured out of me, and I realized I was crying. I stopped talking, wiped my face, feeling pathetic, and waited for Tommy to tell me he'd confront the guy and make it okay.

"Oh, he just did that because he thinks you are pretty, and who can blame him? You're amazing, I'm so lucky to have you as my wife." He paused. "You want to just give me a signed check and I can fill it in and get him on his way? What time do we need him here next Wednesday?"

My whole body felt sour with anger, but I didn't know if it was because of Tommy or the crane guy. I signed a check, shoved my resentment down as far as I could, and handed it to Tommy. He kissed my salty cheek and walked away.

◆ ◆ ◆

By the time I realized we'd made a mistake, it was much too late. We'd been working on the house for months, seven days a week, ten to twelve hours a day. Installing windows, doors, the deck, the stairs, half the rough plumbing, all the wiring. It was grueling work, but it was not the same kind of hard work, the training and climbing, that had helped us thrive in the years since Kyrgyzstan. That had helped me survive in the years since Kyrgyzstan. When it got too cold to camp on our lot, we retreated to a makeshift bed in the entryway of our friend Hans's house nearby. I drove an hour each way to the lumberyard every day. Sometimes I had to go twice, one sad day three times. I lived on Trader Joe's frozen meals, Joe-Joe's, and Diet Pepsi. My fitness was long gone, I got winded walking up our fifty-foot driveway, and the bass note to all my labored breathing was a growing, persistent resentment toward my husband.

The grim voice in my head that always questioned my choices and their falling-domino effects grew louder. Sure, we were at the top of our industry, but in those days even the best climbers were paid very little compared to mainstream pro athletes. Ordinarily I was so proud of our frugality, our ability to do a lot with a little: the climber's dream. But now our limitations were chafing. If we'd gone to college, I thought, we would have better jobs and we could hire out more of the work. If we'd waited to build, we could have saved up more money. If we'd broken the project up over several years, like we had when we remodeled our cabin in Estes, we could be climbing right now. I wouldn't be cooking and cleaning for Lance, who grated on me, because we needed his experience. I wouldn't be losing the regimen, the control, that had kept me safe since I had started to come back to myself after Kyrgyzstan.

It wasn't fair or right, but I blamed Tommy for the choices we'd made together, the choices for which I was equally responsible. I was angry at him, and I couldn't explain why. I'd wake up every morning at Hans's hoping to feel different, wishing for the desire to roll over and snuggle into Tommy's chest. But instead I'd creep quietly upstairs so I could eat my breakfast alone.

I hadn't enjoyed being alone in almost a decade. But now I loved the peace and stillness. I'd never thought of Tommy as loud, but suddenly everything around him was cacophonous. His snoring, his eating, his laughing, his walking. My head started to hurt as much as my back. I took Advil, but it did not soothe my mind.

The tradesmen exhausted me. I told Tommy about them sometimes—the asshole at the lumberyard, the chauvinist at the dump, the condescending clerk at the hardware store. He was so focused on finishing the house, and he had no idea what I was talking about, and that made me resent him more. There wasn't much he could have done, anyway. It wasn't like I expected him to drive down to the dump and stage a confrontation. Still, I wanted more outrage. I wanted Tommy to understand. But that wasn't how things really worked between us—we were long on love, short on empathy.

This was the first time we had been together and not focused on climbing. I was a professional climber, living on the edge of Yosemite Valley with my professional-climber husband, and I'd hardly touched rock for months. What had gone wrong? Here we were, dreaming big, working hard. But I had stopped saying *See you all night long* to Tommy before we fell asleep.

◆ ◆ ◆

I had just prepared my second cup of decaf Earl Grey tea, mixed with honey and vanilla soy milk, when the phone rang. I looked at the half-eaten box of Joe-Joe's and grabbed one more. My head was still throbbing from the noise of the miter saw and the palm nailer—and the strain of our depleting bank account. We'd always been so responsible. We owned our Estes cabin outright. We'd used the money we'd gotten from a book and a potential movie about Kyrgyzstan to open retirement accounts and a college fund for the kid we did not yet have and to buy this lot for $48,000. We lived incredibly cheaply. We wore free clothes from our sponsors. We ate free bars for one or two meals a day. We'd taken out a line of credit on the Estes cabin to build the house here, but the money was running out.

"Hello?" I said around the cookie in my mouth.

"Well, hiiii, Beth, it's Terry"—the familiar high-pitched voice. Tommy's mom always accentuated the word *Hi*, making it last twice as long as any other word.

I finished the cookie and settled in for a chat, but Terry, unnervingly, asked to talk to Tommy. She almost never talked to him without me—we were BethandTommy, even to her. I yelled downstairs for him to pick up the phone.

I should have hung up once he was on the line. I had tended to be a passive wife where the Caldwells were concerned. I obeyed and stayed silent when Mike laid into us about not climbing hard enough, not training enough, not getting our faces on the covers of enough climbing magazines. I had learned that response from Tommy. He survived all those years in the Caldwell house by just letting Mike be—rant, complain, instruct. He always calmed down by morning. But that was not my world. I grew up with the gentlest father. My skin was flypaper, not Kevlar coated in Teflon. I kept a running tally of everything Mike criticized about our lives, our climbing, our careers.

I held the phone upside down to my ear, the mouthpiece sticking above the top of my head, a cheap "mute" button so no one could hear my breathing or the Joe-Joe's in my mouth.

"Have you talked to Daddy yet?" Terry said.

"Um, not for a few days," Tommy said. I could tell he was distracted, maybe still getting dressed after his shower.

"I've not seen him this upset in a long time."

I pressed the upside-down phone harder to my ear as Terry spoke. Mike had just been here with us for a few weeks.

"Huh?" Tommy said. "Has he not had any climbing partners for the Rock Club?" That was the typical reason for Mike's sour moods.

"No. It was how Beth treated him out there." I stopped chewing. "He said he'd never been so disrespected in his life, and after hearing it I don't blame him." My armpits started to sweat, soaking through my shirt. "She's really trying to break up this family, and I can't stand it anymore."

I waited, expecting Tommy to set her straight. In the long silence I assumed he was collecting his thoughts. But instead, after a minute, he said, "What was Daddy so upset by?"

That got her started. He didn't like that I listened to Top 40 and rap music. That I swore when I dropped something. That I went to bed late and didn't wake up early.

I looked down at the box of Joe-Joe's. I had eaten the entire second row. I did not understand. For once in our nearly seven-year relationship, I had felt relaxed with Mike while he was here. I sang while I ran the miter saw. I cooked him dinner every night. Before he left we treated him to a meal at the Mountain Room, and we sent him climbing shoes once he'd returned to Estes, as a thank-you for helping us with the house. I'd dropped my perfect facade and felt closer to him than I ever had.

I knew he didn't like rap music, but was it really that bad? I bit into another cookie.

I heard Tommy coming up the stairs. He walked into the living room, freshly showered, clean clothes and socks. He looked at the floor, dejected. He didn't know that I had listened in on the phone call.

I wanted to, but I couldn't just let it be. "I heard that entire conversation, Tommy." I rarely called him Tommy if it was just the two of us. It was always *honey* or *TC.*

"You did? I'm so sorry."

"You did nothing to correct them. You did nothing to stand up for me!"

I felt something break down inside of me, crumbling under the weight of anger and hurt. The whole emotional foundation of me, of us, started to shake. I was so tired of gritting my teeth and smiling, of being good and nice, of playing perfect. It had felt so easy to relax, for once. To be imperfect. But if I couldn't be perfect, and perfection was the basis of our relationship, then what was there? What were we?

Tommy came over and hugged me. I hated it.

"You did nothing. You said nothing," I said. I wanted to say: *You are supposed to pick me.* But I didn't. I wanted him to choose me, not to follow instructions to choose me. I wanted us to admit our mistakes and our flaws to each other, to look inward, to acknowledge our problems and work through them together. It felt like we were always looking outward for solutions, papering things over so the surface looked pristine. If I felt fat, we went for a long run. If Mike was upset at me, and

I was upset at Tommy for not defending me to Mike, we didn't talk about it. We just trained harder. I didn't have the words to express it to him then, but I wanted us to go deeper. I wanted us to be more than good-on-paper BethandTommy. I wanted our relationship to be real.

By February I was done. The thought of insulating the house seemed far more awful than admitting defeat. When we'd insulated the Estes cabin, my skin had burned and itched for weeks. The fiberglass had burrowed into every inch of my body—eyes, lungs, hair. We'd suffered through it rather than spend the money on proper protective gear—typical climbers. But I shuddered at the thought of doing all of it again, at four times the size. We got a quote back from the subcontractor: $18,000 to do the house. It was a fortune and worth every penny. Then we hired out the drywall as well. We spent two months climbing at festivals—sheepishly, because I didn't feel like a climber anymore; my arm muscles had leaked away and I was fifteen pounds heavier than my peak performance weight. Still, the change of scene got us over the hump. We came home rested enough to paint the walls and install the flooring.

By then it was spring, nearly a whole year gone. I knew I wanted to have a climbing project again. What was the point of having a house so near the Valley if I didn't climb? It would be like owning a Picasso and keeping it in the closet. Like living on the North Shore of Oahu and being really into billiards. I told Tommy I didn't want something monumental, but something attainable. I picked Book of Hate—one pitch, 5.13d, a good reintroduction.

We left Lance in charge of finishing the decking and hired a trim carpenter. "Most couples are divorced by the time I get on the jobsite," he said. "Good work, you two!"

CHAPTER
TWENTY-SEVEN

Yosemite Valley, California, Spring 2007

Book of Hate is a different type of climb. It's a big dihedral, a corner where two blank walls come together at an almost 90-degree angle, like an open book. There is a faint crack in the back, at the book's spine, where you can wiggle your fingertips in and place the gear that will hold you if you fall. But the meat of the climb is the opposite of most: it's in the legs. Usually, hard climbing is about fighting upper-body fatigue. The holds are so small my fingers might give out, or my forearms, or my upper arms. But this climb was all stemming: placing my feet on either side of the dihedral and shimmying up the wall. It's like when little kids try to climb the inside of a doorway: their feet and legs are mainly holding them up, but their arms provide balance.

We left the jobsite behind and headed down the highway. We parked on a dirt pullout and meandered down through a forest of oak and pine before coming to the steep, poison-oak-infested gully that led to the base of the route. I felt like an ex trying to weasel my way back into a relationship that I had left. It had been nearly a year since I had trained seriously, and I hadn't done a big-name route since the Nose a year and a half earlier. Would I feel that same giddy joy but also the intense drive that had always simmered in me? Things had always been happier between Tommy and me when we were climbing. Even he, usually so patient, was wearing thin on building instead of climbing, though he shrugged off his frustrations more easily than I ever could. I was hoping this would help.

The first time I started up the route, my hands and feet knew what they wanted to do. My mind knew what it needed to do. But nothing worked in unison. It was like trying to ride a bike again after a long layoff. They say you never forget how, but with enough time you do lose that sense of balance and timing, of knowing precisely how to merge the physics of your body with the machinery of your bike. I was unsure of how to try hard, when to try hard. The granite felt rough and slippery at the same time. It tore up my skin while I simultaneously slipped off it. Tiny muscles in my back and shoulders quivered.

Sometimes the frustration of knowing how strong I used to feel consumed me while I climbed. *Think of how great you could have been by now. Think of how hard you could be climbing if you weren't so lazy, Beth.* But at other times, I granted myself a little grace. Each day I made progress, and it reminded me of being a beginner again. That early journey is a linear progression, because when I was that far down, the only way to go was up.

Tommy belayed me for each session. He would yell suggestions and encouragement up to me as I worked, and I remembered how much I loved collaborating with him. This was our old, familiar duet. The house had been the problem, I told myself, trying to let the hurt and resentment that had built up between us ease away. The house and the labor and the workmen.

After a week I felt my old granite wizardry return. I loved the mundane act of hanging on my rope, staring at the wall, looking for bumps or weaknesses that I could stand on. Some would be tiny, the size of a Tic Tac or smaller, and others would be smooth changes in angle that I could only see from a certain position, so subtle my eyes might miss them, like the gentle fluctuations of a seashell. While the tedium of nailing hundreds of nails with a palm nailer had drained me, this work fed me. It was meditation, satisfying and serene.

Because the climbing was different, the training was too. We had designed our house around the gym in the garage: an improved version of the Caldwell gym in Estes, because we knew it had already produced success. (We'd built it before finishing the plumbing or installing the lighting. Priorities.) Eleven-foot ceilings, two big climbing walls at varying angles, a lat pull-down machine, a bench and weights, some new machines for ab work. I knew how to beat myself up in there, to train until my arms burned and the skin on my palms was raw and thin. But my arms weren't the main act in this climb; my calves and quads were. I had always ignored these parts of my body. I had even thought I should neglect them intentionally so they wouldn't bulk up with muscle to weigh me down. Now I had to rely on them. But that was just part of the challenge, part of this new puzzle that needed to be solved. I started riding my bike on a trainer in the garage and always offered to be the one to walk up the steep hill to our mailbox. Already, things felt better between Tommy and me. At night, we'd talk through the moves I'd worked on that day while we ate vegan lentil soup and unbuttered bagels, or snuggled on the couch and watched *CSI: Miami*.

After a couple weeks I was near completion. My mind was a twist of excitement, nerves, anxiety. I knew I could do it. This was the point where I just needed to put everything into place.

I tied into the rope, now as familiar as tying my shoes. (I laced those up too.) My mind wasn't on the prep I was doing, it was starting to quiet, to get into the space where I knew I had to try hard, to put aside fear, to silence the doubting, negative voices in my mind. Suddenly, on the brink, it felt scary to give myself over to that sending mentality again. I didn't know if I was quite ready yet. Could I put my faith entirely in the gear? In my physical ability? Could I just let go? It felt so perilous, even though it was exactly what I wanted.

I started up, making one move after another. Soon my calves were burning, my quads were burning. There was no more room for doubts.

Halfway up, I paused, dropped my legs, and shook them out. When the burning had eased to a tolerable level, I kept going, mind quiet, focused on getting to the top.

When I reached it, I clipped the anchors and smiled. I let myself soak briefly in the pleasure of a small win. I had done it: the first ever female ascent of Book of Hate.

But that kind of thing was hard to feel, to hang on to, and soon I was telling myself it hadn't been hard enough. Sure, it had gotten me into the magazines for the first time since the Nose. It reminded my sponsors that I was still here. But Book of Hate was easier than other climbs I had done before, and therefore I shouldn't find it worthy of true celebration. First female ascents were a double-edged sword: they got me accolades and raises from my sponsors, but I also knew they would always carry an asterisk. In the end, I would be judged against the accomplishments of the men, and I needed to do things none of them had ever done to be recognized among them. (Even then, I might still be undermined: *Oh, she only sent that because she has such little fingers.*) This was just a stepping-stone to get me back to harder and bigger objectives.

CHAPTER
TWENTY-EIGHT

Yosemite Valley, California, April 2007

Thin, hard cracks are difficult to find. Nature has to align in the most mundane and extraordinary way. I'd walk around, searching for a delicate, nearly invisible line: a thin gold chain on a wide sand beach. What are the odds that a firm enough type of rock (nothing too soft or flaky) would yield a crack in it at the right angle? With enough of a gap to slide a small part of my fingers in but not a big enough space to be able to fit my whole hand (that would make it too easy)? And that the crack would extend far enough to be considered a route, longer than a few feet, continuous and maintaining enough openings throughout to actually be climbed?

I wanted and needed something very particular, the physical manifestation of a certain kind of test. A long, tiny fissure to create a precise athletic riddle—just the right degree of difficulty, requiring mastery of the body in a true sense to overcome. The right crack for a climber is one that requires them to learn the same hard lessons, every time. How to get a handle on yourself physically and mentally, how to know what to accept and what to push through.

Our friend Corey, the photographer, first showed me the crack that would become my new project. He made the trip down to Yosemite to shoot me on Book of Hate for a La Sportiva ad, and before he left town, he suggested we take a walk up to an old, unnamed project that the legendary Yosemite climber Ron Kauk had started but never finished. The etiquette around picking up another climber's unfinished project is a little murky—even now, writing those words, I want to look over my shoulder and see if Ron is watching. But it had been nearly a decade since he had worked on this one, and Corey and I joked that the statute of limitations on it had expired.

You could probably throw a ball from where Corey parked his car along the side of Highway 120 to the base of the route. (Or someone could, not me; there's a reason I didn't pursue ball sports.) We ran across the two-lane highway and started up a very steep hill. It was covered in pine needles with no trail: nature's Slip 'N Slide. We wove our way up the short, dry slope, passing the odd patch of manzanita, until we started to see some outcroppings of crumbly dark granite popping out of the hillside. We were on the west side of the Upper Cascade Creek drainage, and the waterfall became deafening as we got higher. After about fifteen minutes we stood on a granite outcropping and looked across Cascade Falls, raging with the spring melt, to a thin discontinuous crack that crept up an otherwise solid wall. The crack was less than fifty feet away, engulfed in frothy white water, the falls loud as a passing freight train. Even at a distance, my hair was damp and the front of my shirt got soaked.

The place was beautiful, the crack had never been climbed, and, I realized, it was tucked away from sight, so I could work on it without anyone knowing or watching. What could be better?

◆ ◆ ◆

After we finished the house, early in the summer of 2007, Tommy and I got back into our old rhythm: his turn, my turn, our turn. Even during the times when we weren't climbing, we had rediscovered an easy coexistence, a comfortable routine.

In May, we'd completed another El Cap route together: the first free, ground-up ascent of El Corazón, meaning that we free climbed it without rehearsing the hard pitches at the top ahead of time. In August, I made the first female ascent of a 5.13c called Peace, up in Tuolumne, the high country of Yosemite National Park, and Tommy started working loosely on freeing an El Cap line called Mescalito. (Later, his new route would become known as the Dawn Wall.) He'd made plans to attempt yet another El Cap route, Magic Mushroom, beginning in the spring. So that winter it was my turn.

We came back to give the project by the waterfall a try in September, when the water was low enough to make climbing possible. Tommy strung a rope on the anchors Ron had put in a decade earlier. For a professional climber, I never feel that brave: I like having the rope secured to an anchor above me. I like being able to dissect everything, slowly and up close. If I'm leading, meaning that I am placing my own gear as I go, and then climbing above it to place the next piece, I have all these extra worries and fears spinning through my mind: about falling, about the gear holding. It feels easier to decode the climbing first, knowing I'm secure, and then face the fear later.

The route was about seventy feet tall, which is not long or sustained by any stretch of the imagination for a rock climb. (Modern routes are often two hundred feet or longer.) But the first time I tried it, I only managed to climb about five of those feet. That sounds defeating, and I guess it is, but I liked the challenge of it. There was seventy feet of rock, and on that rock were some number of holds (bumps, cracks, indentations, or other irregularities). It was up to me to figure out if I could contort my body, grab the holds, move my feet in the correct way to get to the top.

Over the first few days, Tommy tried a few moves and had just as hard a time with it as I did. That was one of the ways we worked so well together: giving each other perspective. He had done so many hard routes that if he thought it was hard, then it had to be hard. But I was able to do as many or more moves as he could in the beginning, so I knew it was a candidate. All I needed was a small seed of hope or confidence or possibility to think that if I got stronger, if I unlocked a better sequence, a better body position, there would be a path for me.

The rock in that area is black, which is weird for Yosemite. Usually the good, bullet-hard rock is white, or light gray. But this almost looked like obsidian, and it was slippery as wet moss thanks to the eons of waterfall spray that had polished it. I remember the first time I pulled on it, the inside edge of the crack was so pronounced it felt like driving a butter knife into my skin. Sometimes in crack climbing, the texture of rock can be used to a climber's advantage by hanging fingers or skin off of it: like a sheet draped over a stiff hedge or bush to dry, it just sticks. And other times, if the rock is smooth or polished, it's not sharp. So the climber can tense, expand, wiggle their fingers to find the perfect, most comfortable spot, and sort of muscle their way through it. This rock, unfortunately, had none of the good and all of the bad. It was sharp and polished at the same time, meaning I had to tense and flex my fingers and literally dig in to the pain of dull but intense jams.

Handholds in crack climbing are called jams, because a climber jams their fingers, hands, or feet into the gap in the rock. Imagine sticking your first two fingers into the mouth of a glass bottle and then hanging your body weight from them. Imagine that the lip of the bottle was cracked, but it had been tumbled in the ocean for years, so the crack's dangerous edges had been dulled. That lip was still sharp, but no longer immediately lacerating. Still, the more time and weight I put on each hold, the more urgently I wanted to get off. It was like I had a stopwatch ticking each time I slid my fingers in and slowly and methodically twisted them downward, feeling and accepting each indentation.

The first few weeks, just as I had on Book of Hate and the Nose, I spent hours of each climbing day hanging on the rope, swinging slightly from one side of the crack to the other. I'd press my face so close to the rock that I could smell the musty green lichen. Staring down toward the ground, I hoped I might spot a nub or weakness in the rock that I couldn't see when looking straight on. I felt like a treasure hunter poring over obscure clues, or one of those people who wanders the beach with a handheld metal detector, scanning the faceless sand. Whenever I found even the possibility of a hold, I would put my hand in my chalk bag, remove a tiny piece of white climber's chalk, and dot the place with a tick mark. Most of the holds were no more pronounced than the texture on the drywall at my parents' house.

While I worked, my mind zigzagged from one thought to the next. Had Ron, one of my idols, figured out this part of the sequence before he let the project be? If I sent it, was I besting him? Stupid idea, I could never be better than Ron Kauk—he was a granite genius. Then I'd make a mental note to add another hour of training at home that night and to make sure I only loaded my plate half full at dinner. Or I'd count up my *Rock and Ice* covers, setting my total against the handful of other female climbers I always, back then, saw as my competition for a seat at the boys' table. Would this climb get me another cover? Would it get me a raise?

Searching out the holds, nose to granite, I was totally focused, while at the same time my inner narrator had no focus at all. But that tension worked for me. Soon the wall was covered in chalk polka dots, and the crack had little tick marks next to each of the best openings to stick my hands in. All the possible options were marked, all the things I wanted to remember, all the things I wanted to consider for my final formula. I would erase these at the end of each session, but after a few weeks, my mind and body knew each one. Each single move contained dozens of muscle memories: my body needed to know how to tense the abs, how to hang, when to breathe, when to flex. Maybe that was why I loved it so much.

Until I found climbing, no sport I'd tried had aligned with my drive. In swimming, I was competing against girls twice my height and weight. Tennis was the same: I tried hard but didn't have the mass to back up my swing. With climbing, my body could fit itself to the task while my mind attacked the puzzle. At first I could focus my drive only against the route and with myself. I just wanted to get to the top. I'd climb, feel my fingers opening up, clench harder, hold on tighter, and will myself to the top. It was like that on every move if I felt myself failing. I dug deep, pushed past any fatigue or pain or doubt. Then I started to feel triumphant, like I was better than people who fell or let go early. I started to think of them as weak. I wondered why they didn't just hold on longer. What was wrong with them? I liked that feeling of being on the brink of puking. It made me feel worthy.

CHAPTER
TWENTY-NINE

Yosemite Valley, California, Early Winter 2007

Training for a project again put me back in control: of my body, my schedule, my mindset. No more boxes of Joe-Joe's, no more tea with honey and soy milk every night. I believed that successfully restricting myself was part of my competitive advantage over other people with less discipline, less commitment. I lost most of my "building pudge," as I called it, and soon I could fit into my old harness again. My fingers were strong.

My project was an easy approach, a short pitch, and not far from our house. Tommy would belay my burns on the crack in the mornings, which left the second half of the day for him to boulder. More and more often, that meant meeting up at Camp 4 with the group we had started calling the Bay Crew.

"This is Courtney, Lyn, Paul, Tim, Patti, Nora, Ingar . . . ," Randy said one afternoon when I'd decided to tag along. The names seemed to go on forever. I could not relate at all to the desire to climb in a group. A short walk away, up the hill, they'd only hear birds and wind, with no one else around. They knew that, right?

I'd heard of Randy for years, but until I reencountered him through the Bay Crew, I'd forgotten that we'd met ten years earlier, when Randy was twenty-four and I was sixteen. He was the quiet guy flying under the radar, the one with loose-limbed ease and a full-time tech job in the Bay Area. He was confident but kind, and he climbed as hard as us professional climbers. He had once considered becoming a professional race-car driver, but he shied away from the limelight. He was handsome, with short dark hair and a warm broad smile that always made me want to smile back.

Courtney was his fiancée. She had shoulder-length brown hair, muscular arms, and a silver bracelet around her wrist; she came up and gave Randy a hug as he ran through the names. I waved hello to everyone, then left to go sit by myself on our crash pad.

Bouldering is climbing without ropes. It has its own grading system, ranging from V0 to V17, and it doesn't require climbers to go very high—generally only as far as someone can comfortably fall on portable foam mats called crash pads. It's the most approachable form of climbing, the one with the least technical knowledge required: no harnesses, no gear. And it's the most social, since no one is tethered to a cliff, with a partner a rope's length away.

Through the trees I saw Tommy pulling on his climbing shoes and jumping into their scene like a kid into a pool, happily and all at once. Bouldering required raw physical power, climbing in front of people, and hour upon hour of hanging out—none of which I was good at. Besides, I did not understand how anyone felt content bouldering. Didn't they pine for greatness? Didn't they see the towering walls directly above them? Didn't they want to achieve?

"Are you climbing today, Beth?" Courtney asked, walking over.

"Oh, hmm, I'm not sure yet. I think I'll just wait a little while. I'm not very good at bouldering." I always tried to say in advance the horrible things that I knew other people would eventually think anyway.

"That's okay, we're all just out here having fun," she said.

But as I watched I realized the women were climbing V9s (the hardest boulder I'd climbed in the Valley was a V5) and working on problems I'd only seen men send before. Randy was playing on a notoriously hard problem that he had established years before, called Stick It. He laughed his magnetic laugh—and climbed like a wizard, smooth and deliberate. His technique and strength were phenomenal. It was funny to watch Tommy trying to follow Randy. Tommy's muscles shook; he looked like a diesel truck chasing a sports car, grinding it out.

And I was fascinated by Lyn and Courtney. They climbed things I couldn't imagine, and freely shared beta (climber speak for crucial information about a route), which, with my competitiveness always on high alert, was unthinkable. I sat there and watched, knotted up inside. I had the perfect life. We were BethandTommy, "the first couple of rock." We owned two houses we'd built ourselves. But the Bay Crew seemed to run their lives on a different set of expectations. And I could not stop watching Randy.

◆ ◆ ◆

Back at my new project, I hung on the rope and stared at the wall. *It should all be here,* I told myself. I had a sliver of a crack and seven or eight potential footholds dotted with chalk, three on the right side of the crack and four on the left. These were the puzzle pieces that made up the crux of my new route. Despite the name, a crux doesn't nec- essarily come at a climb's summit or apex—it's just the climb's most challenging move or sequence. This one was maybe fifteen, twenty feet off the ground. But if the crack was going to be climbable—if it was ever going to become a named, graded route and not just another failed project—I would have to fit these pieces together.

I felt like a kid trying to break into a friend's locker, trying every possible combination. I grabbed the crack with my left hand, thumbs down, and perched my right foot on the worst hold of the route: a tiny bump, the size of your average high-school pimple and the same shape too. Instead of being red and white and shiny, it was black and shiny, but equally loathed. I smeared my left foot on the small edge, tried to do a pull-up, held my breath, but my left foot slipped and I catapulted off the wall. Goddamnit. Why didn't that work?

I pulled back on, left hand still thumbs down, right hand just below it this time, so as not to get too extended, right foot on the nonexistent edge below the pimple hold, and left foot on the same marginal smear. This time, I had time to move my eyes from my right foot to start to look up the crack before—wham! I was hanging on the rope again.

Was it my lack of finger strength? My lack of shoulder strength? Was it my shoes? I tried to find a reason: something to blame, something to fix. My Miuras had never failed me before. My eyes moved over to the dark wall where the waterfall would be raging by the time winter receded into spring. The skin on the sides of my fingers burned from torquing them inside the thin crack for the past hour. But I hadn't figured out what was possible yet. I couldn't go down until I at least had an idea of what might work.

I stared at the pimple hold. It was in the perfect position. Not too high, not too low, just far enough out from the crack to give me oppositional balance. I hated that hold. My foot skidded off it every time. I looked down at Tommy, holding the rope and staring at his shoes, twenty feet below me. I worried that he was bored, or hungry. Was he thinking that all this time belaying me was pointless because I was never going to succeed?

I reached out again. Put my right foot on the hold, the thumb on my left hand pointing down and my right hand in the low position again (that seemed better last time), and then I put my left foot on the slightly higher razor-thin smear. I pulled on. Something felt different. I could tell I was about to fall like a stone, but still, something clicked. My body liked this position. From here, my body knew that I could do this one day. Not today, but one day. If I put in the time, kept up my discipline at every meal, if I built up my fingers and shoulders and abs enough to hold on. I slowly moved my eyes and head from staring at my right foot to looking up the crack. And then—boom. My right foot exploded off the wall again.

As we drove the winding road home, I was only half aware of the Harry Potter audiobook coming out of the stereo. My mind spun from the hint of a breakthrough I'd just had. I headed straight into the garage, to our training wall. I was filled with adrenaline from the possibility that the crux might be possible.

I felt like Rocky in the Russian barn, only instead of running in the snow with a log over my shoulders, I needed to try to replicate the crux's conditions at home. I walked over to our less steep wall—its angle was similar to the slant of the crux. I moved the black-and-red triangle hold to the middle of the wall and the slippery brown Metolius edge below it, tilted at almost a 90-degree angle to simulate the crack. I screwed on a few more edges above them, at equal angles to mirror a crack. That offered a rough approximation of what my hands would need to do. The feet were harder: it was impossible to replicate the minute footholds that were all I had to work with on the route. I found the slipperiest and worst feet I could and screwed them on. Then I practiced over and over until my hands opened up. It was just a matter of building the engrams: If I could do it here, then I could set it on the 40-degree wall. If I could do it on the 40-degree wall, then I could absolutely do it on the actual route.

◆ ◆ ◆

The crux *is* the most challenging part of a climb, physically. But after the crux is where climbers need to keep their heads together. If you let your mind get ahead of itself, it's like nailing a job interview but then blowing it with a bad joke on the way out the door. That's when I need to quiet all the doubt, when I can't let the *Holy shit I'm going to do this* get ahead of me. Everything becomes heightened: butterflies try to fight their way out of my stomach; it feels like my skin has goose bumps everywhere; my whole body feels alert and anxious. I know I can't lose focus, so I usually start talking to myself out loud.

After the crux sequence on the route, there was a huge flake—a piece of rock that is partly detached from the wall. That flake made me so nervous. It sounded like a bongo drum when I tapped the palm of my hand against it. I was terrified that if I fell on the gear I'd placed in the gap between it and the wall, the whole thing would come tearing down, and me with it. (Once, I'd asked Tommy if he thought it could break off, laughing about it to try to mask my fear. He'd replied: "If it did, I would catch you.")

Anxieties aside, the flake was the rest spot, the place where I could catch my breath, fit half my hands in the crack, and try to relax. When I got there, every time, I would go through the same motions, the same ritual dialogue. I'd breathe heavily and audibly. I'd check the gear and recheck the gear. I'd say in my head, *Keep it together, Beth, keep it together,* over and over again. I'd feel the blood pumping from my exhausted and depleted arms and flowing into my head and stomach, filling them with nerves. The balance was so tenuous, so tricky to nail. I couldn't hang out there too long: if I did I'd lose my edge. But if I rushed it, my body would be too fatigued to execute the hard sections ahead.

I needed to keep everything the same. If I did that, I would achieve greatness. I'd put my right hand on the back of my neck one more time to warm up my fingers, then shake it as I slid my hand back under the flake. I did the same with my left hand, chalked up and said, "C'mon, Beth," took a huge, deep, audible breath, and then said, "Okay," to Tommy. Loud enough that he could hear me, but not shouting. I didn't want to draw too much attention. Never mind that it was literally me, Tommy, and a waterfall that was growing steadily with each winter storm, not a pedestrian around for miles.

I am superstitious, and when I started climbing it permeated everything. I'd pack my purple bag the exact same way for each competition. I'd eat the same meal the night before: Olive Garden, penne pasta with red sauce, two and a half breadsticks, one virgin strawberry daiquiri. I'd dress in the same clothes and wear my same familiar climbing shoes down to nubs. When I moved out of the competition scene, I brought my superstitions with me. For this new climb, I was wearing the same black long-underwear bottoms I'd worn on the Nose and Book of Hate, the elastic starting to stretch and loosen. I had the same white Champion sports bra, the same white long-sleeved base layer, slightly stained. But for the first time in my career, I'd decided to switch shoes.

Every other climb of my life, I'd worn La Sportiva's fluorescent-yellow-green-and-black Miuras, but I decided that the small, slippery footholds on my new project needed something softer, more supple, something that would settle around a hold rather than on it. Just like the rubber on snow tires is softer, to hug the icy road, I needed a softer shoe to grab the footholds, not just perch on them. Sportiva had just come out with a new, softer shoe called the Solution, and they turned out to be one key piece of the puzzle.

Each day, after I was done beating my head against the wall, we'd drive home. I'd crawl onto the green couch that used to be Granny's, pull a white waffle blanket over my tired body, and close my burning eyes. I needed to sleep before going into the garage and training for another three to four hours.

At first my mind would spin, full of what I'd learned that day— what I didn't want to forget. *Maybe I should write it down? No, that's pathetic.* I was better than that. I was the best in the world, I could remember it, it was just a rock climb. No, it was *the* rock climb. *The* rock climb that was my life, that my entire self-worth hung on. If I just trained enough, bulked up my pencil arms (why couldn't they be beautifully muscular like Courtney's?), lost a little more weight, did another set of abs, another finger hang, then I could be fit enough to do it.

My mind raced with all of these thoughts. I was good enough; I wasn't good enough. This was the hardest thing I'd ever done—but was it really that hard if I could do it? And it wasn't on El Cap; it wasn't a hard man's route. But this was about pure rock climbing, not chest thumping, not some ego-boosting thing. It was mine, a quiet master-piece. I didn't want anyone to know about it; I wanted to have this as my own, to be able to cry and whine and collapse when I wasn't making progress. To have only Tommy witness my lows. To be able to kick and scream at the rock when I slipped off or my sequence didn't work. To shout at this rock wall and its indifferent lichen. To be able to act my worst. I didn't want to be at center stage on El Cap. There was too much history, too much tied to it, so much bravado and shit-talking and judging. I wanted to be back to just climbing. I wanted to be able to sleep in a bed at night instead of hanging off a wall, to take a hot shower and eat fresh food. I wanted to be alone with the awful simplicity of me and my ability and seventy feet of black granite.

CHAPTER THIRTY

Yosemite Valley, February 2008

One cold morning, between belaying my burns on the route, Tommy said, "I'm going to email Randy and see if he wants to boulder this weekend."

I wasn't really listening. I was in my try-hard room, and the only thing that entered my consciousness besides the rock was the water pooling at the bottom of my route. Soon the pool would start covering my footholds, and that meant the end of my season.

"Honey, did you hear me?" Tommy said. "Is that okay?"

"Huh, what?" I said. "Yeah, of course . . . What did you say?"

"I was going to see if Randy wanted to climb again this weekend. It's been fun for me to have someone to climb with . . . That group energy, you know?"

I stared in Tommy's direction, still not really focused on his words.

"Plus he's the Yosemite bouldering master. It would be neat to see new stuff with him in his zone."

"Wait, I'm not enough motivation for you?"

I was joking, but it was true: I was a bad partner these days. Just the day before, I had made Tommy hike up to work on Shadow Warrior alone while I napped in the back seat of the truck, resting for that afternoon's garage session.

"You are my entire world," Tommy said. "But it'd be fun to try some really hard stuff with someone else."

Through that whole winter, the Bay Crew showed up almost every weekend, developing new boulders in different parts of the Valley and eating the freshest food I'd ever seen. At lunchtime I'd pull out my sad peanut-butter protein bar and they'd unpack bright-green cucumbers, delicata squash, four types of citrus, charcuterie, and fresh bread. They seemed so adult and together: real people, whole people, talking about work, politics, relationships, whether or not to have kids. I was most fascinated by their debates; Tommy and I were so certain of our path, at least on the surface, that we never paused to question our decisions. These conversations felt like a massage for my brain: more intellectual stimulation than I'd had in a decade.

Randy always looked like he was in the center of it all. He'd make jokes with ease, and he was the strongest climber. I was drawn to him, but so, it seemed, was everyone else. I told myself it was just his charisma, why I noticed his every move and mood: his talent, his laugh, his ease.

◆ ◆ ◆

Tommy and I sat at the traffic light as they repaved the loop road in Yosemite. It was Valentine's Day, six years to the day after we'd gotten engaged. Winter in Yosemite (back then) was cold and snowy. Several major snowstorms had stymied any progress on my route. We were still listening to the Harry Potter audiobooks, and we were on book four. Harry, Ron, and Hermione were mired in their first tangled efforts at romance, and the story consumed me more than the climb. I wondered if I should take that as a sign.

A week earlier I'd had my biggest breakdown about the project: a fit of anger and tears. Tommy and I were hiking up, and before we even got to the base of the climb I was wet from the spray of the waterfall. Too much snow, too much sun, too much water. Spring was coming, the melt was on in the high country, and my fate would soon be decided. Standing in the swelling creek bed, staring up at the falls, I started to yell, demanding to know why this was happening to me, and then I started to cry. I wondered how I, the queen of control, had somehow let my life, my career, revolve around something as utterly outside my control as the weather. The tears mingled with the spray that had already soaked my face. The route was soaked too, the polished black rock shinier than ever.

When I was a child, sent to my bedroom, I'd imagined that if I made enough of a scene something would change. But instead, I'd just sit there on my bed, soaked in tears and emotions, more exhausted than when I started. This felt the same way. *Meltdown.*

It's absurd in retrospect: an adult woman screaming for the seasons to stop turning. But I felt so slighted, so angry. Then something switched in me. All the fears and doubts and questions and hesitations that orbited in my mind disappeared. I was burned clean. I wasn't going to let this spray ruin six months of my life, six months of dedication. I knew I could do this route. All the pieces were in place; I just needed to execute. I said under my breath as I turned and walked toward the car, "That's it, I'm over this, I'm doing it next day."

And here I was, on that next climbing day. Some of those burned-away insecurities and doubts had crept back into my mind in the days since I'd had my meltdown, but still the confidence won out. The light turned green, and we started up the hill toward Upper Cascade Creek. My palms began to sweat, and I remembered these same feelings every time my parents drove me to a competition. This was when I would have put on "Eye of the Tiger," to have that added confidence pulsing through my veins. Now I just listened to Harry and Hermione scheming.

At the base of the route, I started by freezing my fingertips, acclimating them to the harsh cold of the rock by grabbing a hold and releasing, grabbing and releasing, until they were beyond numb. I reached under my layers and pressed them against my stomach. This prevents fingers from becoming useless midclimb: freeze them first and then rewarm them rapidly. The change brings the blood rushing back, and then it sticks around for a while. Soon it felt like someone was stabbing a thousand needles into the pads of my fingers. Climbers call this the screaming barfies: as the needles jabbed my fingers, I jumped around in circles on the small dry area at the base of the route, screaming, trying to run away from the pain that I had just inflicted on myself. When the pulses dulled and were drowned out by a warm rush, it was time to climb.

I stood there, shoes perfectly laced, harness cinched tight (but not too tight), chalk bag half full (not half empty). I put my hands behind my back, dipped in, and squeezed the pile of chalk: perfectly broken up, neither too fine nor too chunky. These were deep reflexes by now: even my mania was muscle memory. I rubbed my chalky hands together and stared up at the thin dark crack.

The intensity filled me again. The same intensity of purpose, that certainty and focus, I'd felt as my meltdown receded a week before. I chalked my hands one more time, said in my head, *Just get this done,* and started climbing. No warning to Tommy, no good-luck or zen or flow-state talk. I knew nature's clock was ticking, and I knew I had this in me. I opened the mental door, the one that leads to the place where I leave the safety of self-deprecation behind. For months I'd rehearsed each move: how to tense my toes, how to drape my calloused skin on each hold, when to move fast and when to slow down. This was my time to perform. Now I just had to open the second door to my physical prowess. If I can open both doors, that's when the send happens.

I started climbing, and things felt almost routine. My mind was analyzing everything, like a computer working on hyperdrive. *How did that hold feel? How strong do my arms feel? Are my fingertips warm enough? Should I chalk up? My foot needs to go there next, don't forget to breathe, stand hard but not too hard, steady as you take off that piece of gear, grab the rope, good, that went quickly. I feel strong—better than I did last week, that's a good sign. Keep breathing, don't forget to shake before that next move, it's the last time before the crux, it's slightly damper out here today—don't let that bother you.* And yet it felt quiet in a way. This type of analyzing noise was comforting, my own version of a soothing ocean soundtrack. The good noise was like a well-oiled machine. It was invigorating. It aligned months of work into one final act. I loved this. This was like my competition days: I always climbed my best when it was go time. When I could open that door, be fully present, not project failure onto the future or dwell on the failures of the past. All those past failures were now the stepping-stones on which I was sending.

Just before the crux, there was a spot where I could stop and shake and warm my hands on the back of my neck once or twice, chalk up, and go. Everything before then went perfectly. I felt strong—the extra sets I'd added to my training were paying off. I took two deep breaths and then reached up with my right hand to the worst hold on the route. It was a quarter of a finger pad deep. I stuck my right index finger into it with my thumb facing down. The friction felt good.

I stepped my right foot onto the pimple, stabbed my left foot out to another terrible hold—these two footholds were the reason I'd switched to a softer, more supple shoe. Now I stood on them with complete accuracy, no room for doubts. I weighted my right fingertip and pulled with my arms. As I reached up I had only a second before my body would start to succumb to gravity and pull me over backward, off the wall. But I felt strong. I pulled up and grabbed for the next hold with my left hand. I grunted a deep scream. I often scream if there's a hard move; it distracts from the pain, lets my natural state take over, and makes my body do what I know it can do.

I was above my gear now, and I'd never fallen from here, but if I did, it would be a big fall. Maybe a bad one.

But I only let in those thoughts when I'm not in my zone, when I can't open my doors. This was different. I had two more moves before I could place another piece of gear—not the hardest moves, but hard. I needed to focus and climb my best. I felt myself open that second door, felt myself stepping in, felt myself pulling on the rock, analyzing the friction, how I was grabbing the hold. My left hand went up, and then my right hand. I couldn't hear the raging waterfall to my left anymore, couldn't hear Tommy shouting in excitement below. It was like I was in a tunnel, no detours, no options to distract me. My body took over.

I grabbed the good hold after the crux, and I heard myself take a breath, the first sound I'd heard in several seconds. I placed my piece of gear, and the noise of the waterfall returned to my awareness. It was a loud, awful reminder that this was my chance, and I wouldn't have many more. Shaking that off, I grabbed the next tiny razor holds. They didn't cut my skin anymore; I'd built up enough callus, enough knowledge and resilience. The next thing I knew, I was at the resting place, the most anxiety-provoking part of the climb, where I let my physical body rest but had to concentrate on keeping my mental state quiet.

"Okay," I said to Tommy as I started climbing again. I was jittery, knowing I was close, knowing this was mine to have today. If I did it I would make climbing history. This was my pinnacle. I'd worked harder on this than on anything before, so much harder than on the Nose or anything else on El Cap. I wanted this, but I couldn't say that out loud, not even to Tommy. That would break my golden rule of being the good girl and downplaying everything. But inside, it raged: I wanted this, and I knew I could do it.

I told myself to breathe. I was getting ahead of myself. I needed to get back into my zone, where there was orchestrated chatter: the conductor, not the heckler in the audience. I quieted my mind, started focusing on the feel of each hold again, the sharpness of the edges, the sequence of movements that I knew with my eyes closed.

There was still one hard part before the top, one with a blind gear placement, one that if it pulled out meant I would be falling onto the hollow flake. I grabbed the edge of the crack, took off the minuscule number 4 nut, and reached as high above my head as I could. I dragged it along the rock until it hit a tiny opening, just wide enough to accept a piece of gear that was less than a quarter-inch in size. I paused there and pressed the piece inward, something I had practiced hanging on a rope hundreds of times. I wiggled it, and it went to the back of the crack and set down inside, perfect, exactly where I wanted it. Placing that piece gave me a shot of energy in my arms. I grabbed the rock and held on tight, but not too tight. I still needed my reserves. I lifted my right foot up to my belly button and pressed it firmly on a tiny ripple in the rock. I engaged my shoulders and my hands and weighted the foothold. I grabbed above the nut, moved my left foot higher, and crossed my right hand above my left. I wrapped my thumb over the top of my right index finger to help hold it in place, adjusted my feet one more time, and then tensed and lunged for the subtle left-hand jug. I latched on to it, and my feet blew off their holds. My instinct was to let go, but my two remaining points of contact, my hands, clenched and doubled down. I let out a primal scream, reeled my feet back onto the wall, did a pull-up, and grabbed the next right-hand jug. I had done it. A few more obligatory moves and one more piece of gear, and I pulled over the final dark-gray slab.

I stood there, pulled up the rope, and clipped it in. I looked down at Tommy, smiled, and said, "Take!"

CHAPTER
THIRTY-ONE

Yosemite Valley, Spring 2008

The route I named Meltdown lit up the climbing world. I graced magazine covers all over the globe, had a spot in the annual Dosage film series—that was as big as it got for climbers back then. Its grade made it the hardest established route in Yosemite at the time, and one publication, *UKClimbing*, called it "one of the very hardest routes in the world." (Elsewhere, it was called "a masterpiece" and "nasty.") Despite many attempts, it would be more than a decade before anyone else was able to repeat it. But the certainty I'd felt on the send had leaked away, and it was so easy to doubt the strength of my own accomplishment.

I knew Meltdown was hard for me, and that Tommy had struggled with it too. But climbing is so subjective, I didn't know how hard it would be for anyone else. It's not like knowing you put up the fastest time in a hundred-meter dash down a standardized track. It's more like finding the way to a distant finish line and wondering if it only seemed so hard because you got lost along the way.

Ordinarily, when a climber puts up a first ascent of a new route, it's their prerogative to both name and rate it. I'd always been intimidated by that ritual—the pressure and the permanence of it—and on the Optimist, my other named route, I'd taken my friend Josh's suggestion of a name. I was even more reluctant to issue a verdict on the grade. I knew that Meltdown felt much harder than the Optimist, which I'd rated a 5.14b when I did the first ascent back in late 2004. It felt harder than the other 5.14as I had done too. But did that really make it 5.14c? I was wary of claiming something that could easily be stripped away. What if someone else came along and found an easier sequence? What if I had totally missed a hold? Tunnel vision is easy on a first ascent. And I knew people would be whispering, *It can't be that hard if a girl can do it.* Claiming to do the hardest trad route in the world, as a woman—as a shy, quiet, good girl—felt too brave, too loud, for me.

I was proud of myself. On my better days, I could feel a sense of accomplishment, the feeling of victory that fed the competitive hunger inside me. I had done something big. I wanted it to mean something. I wanted to have established the hardest crack climb in the world, eclipsing my idols, propelling me to the top of a sport I had been drowning in for fifteen years. I wanted to feel like I had reached some kind of finish line—that I was safe. I wanted to feel some peace about my place in climbing, finally. But I was also always waiting for the other shoe to drop. I knew that the interviews, the magazine covers, the attention were all fleeting—that I would have to send again to get my next hit. Meltdown had bought me some time, held my seat at the table, but I worried that inevitably I'd be outed as a fraud. Someone who was always scared on El Cap, who still preferred to toprope. The constant self-criticism in my head was barely muted even in the moment that my career reached its pinnacle.

I was also tired and hurting. The years of climbing had abused my body, and Meltdown had taken a particular toll on the ligaments in my fingers and hands. I needed a break, mentally and physically, from the climbing and training and the pressure to perform, to excel. The endless cycle of setting a goal, chasing it, achieving it, basking briefly in the resulting praise, and then immediately choosing a new, even harder target, rinse, repeat. I wanted to sit on a beach, eat ice cream, be normal. But I had no idea how to take a vacation; neither Tommy nor I did. We were so focused, we had never even bothered to get a Christmas tree. We didn't know how to be BethandTommy without an intense goal. The last time we'd taken a break, to build our house, we had almost unraveled. Climbing was all we knew. I longed for the lightness and ease of Randy and the Bay Crew.

That spring, Randy and his friends were supposed to vacation in Hawaii for a week. When the airline they'd bought tickets from folded, the rest of the Bay Crew decided to save their vacation days. But Randy spent his time off at our house in Yosemite instead, and that was my first chance to get to know him outside of the group bouldering sessions. He and Tommy climbed together each day and night. Randy chopped vegetables at our big kitchen island and wore J.Crew sweaters, which I thought was just amazing. Tommy and I only wore sponsor clothes and event swag that we'd gotten for free.

On the day I went back to Meltdown to re-create the climb for a filmmaker's camera, Randy and Courtney came along to watch. Afterward, they'd planned a quick bouldering session with a group at Camp 4. When we walked into the warm-up zone, the crowd was a shock to my system—even more so after six months of solitude on Meltdown, just me and Tommy tucked in next to the waterfall, hidden from the tourists gazing up from the road below.

I assumed my usual position: away from the crowd, on our folded-up crash pad, just observing. I had just completed my hardest climb ever; I didn't need to hide. But I was glad to have the excuse of having worn myself out already that morning.

Stephanie was a newcomer to climbing and the Bay Area, a traveling nurse who'd just moved from North Dakota. She'd started dating Daniel, one of the crew, expecting a summer fling. But the Bay and Daniel stuck, so she was trying this climbing thing for the first time. The whole crew was there to encourage her, even the ones who should have been off climbing their V12 projects.

I watched Randy climb. He bounced around the boulders as easily as he bounced from person to person, laughing, climbing, the life of the party. Normally I'm turned off by those people, because they usually bring ego or showiness with them. But Randy just seemed so earnestly eager to interact with the world around him. His curiosity and playfulness were genuine. Asking Lyn how Melody's soccer game went. Talking about programming ideas with Ingar with the same excitement he would have for beta on a boulder problem. It all seemed so light and free and fun.

Stephanie started climbing on the warm-up. I wondered if she was overwhelmed by all the people giving her tips and ideas on how to get up the rock. Randy was chiming in with everyone, giving ideas here and there, spotting her. But what struck me the most was when she did it, when she finally stood on top, how genuine and long-lasting Randy's enthusiasm was. In the days and weeks afterward, he continued to encourage her, reminding her and all of us that her accomplishment was worth celebrating. His earnest positivity—never my strong point— was infectious. I wanted to find a way to be like that: less judgmental, of myself and others. I wanted his joy around me, wanted to let it wrap me up and make me joyful too.

◆ ◆ ◆

Later that spring, Tommy was ready to make a big push of his own. Free climbing most El Cap routes had become routine for him. He teamed up with our friend Justen to attempt the first free ascent of Magic Mushroom, El Cap's hardest route at the time. For weeks he spent long days on the wall, gone before sunrise and home after dark. That left me alone, which pulled me out of my shell. I did a lot of hiking and climbed in our garage by myself, and on weekends I often bouldered with the Bay Crew, savoring the lack of urgency: no immediate projects, no big push on the horizon.

When I did get the itch to do some bigger routes again that spring, I started calling around to find partners. Spring was my favorite time in Yosemite, and there were a few classic lines that I'd always wanted to do, routes that weren't "noteworthy" so I hadn't let myself waste time on them. I called Corey, but he was too busy with work. I called Marko, but he was focusing on biking. Kelly had hurt his back. Luke said he wasn't sure it would be appropriate to climb with another man's wife, while Tommy was on the wall and Caroline was at home with their baby. His implication felt insulting, but there was no way to argue without making an awkward conversation even worse.

That left me with the Bay Crew. I thought through my options there. Randy was a great climber, but he was engaged to Courtney, and Courtney was so confident and beautiful and normal and smart, and a good cook with a real job, obviously so superior to me . . .

I caught myself. Why was I so concerned about Courtney? I told myself that Luke's weird rules about intermarital climbing had gotten into my head.

Randy started coming up to Yosemite midweek, working four tens, as he called his ten-hour days, and taking Wednesday or Thursday off. He would sleep near the park, or drive in from the city early, and meet up with me for morning sessions. Some days other people would join us too—Lyn and Patti, or Tommy if he finished up early on the wall— and I would paper over the disappointment I felt with forced smiles and laughter. But when it was just Randy and me, I never had to force anything. I wanted to know everything about his life, and we could talk constantly while we climbed. I always felt giddy on those days, like I was floating. Sending easily, never needing to eat or rest or drink. I wondered if I was going crazy. I wanted to ask him if he was going crazy too.

In May, Randy emailed me. He was going to come up the following week. We made a plan to do multipitch routes on a couple of days, a departure from our usual bouldering sessions. A more sophisticated woman might have read the subtext in this, but I just thought everyone wanted to do long routes. We lived on the doorstep of Yosemite Valley, home to the greatest big walls in the world. And I had offered to climb on bigger routes with any of the crew who wanted to join me. Did it mean something that Randy was the only one who'd taken me up on it? I suggested we do Astroboy, the soft, shorter version of Astroman. I felt confident that I could lead him up that.

I packed up the rack, sunscreen, and food the night before. Tommy was still up on Magic Mushroom with Justen, and for once the gear was my job. Tommy and I always had unspoken tasks: I packed our water, food, and clothes, while he handled our gear. As I fumbled through the cams in our garage, the weight of having to be the stronger partner this time felt like it might flatten me. For years, I had climbed almost exclusively with the most competent gearsman in the world and one who defined his role in life as caring for and protecting me. If I didn't want to lead, Tommy led. If I felt insecure, he took care of things: ticking holds, carrying the pack down. I was one of the most accomplished female climbers in history, but I still felt like a newbie on relatively easy routes. I relied on Tommy's incredible instincts, his excellence in the vertical realm. I always had a guide in him; now I had to be the guide. Could I keep Randy safe?

Randy was better than Tommy and I were at intricate boulders, a master at finding ways up blank rock faces. Like all the best boulderers, he combined explosive power with extreme finesse, and he had the vision to find holds that other climbers couldn't see. But more than twenty feet off the ground he was a relative beginner: he didn't know our rope management and tactics. Leading him up a route would be a leap into a new-to-me sense of responsibility, of independence. It was thrilling and terrifying.

We'd agreed to meet at 9:00 a.m. My hands drenched my old Civic's polished gray steering wheel as I drove to meet him. On my way to the Valley floor, I drove past the top of the Rostrum and saw the branches blowing in the wind like they always do. I drove past El Cap, knowing Tommy was up there with Justen. My stomach hurt. My hands trembled. Tommy and Justen had been climbing since 5:00 a.m. I knew they were working on one of the crux pitches up there today. I felt no envy, could almost feel in my hands the pain of all the rope work they were doing. I hoped they succeeded.

Driving by my husband, up on the wall, to meet Randy was surreal. The symbolism was almost too much. I felt an awful mixture of desire and excitement and guilt and shame. And then . . . there was Randy, standing next to his silver Audi station wagon in the Ahwahnee parking lot. That smile on his face, those squinting soft brown eyes. He was five foot six, taller than me but not too tall. I liked that.

"Good morning," he said as I tumbled out of my car. I wanted to wrap my arms around him immediately, but I refrained.

"Hi," I said, looking down at my blue Sportivas so I didn't stare. "How was the drive?"

I asked this in lieu of the question I really wanted to ask. *I can't stop thinking about you; can you stop thinking about me?* I felt lost and hopeless and thrilled. I was married to a wonderful guy—a perfect guy, really. Tommy was loving and supportive, more than I ever could have hoped for in almost every way. We had this extraordinary life. And there I was, drowning in feelings. Randy was engaged to a woman I admired. I knew life would be simpler if he had no interest in me. But I wanted to know. My cheeks turned scarlet.

Randy just stood there, calm, and asked, "What can I carry?"

I handed him the bright-yellow rope and awkwardly stuffed my jacket and water in my pack. "You ready?" I asked.

"Ha! I don't think so," Randy said. "But I'm excited to try."

Spring was always so alive and vibrant in Yosemite, everything just waking up: each drop of glacial water, each blade of fluorescent meadow grass. It soaked into my body and rustled me awake, like the wind through the new leaves on the trees. The river was full and fragrant and raging. The waterfalls roared, the tumult bouncing off the Valley's big rock faces. It felt like a symphony performing the opening act of the season.

I didn't really know what to say as we walked along the road, but I felt like I had to say something.

"What's Courtney up to today?" I asked. *Why did I have to bring up his fiancée?*

"She's at work. I think she's heading to the gym afterward."

We settled back into an awkward silence that continued even once the trail ended and we started scrambling up rocks. I kept waiting for a sign, any sign. We finally managed to make small talk, going over details of the route—what to expect, what kind of climbing it was. I'd done this same hike so many times with Tommy: the road, the rocks, the steep grassy hill near the base of Washington Column. By the time we got to the trees at the start of our route, I was soaked with sweat.

"Oh no," Randy said, in a sort of desperate tone, after we'd set down our packs and started getting ready. "I only have one shoe." His face went as red as mine so often was around him. *He must have been frazzled at the car to forget it,* I thought, snatching at the possibility that he was just as off-balance as I was. *He's the most organized person I know.*

"Are you serious?" I said, laughing. "What happened to the other one? I saw you had it by your car this morning."

"Yeah, I totally did. I have no idea, I'll run back and try to find it." His embarrassment was adorable. But I knew if he'd been Tommy in that moment, I would have been annoyed that he'd made me wait.

While he went to retrieve his lost shoe, I lay down on the prickly green grass, put my head on the backside of my sweaty backpack, let the sun warm my body. I shut my eyes. The old thoughts, my mantra in my hardest times with Tommy, resurfaced: *You have an amazing life. You are lucky to have him. People would give anything for a man like Tommy. Just focus on the good, just focus on the good. Don't ruin this, Beth.*

Then a moment later all that was pushed aside by a desire I hadn't felt before, a level of attraction I couldn't deny. I wanted to follow that feeling, but I didn't know how, and the idea of trying was terrifying. I wanted a fast-forward button, to skip to the end of this story so I'd know where it landed and which plotline I should pursue. I didn't want to wade through the messiness. I didn't want to choose the wrong path.

I heard Randy's footsteps coming back up the grass, crunching the prickly parts and squashing the soft ones. "Got it!" he shouted, laughing and holding up his bright-red-and-black climbing shoe. "I must have been so flustered and excited I forgot it. You must do that to a lot of people."

My face turned beet red.

When we got to the base, I started my routine of putting on my harness and chalk bag and climbing shoes. I also added in the unfamiliar routine of racking the gear on my sling and harness. It was weird to realize that while I had been a professional climber for over ten years, my partnership with Tommy had a cost. I had some learned helplessness: I didn't entirely believe in myself. I always gave myself an out.

"Okay," I explained to Randy, "so when I get up there, I'll yell, 'Off belay.' If you can't hear me, you'll know that you can take me off when I pull the rope three very distinct times in a row. You'll know you're on belay when you either hear me or I pull the rope again three very distinct times in a row." Tommy and I hadn't had to articulate these cues to each other in years. It was part of our history, our unspoken shared language. Having to explain it was like telling someone *When I put on my left turn signal, it means I'm turning left.* It felt strange to spell it out. Everything was new with Randy.

I was nervous, but if we were going to do this, I knew I had to set those doubts aside. *Suck it up, Rodden,* I told myself, as I had before so many other climbs. And I reached out to the rock wall and started up.

I felt proud as I led the first pitch, which was weird because I'd climbed this exact route at least five times before. But I was doing it myself, for myself, without the help or support of Tommy. I felt competent and light in a way I hadn't since before Kyrgyzstan.

After two pitches we reached the hard one, a long right-facing granite corner, mercifully in the shade. The rock was yellow and gold with black and gray streaks, slippery but with perfect cracks to slot my fingers and toes into, so I could use my whole body—arms, shoulders, legs, butt, hips—to wiggle my way up the climb. I racked up my gear and sighed with relief that I was about to climb over a hundred feet away from Randy. For the past ten minutes we'd been smashed up together on the belay ledge. It was too much for me to handle, this beautiful person who I was not supposed to want in my life, right there, inches away. As I climbed I started singing Bob Marley's "Three Little Birds." Then, out of nowhere, I was muttering again: "You can never leave Tommy. He's the one who gave you this gift. He's the reason you are able to do this."

I didn't know where that voice came from. Did I really think so poorly of my own ability? Of course, Tommy had given me so much, but I was coming into my own, getting myself back. My arms and fingers and hands moved in perfect coordination, fell into their places seamlessly. I felt like I was a prima Russian ballerina, performing at the Bolshoi for the czar. Nervous, but knowing exactly what to do, executing each move perfectly.

CHAPTER
THIRTY-TWO

Berkeley, California, May 2008

The city had been a part of my world once. I had spent my teenage years driving to the Bay's mega-gyms each weekend with friends. After a full day of training, we'd go out to dinner at Chevy's on the bay and then get drive-through Baskin-Robbins on our way home, and I'd feel so urban and fancy. But that girl, that life, seemed so far gone: pre-Kyrgyzstan, pre-Tommy. I had this other life that I loved, but it came with a particular narrative—one that was beginning to feel restrictive. Tommy hated cities, all that cement, and I had embraced that aversion. But spending time with the Bay Crew was seeding something in me, or maybe uncovering something that I had neglected for too long. Maybe it was about cement not being that bad, maybe it was about climbing for fun, or maybe it was just a part of me that I had buried over the past decade, resurfacing to remind me that another Beth was still here.

When Courtney suggested I visit them in the Bay during Tommy's next stint on the wall, I surprised myself by accepting. I really liked her. Though I felt guilty about my lurking feelings for Randy, I wanted to be her friend. She was so sure of herself, so warm and genuine, and it seemed like if I could hang around her long enough, some of that confidence might stick to me.

The drive into Berkeley revived my memories of those teenage gym sessions. The old me, the one I'd left behind after Kyrgyzstan, felt so distant. It had seemed too hard to balance the before-Beth and the after-Beth, so I'd dumped the person I'd been and tried to move forward.

Arriving at Courtney and Randy's house, an old Craftsman with dark-wood trim and hardwood floors, I pushed those thoughts aside—his presence left little room for me to feel anything but desire and confusion. I kept waiting for that response to fade, but it never did. Along with some of their friends, Randy and I went on a bike ride through the Berkeley hills. Then we went to the climbing gym, where Courtney joined us, and on to the famous Chez Panisse for dinner. The meal was wonderful—almost good enough to cut through the storm cloud of emotions swirling inside me.

I wanted to be close to Randy all the time. And something else had broken open too. I was starting to acknowledge a voice inside of me that had been buried since Kyrgyzstan. A voice that wasn't ruled by fear. It was the voice I had heard when I'd decided to leave college for climbing, the one that told me to chase the things I wanted. Now it was telling me to listen to my feelings for Randy, that they were real and valid and that I didn't always need to do what I thought Good Girl Beth should do. That I could listen to my heart and follow it. I was starting to hear that, but usually only for a couple seconds at a time. Then I'd shake my head like a dog getting out of water: back to reality, back to doing what I thought was expected of me, back to remembering that I loved Tommy and we had a wonderful life that I had worked hard to build with him.

Late that night, after dinner, I rolled out my sleeping bag and sleeping pad on Randy and Courtney's shaggy white carpet. (Yet more proof of their grown-up-ness: there was zero way I would have ever bought a white carpet.) Somehow, whether despite or because of the day's swirl of emotions, I fell asleep.

I woke up to the sound of trains. It sounded like they were in the front yard. It was 4:30 a.m. I forced myself to stay in bed until five, but then I had to pee. To reach the bathroom, Randy had told me the night before, I would have to walk through their bedroom. ("We're both sound sleepers," he'd said, apparently oblivious to how horrified I was by the idea of walking by them while they slept in bed together.) I seriously considered going in the backyard, but I didn't know if that would be frowned upon, either by them or by their neighbors.

I stared at the round bronze doorknob for what felt like days, wondering if I should turn it left or right, wondering if it would make a noise as it turned or if the door would creak, if the hinges would squeak. I didn't want to look at them in bed. I didn't want to see Randy sleeping, in such a vulnerable state, didn't want to see him sleeping next to another woman. (I know how backward that sounds, because if there was another woman, it was me.) I didn't want to see Courtney in bed either.

Finally I opened the door, as quietly as I could, stared at the dark floor, and crept like I was walking on nails all the way to the bathroom door. I opened that door, shut it as quietly as possible, peed as quietly as possible, then reversed the entire scenario. I managed not to look at the bed. The only thing I saw was a dark wood floor. I felt proud, like somehow I'd managed not to cheat, not to see something I shouldn't. I crawled back into my sleeping bag and stared at their elegant curved white ceiling for the next hour until they woke up.

◆ ◆ ◆

A week later, Tommy was up on El Cap, working on a different section of Magic Mushroom with Justen, and I, happily, was not. It felt so freeing to have no project that season. I wasn't getting back on the horse or thinking about sponsors or crossing another route off the must-climb list. I was just bouldering, exploring the Valley, and falling in love.

A friend who worked in the park had told me that Tioga Road would open for bikes a week before it opened for cars. (Back then, before social media, this was a park secret passed along only by word of mouth.) Randy and I had decided to grab the opportunity and came up with a plan: a short, hard climb in the morning and a ride into the Yosemite high country in the afternoon.

I pulled up next to his Audi wagon, and there he was, leaning against his car again, his harness and climbing shoes dangling in one hand. (Both shoes, this time.) He was wearing shorts, revealing his bowlegs (not as bad as mine), which I found adorable and attractive. I liked looking at his legs. I really liked looking at any part of him—he was lithe, athletic, and strong—but his legs seemed less conspicuous than staring into his eyes. So I focused on the bows just below his knees.

"Morning!" he said in his usual upbeat tone. "Are you sure this is a good idea?"

No, of course I didn't think this was a good idea. None of this was a good idea, yet it was also the best idea. I gave Randy the rope, threw on my pack, and started walking down the trail.

We climbed for a couple hours on Cosmic Debris, a beloved Valley crack climb that was rated 5.13b. I wasn't nearly as nervous as I'd been on Astroboy. Maybe that was because this route was only one pitch. Or maybe the earlier climb had given me confidence, and the whole situation was a little more known—which was scary in its own right, in that maybe it was progressing? Or maybe not?

I came desperately close to sending, trying to impress Randy. I belayed him a few times, and it all felt like a fairy tale. I only started to get nervous again on the return hike to the cars. Climbing, we were usually separated by a rope's length. Cycling, we'd be side by side, no people or cars around, just us and our spinning legs and the entire forest, breathing quietly around us. I couldn't deny that I had real feelings for him anymore, couldn't pretend this was a passing crush. Would I panic-fill the silence by confessing my love? Was I brave enough to do that? When we got back to the cars my mouth was dry, but my palms, even covered in chalk, were soaked.

"I need to keep warning you—I'm not that good of a bike rider," I said as we loaded my bike into his car. "I'm like a turtle, I just keep on going, but I'm really slow. I mean, I love it and I try hard, but I'm just not fast . . ." I couldn't stop talking. I felt the urgent need to dampen his expectations. If he did have feelings for me, maybe they were just because I was a good climber, and now he would see that I wasn't a good biker and that would be the end of that.

"It'll be fine, we'll just go as far as we want and then turn around." Randy sounded upbeat and comforting, as always. "You said it's like twenty-five miles or something round trip to the lake?"

I nodded.

"That'd be cool to try and get to," he said.

We drove separately to El Cap meadow. Then I stashed my car and hopped in Randy's for the last stretch of the drive. The Audi had black leather seats and was clean, really clean, like it had been vacuumed recently. Our cars were constantly filled with Diet Pepsi bottles, chalk, random climbing shoes, construction pencils, chaos. Randy's car felt like a limo. I was afraid to settle my chalky shorts on the seat.

Soon my leg sweat was soaking through its dusting of chalk and forming a lake on those black leather seats. We started talking about nothing, but before long the conversation was about everything. I asked him if he liked living in the city or if he wished he lived closer to the mountains. He asked the same, and I said, "I could never live back in the city. I mean, if Tommy wanted to, then I would for him, but he's more allergic to pavement than I am." *Idiot.*

We parked and walked our bikes around the *ROAD CLOSED* sign, already feeling like VIPs, the world opening just for us. As soon as we started pedaling, the tension grew thick again. All those thoughts, riding along in the four feet between us, here on this gorgeous quiet road beneath these fragrant old trees.

"Are you like this with everyone?" Randy said, breaking the silence that had grown between us.

I stared at the double yellow line, then glanced over at him and laughed uncomfortably.

"Like what?" I said. "Terribly slow on a bike? Yeah, probably."

"Ha, no, like you make everyone feel really comfortable and everything feel fun."

This was it, right? It was starting. I deflected, my default. "No, it's just you. I've seen you, and you bring this out in all your friends." My heart was pounding. I wanted to tell him that I adored him, that I thought about him all the time, that I yearned to be with him, that I had never felt things like this before and I could not deny them.

"Well, that's kind of you to say, but I've never felt like this before. I can just say that." He said it quietly, this leap ahead. He'd summoned his courage and named his feelings. How I responded was up to me.

Should I be as honest, and tell him I felt the same way? Should I listen to the little superego chattering in my brain, reminding me I was married, this was wrong, he was engaged? So many people could get hurt. Why couldn't I just stay on the path? Keep the promise I'd made in Kyrgyzstan, focus on all that worked with Tommy?

We had a great partnership, if not a great marriage. There are things missing in every relationship. I could just continue being the goodest girl out there, but I also wanted to live. I wanted to relax, enjoy the small things, make room for more depth and dimension in my life—with someone who made me want those things. I wanted to know real love, even if it meant real heartache. I wanted to have real sex.

I stayed quiet for a long time. The familiar—the good path—felt so safe. But I wanted to try. *What's the worst that could happen—I die of embarrassment?* So I blurted it out: "I've never felt like this either. It's so amazing and weird and scary and exciting and it's been eating me inside for months now!" I stopped and caught my breath. What had I done? Saying it out loud felt so good. A voice in my head was cheering. Another one said: *Well, shit, you've done it now.*

I looked over. Randy was smiling, but with caution. He understood that this wasn't just two people falling in love.

For the rest of the ride to the lake we talked freely and openly, the rawest questions and answers flying back and forth between our bicycles as we soared along, wheels spinning. *When did it start for you? How did you know? What did it feel like?* I couldn't stop blushing, but somehow I ripped off my usual filter and told him everything. How amazing I thought he was, how I couldn't get him out of my head, how I'd never had these feelings before, how I wanted to foster them. They were so exciting and warm and powerful, they shook my entire body. I couldn't believe he felt the same way. It felt so good to get it out in the open, such a relief, and somehow it felt safer to say it all up there, with no one around, with the vastness of the high country all to ourselves. Like we could be shouting these feelings and no one would ever know.

As we neared the lake, the landscape started to change. We emerged from the thick canopy of tall, fragrant pines and out into the famous white rock of the High Sierra. The openness and the grandeur of the high country takes my breath away the first time I see it each season. Clouds Rest and Tenaya Peak and Mount Hoffmann and the endless views of the round granite domes that make Tuolumne unique and my favorite place on earth. Our conversation slowed, and it felt like we could really just enjoy this time together. Everything had been spilled, and we got to just soak it in. Occasionally I could feel my legs burning from the exertion, but mostly I felt like I was floating. I'd thought I would be hungry, but I didn't seem to need any fuel. I enjoyed that too.

We crested the corner at Olmsted Point and saw Tenaya Lake. Its vibrant blue seemed even brighter than when I'd seen it from a car. It was so quiet, aside from the wind in our ears as we biked, and so still, like we could just stop and sit and not have to move, ever, because no one was there and we weren't needed anywhere for anything. This was ours to enjoy that day, to soak in, to relax into everything we had just said. To not worry about the repercussions until another time—later that day, or in another life.

We coasted down to the rock slabs on the north side of the lake that slant all the way down into the water, like a nature-made ramp. We set our bikes down, and I said, "Look at this!" I walked to the double yellow line and lay down right in the middle of the empty road. It felt so freeing and crazy and good. A little *This is for me* moment. A small external rebellion to match the one I felt inside: I was finally choosing something that might be dangerous, but that I wanted.

I lay there, staring up at the amazing blue sky, hearing the birds singing a chorus and the wind whirling through the stocky trees by the side of the lake. I heard the water lapping up onto the shore. I breathed deeply in and out. And then, all of a sudden, I said, "I'm going to jump in!"

I remembered, a few weeks earlier, meeting Randy and Lyn and Patti on Cathedral Beach in the Valley. They had just finished breakfast and were all laughing hysterically. Lyn said, "Good timing, Beth, you just saved yourself from seeing Randy skinny-dip in the Merced. We're all still recovering!" I had tried to keep my face still while my heart sank.

"Do you have a suit? Or a towel? It's freezing in there!" He laughed, but I could tell he was intrigued.

"Nope! It'll be fine. I'll air-dry. But you have to do it if I do it." I smiled. The butterflies in my stomach were flapping in a frenzy, but it felt so right.

"Don't look," I said as I moved toward the water, stripping off my biking clothes. I didn't know why I'd said that. Maybe I was embarrassed. Maybe this was where he would see something he didn't like—like, should I shave? Didn't city girls shave and take care of their lady parts in ways that I was oblivious to? Make themselves more "presentable"?

I jumped in. The water was so cold my breath immediately shot up into my head. I leaped out and put on my sweaty orange T-shirt as fast as I could. I was laughing but mainly just excited. "You are crazy!" he said, laughing too, but with a hint of fear. He stripped down, facing away from me, and jumped in. I stared at my bare feet on the white Sierra granite. I heard him gasp and then run up onto the slab as quickly as possible. He threw his clothes back on and shouted, "That was freezing! You are so tough." That was the best compliment I could hear. We sat there for a little bit, not saying anything. We'd said so much earlier, it felt nice to sit and listen to the high country, to really hear everything.

After we'd warmed up in the sun for a while, I said, "Let's do a couple boulder problems so we can have a three-sport trip up here—biking, swimming, and climbing. But we should probably head back pretty soon. It'll be dark in a couple hours." I hated the words as they came out of my mouth. I felt like the mom telling lovestruck teenagers about curfews and rules. I didn't want to go back. At the car reality would be waiting: there was the weight of what we had said, there was my marriage and Tommy—oh, poor Tommy—and the unbearably awkward fact that we were all—Randy, Courtney, Tommy, and I—supposed to be heading to South Africa that summer to climb together. I didn't want to think about any of that. I wanted to immerse myself in this new, fresh love.

We rode back and both got a little quieter as we approached the car. The day had been beautiful, perfect—something unimaginable, and just for us. For once, I hadn't been stewing over the past or worrying about my next ten steps forward. I had spent this one day, with Randy, living entirely in and for the present. It had felt good to throw away the plan. I had done it once before, when I had listened to my heart and dropped out of college, abandoning conformity and—some would say—common sense to chase a dream of climbing. Today I had listened in that rare, powerful way again. But at some point, I would have to face what this day and my choices meant for the future.

CHAPTER
THIRTY-THREE

Estes Park, Colorado, June 2008

Tommy and I were back in Estes. It was June, a month after my bike ride with Randy. I sat on the futon in our tiny office, working on our laptop, while Tommy sat at the desk, typing on my purple iMac. He was dealing with La Sportiva, our shared sponsor in Italy, about the new shoe we were designing.

Tommy typed by hunting and pecking, hitting each key as if he were up on El Cap and his life depended on it. The sound of it always made me smile. It almost felt normal being in that office together, in the little cabin I loved. With the walls that I painted, the trim I stained and nailed up with Tommy, the cheap laminated desk that we picked out at Office Depot in Fort Collins. It almost seemed like we were back in our rhythm, our routine, that I could relax into our relationship. I was on an intermission from the swirling, confusing emotions that had consumed me for the past two months.

After the ride to the lake, Randy and I had made a pact that we weren't going to talk for a while. He had told me that there were long-standing issues in his relationship, beyond his feelings for me. We hadn't made any commitments to each other—he'd said he would leave Courtney, regardless of my choices, if that was the right decision for him. He needed to figure that out sooner rather than later, because they had a wedding coming up, and I . . . I couldn't even believe I was involved in a situation like this. I was the girl who prided herself on being drama-free. I was the reliable one, the nice girl. It was incomprehensible.

An email from Randy popped up in our inbox. It was as if a switch had been flipped on a blender; I was suddenly nervous and terrified and giddy and excited and elated and ashamed all at the same time. I wanted to dive through the screen, travel through the tubes of the internet, and emerge into Randy's arms. I still could only imagine what they felt like, and whenever I let my mind loose, I did. I looked at Tommy. He was hunched over, jamming his fingertips against each key. He hadn't seen the email yet, but he would. It had been sent to info@bethandtommy. com, and he was an equal half of bethandtommy.com.

I shut the laptop. I couldn't have an email from Randy staring me in the face. I wondered what it said. But we'd said we weren't going to communicate, and this felt like it was communicating. Maybe that was arbitrary, even absurd, but with everything that had already been said between us, somehow, opening the email was a line I wouldn't cross.

I walked into the gear room, pulled out my road bike, and biked up Trail Ridge Road to take my mind off those bits of data in my inbox. An hour or so later I walked into the house, and Tommy had moved on to researching climbs he wanted to do in South Africa. I took off my sweaty spandex and sat down on the floor in front of him to stretch.

"So it looks like it'll just be us and Courtney, I guess," he said casually. I stared at him, wondering what he meant exactly.

"We got an email from Randy saying that the wedding is off."

I felt a hot, nervous sensation pulse through my body. It started in my stomach and went to my teeth. My face flushed, and I felt slightly lightheaded. He'd canceled his wedding. He'd canceled his wedding to someone he'd been with for eight years. Even if he had other reasons for doing it, surely it also meant this wasn't some sort of passing feeling, for him. I felt like I was going to black out. *Does he regret it? Is he freaking out? How did it happen? What did she say? What will happen to the venue and the plane tickets and the suit he had tailored? Why am I worrying about trivial things?*

Tommy passed me the laptop. The email was vague. How could he tell over a hundred people the truth of why he'd canceled the wedding? How could he say he fell in love with Beth Rodden, even though she was married to Tommy Caldwell, and that it brought up all these cracks that he had covered up in his relationship, and that he didn't know what was going to happen, but he knew that he couldn't go through with a marriage to someone else once he'd been forced to acknowledge those cracks, so he was canceling the wedding, and he felt awful, but it was the right thing to do?

As I read, I felt hollow. I thought of Courtney, how happy she'd seemed and how sad and confused she must be. Where was the handbook for this? I had no girlfriends to talk to; I didn't even have friends that weren't BethandTommy friends. I liked and respected Courtney, and I had always thought I was a kind and good person. But now I had all these feelings, feelings that were the most intense and wonderful I'd ever felt, and they were shaking my own belief in my goodness—the foundation of who I was and how I'd built my life with Tommy. I knew I was supposed to work hard at marriage. And I was very good at working hard. But should I? Or should I try to give life to the curiosity and the desire for independence that I felt growing inside me? I had no idea what I was supposed to do next.

◆ ◆ ◆

We'd planned the trip to South Africa a while earlier, in our Yosemite house: Tommy and me, Randy, Courtney, and some other climbers, all gathered around the big kitchen island, elbows on the cool granite countertops. It was exactly what I had wanted when I designed the house. Friends and family would come; we'd make plans and memories. The kitchen island as the gathering point.

The trip was still on—minus Randy. He'd told me ahead of time that if he broke off his engagement, he would bow out, let Courtney go instead, and he did. After we heard about the breakup, Tommy emailed Courtney and offered to share our rental car. She accepted right away, and I figured Randy must not have told her anything about me, about us. I would be the only one who knew how surreal our little trio was. We wouldn't just be BethandTommy in South Africa but BethandTommyandCourtney, which was downright perverse.

Despite my feelings of guilt, I was excited to travel with Courtney. She was into good food, so she had been researching the best restaurants and cafés; even before we left, our prep felt so grown-up and cosmopolitan. I knew it would be unlike any other climbing trip I had been on, where we ate pasta with red sauce from the grocery store every night and never explored anything beyond rocks and trails.

Our lives were going so well. Meltdown was still everywhere in the climbing news. Magic Mushroom was too. Tommy and I were literally at the top of the sport: magazine covers, movies, thriving sponsorships. We had everything we'd been working toward for so long. And I was falling in love. But with the wrong man.

I started running a lot. Sometimes everyone else would drive to the crag and I would run. My weight dropped to its lowest since Kyrgyzstan. My hip bones stuck out. It felt both strangely familiar and, if I'm honest, empowering. My body was one thing, in my fast-spinning life, that I could still control. I replaced binges with bike rides and sit-ups. I felt like I was sixteen again, light and free. I had no appetite. I felt like I could go for days with almost no food. I felt like I could run forever.

I knew that Tommy had noticed how much fun I'd been having with Randy—how I'd gushed about the dinner at Chez Panisse, how animated I'd seemed when I talked about the things I'd been up to while Tommy was up on the wall. But it wasn't until after Randy canceled his wedding that Tommy asked me directly about it. Had I known this was coming? Had Randy said anything to me—had I said anything to him? Did it have anything to do with all the time we'd been spending together? I had denied it, and he seemed to believe me.

Randy and I still weren't talking when BethandTommyandCourtney flew to South Africa. For the first part of the trip, the three of us sang rap music in the car and cooked in the kitchen of the farmhouse where we were staying. We climbed every day, bouldering in Rocklands, a gorgeous landscape painted in sandstone reds, browns, and golds. Our tiny, ancient rental car had no air-conditioning, no power steering or power windows, and no central radio. We played music on a little external speaker that Corey, one of the dozen friends we were traveling with, had brought along. We set it on the dashboard, and I impressed everyone with my encyclopedic knowledge of Eminem. Then it started raining, so we couldn't climb, and everything grew a bit tense. Everyone wanted to be outside, climbing, and I was struggling with the lies I was telling, the truths I was holding back.

Earlier in the trip, Courtney had asked me about her breakup: what I'd known about it, whether I was involved somehow. Just like when Tommy had asked me the same sorts of questions, the moment felt like a kind of awful threshold: when I passed through it, I was leveling up, attaining a new degree of deceit. I felt terrible. But again, I had lied, told her no.

When the rain didn't let up, half of us went to Cape Town to enjoy some city time—good food, cafés, a few days outside my comfort zone. It was fun, exhilarating even, not to focus on climbing. But I felt like I was plugging a Yellowstone geyser with my thumb. I wanted to stop lying, stop hiding.

I decided to tell Courtney first. If she hated me and shut me out of her life, it would be sad, but not crushing. Tommy, on the other hand— no matter what happened, there would be so much fallout. We were a life-sized Jenga game on the teetering verge of collapse. Our careers, our homes, our families and friends—when the moment came, the blocks would go flying every which way. Knowing I was only postponing that moment of collapse a little longer, I asked Courtney to come down to the hostel bar and talk.

Tommy jumped in the shower and said he'd meet us in a half hour. Great. I had thirty minutes to upend our lives.

We took two seats at the bar. She ordered wine, and I ordered rooibos tea with soy milk. I took a few sugar packets and dumped them in. I was on the edge of an affair and on the brink of blowing up my life, but still, alcohol was too out of control for me.

Courtney and I had been having fun together on the trip. Had she believed my denial, a week earlier? She'd seemed a little hesitant, maybe, when I told her I wanted to talk. I spun the cup in circles on the saucer, thinking of all the excuses I wanted to make, and then I just blurted it out.

"I do have feelings for Randy. I'm so sorry I didn't say anything earlier. I know it doesn't help anything, but I didn't mean for this to happen, it just did. I don't know why." My face was on fire, my stomach burned, hot tea was the last thing I wanted to drink. I kept spinning the saucer. It was annoying even to me.

"When did it start?" Courtney sounded calm.

What did that matter? Didn't she want to punch me? Yell at me? I couldn't imagine how to answer the question. *It started the first time I saw his bowlegs. It started the first time I heard him laugh.*

"Um, I don't know exactly, but maybe on our bike ride? I mean, that's when I said something, but I guess I've had feelings for a while?" I felt like a kid trying to guiltily explain something to a parent, knowing it didn't matter.

"Was that before or after the Bay trip?" she asked.

"No, the bike ride was after the Bay trip." I met her gaze, forced myself to. It was awful. She looked at me, then at her wine.

"Okay," she said. She sat a little longer, quiet, her silence screaming in my ear, then told me she needed some time to think and left. I couldn't read her at all. I sat there, stomach in knots, eyes burning, cup still twirling.

Then I felt a calloused hand on my back. "Hey, honey, how's it going?" Tommy said. "I saw Courtney, she didn't look too good."

He was so innocent. I felt like I might vomit. I knew I should go through the ritual: sit him down, tell him I had something to talk to him about, rub his leg. But I couldn't bear the preamble.

"I told her that I had feelings for Randy, and that I had lied when I told you both there was nothing between us. I mean, nothing happened between us—well, we both said we had feelings for each other. That's why she's upset, and it's true, and I'm sorry." I could feel myself getting less apologetic as I went on, just rushing to get this done. Like it was a test that I had to get through. I didn't care anymore if I passed with grace; I didn't care if I failed—I just wanted it over.

I looked over at Tommy, suddenly feeling spiteful. He was biting his lip, with a look on his face like he was on a roller coaster and desperately wished the ride were over. "Say something!" I said.

"When? Why?"

Why did they keep asking that?

"I don't know, it just happened. I'm sorry, I really am, but I don't know what to do," I said. He was quiet, so I kept talking: "There's something wrong with me—I need to go to therapy." I wasn't sure exactly where those words had come from, but I found myself repeating them into the silence. *There's something wrong with me. There's something wrong with me. There's something wrong . . .*

Maybe I thought it would be easier for Tommy to hear—that I was broken, but we could fix me. It seemed like the easier path to me, a simple story instead of a complex problem. I looked at him. His strong body looked like a balloon that had been popped. I felt a dizzying mix of terror, sadness, defeat, impatience to move ahead now that I'd made the leap. And, somewhere in there, under all the fear, a little flame of curiosity burned about where this road might take me.

The next morning, I was sitting at the hostel's kitchen table when Tommy walked in. We hadn't talked much more since my confession the night before. He headed over to the coffeepot and poured himself a cup. He never drank coffee. Apparently we were both remaking ourselves. He added milk and a few packets of sugar and then picked up a few extra sugars to bring back to the table with him, lingering a little as he stirred. When he finally sat down I couldn't look at his face and all the devastation and anger I imagined I'd find there. He put his hand on my knee. I shuddered.

Tommy had always been my comfort, my safety. Now his touch only made me feel that much more guilty. He slid one of the white packets of sugar across the table until it rested right in front of me. I picked it up. On the back it had a printed quote: *When we forgive someone, the knots are untied and the past is released.*

The past is released. I knew he probably meant it to say: *I can forgive you, and we can move past this together, leave it behind.* But instead, it felt like I was being granted a kind of permission: to release myself from the good-girl script, from my wedding vows, from the promise I had made in Kyrgyzstan. To jump into the abyss alone and see where I landed. To follow that flash of lightning I felt with Randy. A voice inside my head, so different from the usual voices demanding obedience to the safe choice, whispered: *You don't need to be good all the time. Or maybe being good can mean being honest with yourself instead of following the rules. It's okay to be messy. It's okay that this hurts. You'll survive this, and Tommy will survive this, just as you've survived everything else.*

PART THREE

CHAPTER
THIRTY-FOUR

Yosemite Valley, November 2008

When my alarm went off at 5:00 a.m., I had already been awake for twenty minutes. A Steller's jay was squawking outside the open window again—I hated that bird. (I'd named him Lester, the most annoying name I could think of.) I went to the bathroom, tiles cold on my feet, and then stepped on the scale. Ninety-seven pounds: perfect. I was always lightest first thing in the morning. I put on my brown Prana pants, white sports bra, and green T-shirt, the same clothes I'd worn every climbing day for the past two weeks—never washing them, because that would also wash away their luck. Then I poured Kashi cereal into a bowl with vanilla soy milk and frozen blueberries— defrosted in the small stainless pot. The next step in the ritual. I turned only the island lights on, the circumscribed circle of brightness granting me the illusion that the massive house was smaller, that my thoughts didn't have such a big place to swirl. It was mid-November; I was on my own for the first time since before Kyrgyzstan. The first time in my life, really—I'd gone straight from living with my parents to living with Tommy, who had moved out three weeks earlier. My sudden independence was exhilarating and intimidating.

It was a training day. I packed an energy bar in my blue backpack, already loaded with gear from the night before. In the garage, I hit play on my iPod, did two songs' worth of warm-up moves (always the same two songs, Jay-Z's "Run This Town" and Rihanna's "Umbrella"), then exactly twelve boulder problems. On the winding drive to the trailhead, it was still dark. By the time I pulled into the gravel parking lot, the day was just starting to brighten.

I loved the early mornings in Yosemite. Just a little effort, an early alarm, and some discipline, and I could elude the crowds, have the park to myself. More importantly, I could have Magic Line to myself.

From the parking lot it was a thirty-minute uphill slog to the route. I had gotten into the habit of sprinting it, music pounding in my ears, legs burning, arriving at the wall sweaty and amped. Vernal Fall had quieted to a trickle by now, as fall slumped into winter, but it was still beautiful. From the bottom of Magic Line I could hear the water tumbling and see the turquoise pool at its base, the boulders around it polished by years and water and tourists. My blue static line was hanging above my head, perfectly coiled from two days earlier. Randy could only belay me on weekends, and my friend Justin helped me out a few times, but he worked for the park and wasn't always available. So I'd hiked around and hung the rope by myself two months ago, the first time I'd started a route on my own in over ten years. The first time I'd had to do the grunt work. The first time I didn't have Tommy holding my hand. My chest puffed up when I thought of it: hanging the rope was a simple task that most professional climbers wouldn't blink at, but this was mine. I didn't need any hand-holding anymore. I clipped in my mini tractions, put Jay-Z back in my ears, and started climbing.

Magic Line is about ninety feet high. It had only been sent once before, by Ron Kauk back in the 1990s, and he had given it its name. If I could make the second-ever ascent, mastering the route in a matter of weeks—well, take that, climbing world. Take that, friends who told me I was a petty little girl, a sinner, a terrible person, for leaving Tommy.

Things hadn't been as simple as a confession, a packet of sugar, and a clean break. Coming home from South Africa felt heavy and strange. Neither of us knew what to do next. Eventually I decided I needed to step away, physically, geographically, to get some perspective. In mid-August, Tommy stayed in Colorado while I went back to California alone. We had so rarely been separated—I could probably count the number of days we'd been apart in the last eight years on my fingers and toes. I was back in Yosemite, in our brand-new house, alone. The sought-after silence that brings people to the mountains was deafening, but it slowed me down. I hiked to the base of Lurking Fear, sat in the back of El Cap meadow, trying to remember how I felt when our relationship began, up on that wall, in another life. I had never really sought out reflection and stillness that way before. I had spent so long trying *not* to feel, to replace feeling my feelings with action, with training, with doing everything I knew I should. It was weird and reckless to try to let my thoughts and emotions loose now. But I also found that I liked this small taste of independence.

Hiking, cooking, camping, packing climbing gear by myself—it felt so new, so necessary. I started seeing a therapist in Davis, holding up my part of the bargain to "try to fix me," as I'd said to Tommy when I left Estes. I based myself out of my parents' house for my appointments. They were the only people in my life not attached to BethandTommy, who I knew loved just Beth. Surprised but supportive, they remained my closest confidants as I took the tentative, potential first steps out of my marriage.

It felt strange to be so intentional about being alone, taking time to explore my feelings, myself. But all this time alone, all this exploration and hearing myself for the first time in forever, I couldn't help but think about that spark, that electricity with Randy. *Is it real? Is it just fleeting? Does it even matter?*

I was surprised by how much I loved being alone, but I also craved company. I had started going to lunch and dinner with old friends in Davis on days I had therapy. They were people I hadn't proactively reached out to in nearly ten years. And a few weeks after my arrival in California, I started bouldering with the Bay Crew on the weekends. I missed the collaboration and excitement of decoding a ten-foot piece of rock. I knew that climbing with the group would be a good addition to my solo time on Magic Line and training in the garage. I also knew that Randy would be there, which would be awkward but terribly amazing. I still hadn't seen him since our bike ride. If I did, I could see if that electricity was real, from a safe distance, with other people to diffuse the situation.

I knew I needed to figure out my feelings about Tommy and our marriage on their own terms. There were fault lines in our marriage that had nothing to do with Randy; my therapist, Debbie, was helping me explore them honestly for the first time. But after a few weeks and nearly ten sessions, she said, "I think you are doing great work in here, Beth, but there's really not much more we can do in regards to your marriage without Tommy here." If I really wanted to give our marriage an honest try, Tommy had to be there. I called Tommy, and we made a plan for him to come out in two weeks to attempt couple's therapy. Part of me wondered if, even hoped that, we would experience some tectonic shift, a change powerful enough to fix things between us. At the very least, I wanted to be sure we had tried everything.

The weekend before Tommy was set to arrive, I climbed with the Bay Crew in the alpine boulders of Way Lake, above Mammoth, on the eastern side of the Sierras. It was just like every other weekend recently: camping in our trucks, climbing all day until our fingers were raw, and then eating colorful and delicious food cooked on the camp stove. I wondered if my attraction to Randy was as obvious to everyone else as it felt to me. I tried not to laugh at his jokes or stare too long, made sure to ask the others to spot me. I felt like there was a gigantic magnet drawing me toward him, drawing us together—a supersized Acme magnet, the kind that Coyote might use to try and trap the Road Runner.

At the end of that day, Randy and I drove home together. My hands were shaking and my stomach was in knots as we drove through Tuolumne. I didn't want to face therapy and Magic Line and BethandTommy emails. I didn't want to have to keep smiling and changing the subject when people asked me where Tommy was, when he'd be back. I wanted to press pause, to stay in this moment. I knew it was selfish and wrong, but I just wanted a little more time. I asked Randy to pull over, no specific place, just the next pullout he saw. I had no plan, no idea of what to do once he pulled over, but I just needed to stop moving forward, back to the life that was waiting for me.

"Can we just go for a little walk?" I asked, nervous, almost desperate. "I mean, there's no trail here or anything, but just to get out and enjoy Tuolumne a little more?"

He glanced at me and then at the woods next to the car and laughed. "Like, just go into the woods?"

He looked at me with his brown eyes. I stared back. I wanted to tell him everything that was spinning in my head. But I didn't. Instead I just laugh-coughed and said, "Sure, why not, sounds kind of fun to just wander aimlessly into the woods, I guess." We had no plan, no trail to follow.

After fifteen minutes—or was it an hour?—we came to a small meadow, totally hidden by the stout trees of the high country. We sat down at first and then lay down on our backs and watched the clouds race through the sky above us. We talked about nothing, really. Our shoulders nudged together, and all of a sudden I felt Randy's hand over mine. Such a simple gesture—but for us, it was a huge leap. The months of yearning and talking and not talking and wondering and yearning some more had all built up to this. I felt electric, humming with energy and desire, the way I always felt around him, but now that current was amplified by his touch. I wondered if I should get up and walk away. Even though Tommy and I had taken space for the past month, I was still married. But then I couldn't stop thinking: *What if this is my only chance?* To follow these feelings, to dive into this rushing river of emotions filled with lust and desire and passion. To, just for once, stop burying what I wanted and forcing myself to do what I thought

I should do instead. What if, as wrong as this was, it was also just so right? It felt right.

I was so tired of my own whirring thoughts. I was exhausted from trying to reason my way through a situation, a feeling that didn't answer to reason. I don't remember making a decision. I just leaned over and kissed Randy, and once I'd taken that first step, our bodies took over, like perfectly matched partners moving through a dance they'd been made for. Our own rhythm, our own song—it was new, but there was no hesitation, no uncertainty. No insecurity, just raw trust. It was like nothing I had ever experienced before.

Afterward, I lay on Randy's shoulder, feeling so safe, so content, so close to him. It might have been the solitude of the place, the spontaneity of the decision, but for the first time I could remember, I felt content to just lie there, no need for motion or talking or thinking, just being in my body. But soon, grief and sadness found me, and I started to cry. In that meadow, I'd been able to find a different version of myself: one who was honest with herself, who could set aside her obsessing over control and sending and sponsors and success. Someone who could be whole, with a complex life instead of a single-minded one—someone who could pursue her desires without apology, without caring about her image or what anyone else thought. But I couldn't embrace that version of myself without hurting someone I cared about so much. Tommy didn't deserve any of this.

Before Tommy drove out for our final attempt at marriage counseling, Randy told me he would understand either way. Whatever I chose, he said, I would have either the sun or the moon.

◆ ◆ ◆

I'd always told Tommy that I didn't understand people who had affairs. If you loved someone else, why not just leave? I had thought it was simple, clear-cut, just like everything in life: a right way and a wrong way. I was so naive. For me, there was nothing simple about ending a marriage. The bonds between Tommy and me went so deep, and there was so much I loved about our lives and what we had built. My parents and family were supportive, but none of them had ever gotten divorced. The idea felt enormous—and most days it felt impossible. To leave a marriage this way, with infidelity and drama? That was never who I thought I was, who I wanted to be. But still, there was a part of me who was ready to walk away from that carefully maintained facade of perfection and embrace the honest messiness of my desires.

At the end of September, Tommy drove out to California. In the living room of the house we had built together, on Granny's green couch, I told him that I had slept with Randy. The next day we drove to Davis for our first session with Debbie and her therapist husband, Dan, and we continued to see them together for several weeks. We talked, cried, and fought in the cruel way that only people who know each other so well can. At times I couldn't believe how vulnerable and open we both were with each other. Where had these two people been for the past decade? Had we just been two children too scared of our own emotions to wade through real life together? By late October he had officially moved out. There was no tectonic shift to bring us together again, just a chasm and no clear idea how to bridge it any longer.

He went back to the cabin in Estes, and we began the process of untangling each of our lives from the other's. The property and finances were the easy part. I bought him out of the Yosemite house, and he kept the cabin outright. We had started telling the people in our lives about our separation, and it was like telling people that trees were no longer green or that the ocean had turned to sand. No one could believe it. We were BethandTommy; we were "what gave climbing couples hope." Since we'd only had one email address and one phone number between us for so long, I not only heard back from my personal to-tell list but sometimes got emails from people Tommy had contacted too. They were angrily supportive messages, intended solely for Tommy's eyes but registering painfully in front of mine. Other times the criticism was more direct: one person I'd considered one of my closest friends told me I was a sinner when I called. Clearly, he said, I needed to get my shit together and figure this out. It made me question the openness and vulnerability I had been practicing with Debbie. She'd been trying to show me that I could let go of the perfect facade, that I could trust people and feel safe to show them my whole self and all of my feelings. But the hard moments made me think it was all bullshit, and I retreated into my shell.

A lot of people, the industry acquaintances who'd always been quick to get in touch and praise my latest send, just disappeared from my life. Even the few people who remained supportive of my choice still seemed shocked by my wild deviation from the script. One exception was Steph Davis, an extremely accomplished pro climber I'd known for years. Often, we found ourselves on the same very short lists: at the time, we were among the only women ever to free climb any route on El Cap. We'd always been friendly, but I had kept my walls up, never gotten too close or been vulnerable—she was my direct competition. When I called her, I'd started into my rehearsed, apologetic speech about how I got together with Tommy when I was young, and then Kyrgyzstan had happened. And how I'd loved him but maybe not ever had the right kind of strong feelings—and then Steph cut me off.

"Beth," she said, and I braced myself for the disapproval, the chastising I'd gotten from so many others in our lives. "Did you fall in love?!"

I had no idea how to answer. I didn't want to lie, but I didn't want her to hate me either. I said, "Yeah, kinda . . ." in a feeble voice.

"Me too!" she said. *Wait, what?* I was shocked, excited, a little unnerved. For a moment it felt like it might be safe to set aside my shame and my self-hatred over what I'd done. *Someone is actually happy for me?* Then she started to ask me all the questions that people ask when someone is falling in love. *When did you meet? What do you love about him? Is he cute? Describe him to me. Isn't it so great to be in love?* It was the kind of giddy girlfriend conversation I'd never really had before. The kind that I'd watched as a fly on the wall but never actually participated in.

She had fallen in love with Mario, she told me. She and her husband, Dean, were getting divorced. And as we were laughing and blushing and gushing about our new relationships, she said, "I'm getting out of a very destructive marriage, so no one is questioning me at all. But you married the nicest-seeming guy on earth, and you two always seemed so perfect. That must make it so much harder!" She was right. I'd heard that from so many people: We were living the dream. Tommy was the nicest guy ever. Who would walk away from that?

Then Steph said the thing I needed to hear, the thing almost no one else had said to me yet: Yes, Tommy was so good and kind. "But that doesn't mean it isn't right to leave. It's totally right. You need to listen to you, to understand what's best for you."

On the hardest days, when I felt as though I'd been marked with a scarlet letter and cut out of nearly all the old social and professional circles I'd known, I tried to hang on to that.

◆ ◆ ◆

I had chosen Magic Line to be my public declaration of independence. In the heart of the park, the crack is a tiny right-facing corner that varies in size from a couple inches to a half inch or so, except at the crux, where it pinches down to less than a quarter inch. There, I could only whittle in a small nut to protect myself, and since no one's fingers (not even mine) are small enough to fit inside the crack at that point, I'd have to crimp as hard as I could on its outer edges. After the first seventy feet of hard crack climbing, I'd get a no-hands rest, meaning I could stand on a ledge big enough to take my hands off the wall and let my arms fully recover. The final twenty feet are balance-y and tenuous, but not nearly as difficult as the first two-thirds.

I was good at this type of climbing, really good. It was the technical, delicate climbing that granite is infamous for. That I was famous for. The route was easier than Meltdown for me, loads easier. I had figured out all the moves in the first two weeks of working on it, and six weeks later, I was doing it in overlapping sections. It had taken me four months to reach that point on Meltdown. I felt empowered by my rapid progress, but at the same time, I couldn't help thinking that I was taking a step down. I shouldn't be too proud. It was only 5.14b, while I had graded Meltdown as 5.14c . . . But this was by myself, with no Tommy asterisk. So I mostly ignored the negative voices; I was owning it.

My left hand crimped the crack above my head, thumb curled around my index finger. My right hand shuffled at chest height. My skin stung from the rough granite as it slowly ground down any extra layers I had. I stepped on the cemented hold as I approached the crux; the now-abandoned practice of cementing holds permanently in place was the one blight on this route. But I didn't care about that one imperfection. I had new shoes, and the thick rubber edged like a race car hugs corners. My arms felt tired but ready for the crux.

I climbed a little higher and then leaned back and sat down in my harness. I didn't need to send that day; I needed to refine everything. I needed to master the recipe of my sequence: the angle of each foot placement, the order of my gear on my harness, how long to rest before the crux. I dangled on the rope and looked at the wall. I'd rarely felt this good while working on a route. But I was building a new, independent me. I'd barbecued my own chicken breast last night; Magic Line would go down soon.

I refreshed my chalk tick marks on the wall and then pulled myself up again. I was stronger than I had been since Meltdown. The crux came easily, familiar choreography: left foot on the crumbly hold, right foot on the cemented hold. Even with my earbuds in, I couldn't hear what was playing. I was in the sweet spot that's both mindless and focused. But I was secure, on toprope, and any possible fall was limited by the anchor above me—I didn't need to go through any doors to quiet the doubt or the fear. Nothing bad could happen to me up there. It felt like singing in the shower in an empty house at the end of a dirt road in the middle of the night: no reason to feel fear or self-consciousness, no unwanted consequences.

My arms were tired, but after two more moves the crack started to widen, from half the width of a finger pad to a few inches. I breathed hard, and Jay-Z flooded my head again. I set a pointless goal of climbing to the no-hands rest before hanging on the rope again.

My left hand gastoned—grabbing vertical holds with my thumb pointed down and my fingers pointed in—for the next thirty feet. My feet smeared on either side of the crack, occasionally finding an opening in the crack big enough to stand on. Chalk dotted the wall where I wanted to stand, not necessarily marking an edge or a divot but sometimes just the best position for my body. My breathing became heavy, my arms filled with lactic acid, and my fingers wanted to open. I focused on them, willing them, *Don't open, you have to get to the ledge, that's where we can rest.* We were a team, and I was the captain, calling the shots, giving silly pep talks to achieve a goal and prove my worthiness to myself. *You can do this, Beth. You can do it on your own.* My right hand slowly started opening, my right elbow began rising toward the sky, in what climbers call a chicken wing: the precursor to a collapse, when the arms are too tired to hold on anymore. But I clenched my fingers, moved my feet up, tightened my core, and grabbed the jug ledge with my left hand. My fingers curled around the horizontal hold, and I let out a small whoop as I ran my feet up on the crumbly granite and stood on the ledge.

CHAPTER
THIRTY-FIVE

November 2008

In late November, I hosted Thanksgiving dinner for a group of over a dozen. They were a mixture of old friends from Davis and newer ones from Yosemite, and cooking the meal together felt like a small but vital revelation: food as fun, food as socializing, food as something other than the bare minimum of fuel for my next climb. After that, I had a food and holiday hangover and zero expectations of climbing my hardest so soon after indulgence. Randy was out of town, at his sister's, so Justin belayed me. Ten feet after the crux, my fingers opened up and I lost my hold on the rock, pitching off the route. I swung on the rope and grazed the giant, leafless oak tree behind me. Despite the fall, I was thrilled, disbelieving. Getting past the crux once meant I could do it: the whole route was possible. But I would have to try again.

Magic Line was giving up its secrets to me quickly, but my personal life remained a messier puzzle. Courtney had asked the women of the Bay Crew not to spend time with me anymore, and she had also asked Randy not to climb at their Berkeley gym. Randy was willing to acquiesce, and we did change gyms, but I didn't like feeling that we had to hide—as though we weren't worthy of friendships and a normal life. In therapy I was trying to learn not to shrink, not to fit myself into others' expectations, and here we were, shrinking.

I didn't know how to tell Randy what I needed. I didn't want to dictate how he interacted with his ex, but I also wanted him to back me up, not go along with our shunning. I wasn't ready to show him all of me yet: every insecurity and hurt. And the shunning *did* hurt. In the weeks before Courtney had made those requests, I had confided in some of the other women—I thought I'd bonded with them—about my guilt and shame, my fears for my professional future, and how few friends I had outside of BethandTommy. Their sudden withdrawal from my life was painful, even if rationally I understood that they were in an impossible position. It was hard for me to be vulnerable with women, hard for me to build and trust those friendships. I had taken this brave leap, in South Africa and since then, into honesty and authentic feelings. Now it felt like I was being punished for that leap. I felt isolated, like I had been marked as tainted. Some days, that felt cruel; other days, I felt like I deserved it.

That fall, I cycled through the strangest mixture of emotions. I was depressed and anxious and ashamed; I was excited and empowered and blossoming. I was getting divorced; I was falling in love. I wanted Randy in my life; I was starting to understand that he would only be one piece of the puzzle. Everything was so uncertain, but I held on to one solid thought. I knew I could send Magic Line, and that would fix at least some of the problems that plagued me.

A week after my post-turkey near miss, I was back. I tied into my orange lead line, my hands shaking. There was nothing left to learn, nothing to do but send. With December already begun, my weather window was closing. It was Wednesday. A massive winter storm was forecast for that Saturday. Randy had taken the day off from his Monday-to-Friday job in the Bay to belay me. If I didn't send today, Friday would be my last chance for the season.

I took a deep breath. I was the master of this moment, the go time, the "get your shit together and just send" time. But this project was different. I had done so much of it by myself. The familiarity of having Tommy as my collaborator, to bounce ideas and emotions and tantrums off of, was gone. With Randy my meltdowns were different, suppressed—I didn't want to scare him off, but I was also desperate to unleash my spinning mind and have him tell me that it would all be okay.

I reminded myself that this was supposed to feel different. I wanted different; I had *chosen* different. Debbie wanted me to work on a new understanding: that sending wasn't everything. That I was a strong, independent woman. That being the best at climbing was great, but there was more to leading a rich life.

Most of the time, that still sounded like bullshit. Debbie didn't know what it was like to be a professional athlete, on the cover of magazines and featured in movies. She didn't understand the pressures of the business. Magic Line wasn't Meltdown, but it would land me on a cover, or at least secure a two-page spread. It would buy me some time with my sponsors, who I feared were doubting my future alone. It would prove, to me and everyone else, that I could do this without Tommy.

Get your shit together, Beth. Tie the damn knot and finish this thing.

I looked at Randy and said, "Are you good?" I glanced down at the belay device and rope to make sure. This wasn't his dance; it wasn't something we had done together every day for years. I felt vulnerable, like a brain surgeon who'd been assigned a new scrub nurse. Randy didn't seem to mind my double-checking. He just smiled his radiant smile and said, "You got this." I turned toward the wall, wiped my left foot against the shin of my right leg and then my right foot against the left leg: half superstition, half cleaning my shoes. I chalked my hands with my perfectly crushed chalk and placed them on the rough, dark granite. I took one deep breath in through my nose and put my feet on the wall. This was it.

Magic Line is longer than Meltdown, but I still had every single handhold and foothold memorized. I knew exactly when and where to grab each hold, how hard to hold each one, when I could relax, when

I had to place gear. My left hand led the majority of the twenty feet up to the crux, pinky up, thumb wrapped around my index finger. My feet stood hard and firm on each of the flat, thin edges. My breath was even and automatic. I had chatter in my head, but it was calm. The bottom of the route is hard, but not too hard. After five left-hand moves upward and eleven moves with my feet, I put in my first piece of gear, a small purple Metolius cam, and clipped my rope to it. Relief came over me. My fingers felt flushed with strength, my mind a bit quieter. My right foot was trembling slightly—not tired, anxious. I clenched my abs slightly and put more pressure on it. *Not yet,* I said to myself. *Save that energy, you'll need it up higher.* My foot stopped shaking.

I placed another piece above my head, shoving it in with a little twist of spite for all the people who thought they could tell me how to live or what was right. Anger was easier than sadness: anger was fuel, powering me up the wall, while sadness and shame just weighed me down. So I tried to keep that fuel lit and burning. I clipped the rope in and then poked my nose into the crack to make sure that the small metal lobes of the piece I'd just placed were properly expanded. Part of my mind had already started to go to the crux sequence. I smelled the air to see if the waterfall spray was big today. To understand if the lichen would feel slippery or if it was dry enough to trust the precarious smears up higher. *You know what to do, Beth. Your left hand is feeling strong, your gear is good, your shoes are perfectly broken in: stiff enough to edge but soft enough to grab. This is your chance; this is yours, yours alone. Get this done. You are strong.*

I didn't look at Randy, but I aimed my voice toward the ground. "Okay," I said, quiet yet confident. I wanted to run through a million things with him, a checklist of things to watch out for. The million things that Tommy never needed reminding of, that Randy didn't really need reminding of either, but I wanted to control this situation perfectly. I got hold of myself: Randy was perfectly capable of belaying a single pitch route. I needed to focus. I said again, "Okay," took a deep breath, and moved my left hand to the higher gaston. A sharp edge on the crack dug into the side of my index finger. I winced, pursed my lips. It didn't hurt. Today was my day.

I tensed my fingers harder, tightened my core, moved my foot up onto the cemented hold. I thought about Ron cementing that hold ten years ago, wondered if the route would even be possible without it. *Keep it together, Beth.* I grabbed my thoughts and put them back on track. I was above my last piece of gear. I stepped firmly on the crumbly foothold, almost willing the granite to hold together. My left hand moved up; I looked down at my right foot, tensed my shoulder, and moved it higher, right next to the crack. I let out a scream without thinking about it.

Three more moves and the crack tripled in size, becoming wide enough for a pad and a half of my fingertips. I had made it through the crux again. *Holy shit!* My right foot started bouncing and shaking again. Without thinking, I reached down to the right side of my harness and unclipped another piece of gear. I pulled the trigger and shoved it in the crack and then quickly pulled up the rope and clipped it in.

I couldn't blow it again after the crux. It was hard climbing to the top, but nothing like what I had just done. I had gotten through the test; now I just had to turn my paper in to the teacher.

I breathed, shook out my hands one by one in the cold air, hoping that my forearms and fingers would get rid of the lactic acid and get some strength back. I could hear the roar of the waterfall and Randy's whoops of excitement below. My excitement was bubbling too. This would show everyone that I didn't need BethandTommy. I could just be Beth.

But I still had forty feet to climb.

There were just twenty feet more to the no-hands rest, where I could pause and think about whatever I wanted. I had this. From here the climbing was only 5.12, the same move over and over again. I just needed to endure a slow but growing burn in my forearms. But that was what I'd trained for over years at the Rocknasium, circles and circles on the wall like a mouse in a wheel.

A few moves later I pulled onto the tiny ledge, tired, pumped, but with a smile on my face. I couldn't believe I was there. I could see the crack end above me, where the anchor bolts were. That was where I would be in about five minutes. That was where I could claim another 5.14. That was where I could finally exhale, own climbing as mine, trust when people gave me compliments instead of deflecting. Giddy butterflies started flapping in my stomach. I shouldn't celebrate just yet. There were still twenty feet of precarious climbing left, but I knew I could climb those twenty feet without too much trouble. I took some deep breaths again. I could almost taste the familiar triumph. I wanted to feel that success. After that, I could choose Debbie's path of hooey feelings and peace and love and true meaning without external validation and all that crap I desperately wanted to believe in. I just needed this win, first.

I don't know how long I rested, but my arms and hands felt fresh. They had snap back in them. I climbed up eight feet and placed a higher piece of gear. I clipped the rope in and down-climbed to the ledge for one more rest. I couldn't believe how fresh I felt. I alternated my hands on the back of my neck to keep them warm. I wiped my feet against my calves again, but they felt different. There was a little less feeling in them, a little more dullness and numbness. I wiped them again, hoping that they might feel better, but they stayed the same. My stomach bounced with excitement, my mind spun. I wiped my feet one more time and told myself they were fine, I knew what to do, just press a little harder and I'd be fine.

I put my right hand into an opening in the crack and shoved my pointer finger down into a constriction. The cold granite grabbed my knuckle like Velcro, and the joint held my body's weight. I moved my feet up, first my left foot onto a decent edge, then my right foot into the crack. They felt flat, not supple. I wondered if I should down-climb again and try to warm my feet. I pictured myself standing on the ledge, warming each foot in my hand one by one. But that could make my hands go numb. They were more important. And I might teeter off the precariously small ledge if I bent my body in half. Was I flexible enough to put my toes on my stomach while still holding on to the crack so I wouldn't fall? I'd never warmed my feet on that ledge. I should have stretched more.

My left hand reached up into a higher opening in the crack and crimped the outside with my fingertips. My feet moved into their designated positions, so well rehearsed I could debate the course of action in my head and my body still knew what it needed to do. I only had ten more feet; I didn't need to down-climb. *Focus, breathe, just climb.* I reached down to my harness, took off the last piece of gear, and placed it into the crack. I shoved and gave it a yank to make sure that it would hold me. It was solid, I was solid, this was working. I grabbed the rope between my legs and lifted it up and clipped it into the carabiner. My harness was light now with the absence of gear, but the rope had gotten progressively heavier as I climbed.

I chalked both of my hands and then placed my right foot higher on the crumbly granite face. The rock past the no-hands rest was much flakier and less pristine. It reminded me of the rock on Half Dome, so revered but, to the eye of a discerning climber, so inferior to El Cap's. The top of this route was easier but uglier than the bottom—I wondered, sometimes, why Ron hadn't just ended the route at the ledge.

At the very top the crack angles right, deviating from its otherwise absurdly vertical line. My left hand still led, but instead of reaching as high above me as I could, I would have to reach farther out in front of me, throwing off my balance. My feet would be the doorstop to prevent me from tipping over sideways and out of the crack. I pressed my numb feet onto the rock as hard as I could as I alternated between a pinky-first, thumb-down move with my left hand and a palm-up, thumb-first undercling with my right hand. I pushed my right hand up into the crack as hard as possible, while the left hand pried as hard as it could. It was like trying to open the hood of a car over and over again.

After ten feet, my skin was tacky and sticking to the granite perfectly. I had left all the mental chatter of success and failure behind and stepped into the rare quiet focus and bravery that was key to my sending this route. I placed my right foot on the last foothold, looking up as I did to see where the crack changed, turning back to vertical, and began reaching my right hand for the final jug. The one that I could grab and then clip the anchors. The victory jug. I looked down to move my left foot onto a crumbly hold. I stepped on it firmly, but I couldn't feel anything. I moved my right hand off the crack and reached up for the jug. As my skin wrapped around the textured hold, I felt it scraping, glancing off. I looked down and felt myself falling. I was airborne, stomach in my throat, my eyes closed so I wouldn't have to watch the length of the route flow by me like a diamond ring being washed down the drain.

It felt like minutes before the rope finally caught me. My body jolted to a stop, and my leg loops and waist belt held me in the air. *What the hell happened? I was right there! I was on the last move! Why am I on the end of the rope?*

Where had all that new confidence gone? What about trying to let go of achievement tied to worthiness? That was all bullshit. *I should have sent this route. I'm a failure, a loser. Everyone is right, I can't do it without Tommy. I should have warmed my feet. I'm such an idiot, why didn't I take the time? I hate this route. I hate climbing. I hate myself.* My chalky hands went over my face as I cried. I could hear Randy asking if I wanted to come down. *Why the hell would I want to go back down? I can't try it again today. Or tomorrow. This is it. Why would Randy ever want to be with me now? I'm weak and pathetic.* Again I heard Randy gently telling me that I was amazing, asking if I wanted some food or a jacket. I wanted him to tie me off to a tree and just leave me there, a spectacle for all the tourists hiking by. Beth Rodden: could have been someone, but she wasn't, so here she hangs in infamy.

CHAPTER
THIRTY-SIX

October 2009

Nearly a year later, in October 2009, I went back to Magic Line.

Everything was so familiar: the hard run up the trail to the base of the climb, the quiet of the early Yosemite mornings, the particular smell of the waterfall, reduced to its lowest flow of the season, splashing through the rocks. My body remembered the moves too. I knew how to push myself, where to pull hard, when to rest. Soon I sent the route on toprope—and it felt fairly easy. A true send, freeing the route, seemed imminent, tantalizingly close.

But Magic Line's style of climbing is especially hard on the left index finger, since it requires the same tweaked position 90 percent of the time. A couple of weeks after my success on toprope, on the morning that I expected to send, I tied myself in like I always did. It was a crisp morning; the leaves were yellow on their descent into winter. I had found my brown Prana pants and white long-underwear shirt at the back of my closet, neatly folded after last year's spectacular failure. I wore them now. I wiped my perfectly broken-in Miuras on each shin and checked my knot and Randy's belay device. I dipped my fingers into my chalk bag, took a deep breath, pulled on, and started up.

I was only ten feet up the route when I felt a sharp pain in my left hand. I knew this pain. It was the acute, consequential pain I remembered from my torn shoulder, from the old collateral ligament injuries in my fingers. The pain that is bad but that you don't want to admit is bad. I lost my grip, fell onto the rope, and shook my hand out violently, like the pain was a fly I could shoo away.

When Randy asked what happened, I shrugged it off. *Suck it up, Rodden, it can't be that bad. Just deal with it.* I started climbing higher, putting my hand back in the same position that had caused the first sharp stab. Left hand up, right hand following, again and again. The pain started to become louder, stronger, with each move. Pulling on the rock felt like I was being stabbed with a knife, right near the base of my left index finger. I sagged onto the rope again, tried to give it a minute to fade. But it only grew stronger. As much as I wanted to, I knew this wasn't something to ignore. I lowered down, my face covered in tears, shaking with anger at my body's betrayal. Magic Line had been stolen from me for another year.

◆ ◆ ◆

It turned out that I had torn my A1 pulley, a band of tissue that helps fasten the flexor tendon to the bone at the base of the finger. Most people don't think much about the tiny scraps of soft tissue that bind our hands together and make them work—when they think about an injury that might slow them down, they think about the spectacular ones: a broken leg, or a blown-out knee ligament, or a major concussion. But a climber's fingers are her tools: just as much as the eyes, they let me learn the rock, seeking out the fine grain in its surface, the minute holds— and then (unlike my eyes) they go to work as the tiny levers that send me up its face. The layers of skin and fine little bones are precious. The slightest tear in the smallest ligament is debilitating.

I can map the next four years of my climbing life—four years of failure after failure—on my body. It was as though, in leaving my marriage behind, in shedding the old skin of BethandTommy, I had also abandoned the bodily resilience I had taken for granted: the muscle and tendon and bone that had always been willing to absorb my abuse.

The trouble had begun with my right shoulder and the most ordinary event. On a bike ride in Berkeley with Randy five months earlier, I had reached down for a water bottle and ridden into a large pothole. The impact shivered up my arm. I have loose joints, and I'd been prescribed regular exercises to keep my arm firmly in its socket. But with all the invincible confidence of a young athlete, I hadn't bothered with the exercises in years. Later I would learn that I had torn my labrum. I tore it even further the next week, when I did an easy mantle move on a warm-up problem and felt and heard a distinct rip.

I passed up a photo shoot to a new, beautiful climbing area in Canada, ashamed of getting hurt but knowing that I needed rest and rehab or my arm would fall out of its socket. I was maniacal at rehab, employing all my old training regimens to getting my shoulder better. After two months, I was healed enough to go with Randy and a small group of friends to South Africa again: a strange mirror of the summer before when I was caught between the highs of falling in love and the surreal awfulness of telling Tommy and Courtney the truth.

This trip was a blender of its own emotions. My first big trip without any photographers or any sort of marketing package to present to sponsors, my first big trip that was "only" about the actual climbing in years. It felt lovely and irresponsible, and I wondered if I was failing somehow by not coming up with an angle to sell. But it was also so early in my new relationship with Randy; we were each still learning how the other worked, how to climb and travel together, how to navigate living side by side. After two months of bouldering there, my shoulder held up okay; I was strong and almost back to 90 percent. I felt like I only needed 80 percent to send Magic Line. So I'd gone back to Yosemite once we got home, back to Magic Line, and that was when my pulley tore.

I should have rested. I should have given my finger, and my shoulder, time to heal. But I was frantic to send the route. I needed to show the entire climbing world—and myself—that I was still here. Still worthy. My labrum tear had come around the same time that word was starting to get out to the wider climbing public about my divorce. In articles and interviews, Tommy explained our breakup by saying I'd left him for another man. It was a simple, easily digestible narrative, and it stuck.

It was around this time that I did my first slideshow tour without Tommy. I was nervous to stand up in front of crowds on my own, but it went well at first—at a sold-out presentation in Calgary, I got a standing ovation. I remember looking into the crowd, blinded by lights and applause, and hearing a tiny voice inside of me say, *See, Beth, you can do this alone, and you might, just might, actually be pretty good at it.* A few weeks later, at the REI flagship store in Seattle, I was nearly finished with the Q&A at the end of my talk when I saw two guys walk in late. Chalk on their shorts, climbing shoes clipped to their backpacks. I asked if there were any other questions, and one of them raised his hand. *Strange,* I thought, *when he wasn't even here for my talk.*

"Um, yeah, so, I hear Tommy is in Yosemite working on a hard new El Cap climb?"

"Yeah, I think he's up on Mescalito," I replied.

"So is that weird," he continued, "to, you know, be there with the boulderer bro that you cheated on him with, in the house he built for you, while he's out there making history on El Cap? And you haven't really climbed anything hard since Meltdown."

I froze, somewhere between fear and anger. Would REI record this? Would they send it to my sponsors? Was this the moment when it would all fall apart? If everyone knew about my affair, who would want to see me in an advertisement? How could I be valuable or marketable to anyone or any brand?

It felt like I stood there silently for an hour, but it was only seconds. I was nauseous, I thought I might cry, but instead my anger cleared my head. Somehow, I managed, "Yeah, Tommy is there. I'm sure it'll be rad if he frees Mescalito."

And then I smiled.

The audience was mostly women, and in the silence that followed, one of them, maybe ten years older than me, turned to the two guys. "Hey, this is REI," she said, "but I'm pretty sure there are classes for emotional intelligence somewhere across the street." The crowd snickered and clapped, and I felt a wave of relief. Maybe being my whole self, even in public, wasn't terrible after all.

◆　◆　◆

I needed to send if I wanted to silence the critics myself. I felt like I was running up a sand dune, sinking in and falling back as I tried to scramble higher. Staying still was not an option. My mind spun with plans and ways to fast-forward through the time my body needed to heal. My finger was hurt anyway, so I thought I would just get the shoulder surgery I still needed for my months-old labrum tear. I thought it would be like a minor car repair: quick and predictable, changing out the dirty oil for clean, a faulty part for one that would perform. But the shoulder surgery was followed by complications. Randy's sister's one-hundred-and-ten-pound dog tugged hard on a leash I was holding; later, I slipped on that same dog's slobber and fell down some stairs, landing on my bad shoulder. And my finger wasn't healing. It hurt to type, to cut vegetables. Then, when I could finally boulder again, I fell and broke my ankle. And then I broke my ankle a *second* time—impatient on a warm-up climb, knowing it should be easy for me, I didn't place the crash pad correctly. When my foot slipped, I landed on a large root, and in the ER.

Injuries cascaded through my fingers. In January 2010, a few weeks after my surgery, Randy and Courtney finalized his buyout of their house, and he moved out of the apartment he'd rented and back into the Berkeley Craftsman. I moved in too, splitting time between the Bay and Yosemite. (I had started renting out the main part of the Yosemite house, and we spent our time in the tiny basement studio: a cozy three-hundred-square-foot hideaway that felt a little more like our own.) But I could hardly turn a key in the old, stubborn locks of the Bay house, which was built in 1902, without feeling something pull or snap.

◆ ◆ ◆

In May 2011, during a brief window when I was healthy enough to try to climb, I flew to Catalonia, Spain—the world epicenter of sport climbing. Sport is a subcategory that involves clipping into permanently installed bolts in the rock instead of placing your own gear for protection. Without the worry of gear pulling or rocks falling, the climbing is distilled down to strength, fitness, and problem-solving. It seemed like every day a new 5.15 was being climbed there and a new young hotshot was making their name. But I had never really been drawn to the scene in Spain. The routes were rumored to be soft, nice on the ego, and the individual lines were not very striking, with so many 5.14s and 5.15s crammed next to each other that it was hard to tell which one was which. It was popular, crowded. Everyone who was anyone was here, clipping chains and filling out online scorecards of what they had climbed. And the Spanish lifestyle never really jibed with me: wake up at noon, to the crag at 4:00 p.m., and back at the house by midnight? It seemed even lazier than bouldering.

But the trip was a chance for me to get fit, to come back from my latest injury and be ready for yet another attempt at Magic Line in the fall. I was recovering from my second broken ankle and, of course, another finger injury. Randy couldn't join me, so I'd stepped outside of my comfort zone, reached out to my friend Emily, a professional climber who was a few years younger than me, and asked if I could tag along with her and her then-boyfriend, Sam. They were going to be staying in a rental house near the Santa Linya cave, not far from where my childhood climbing friend Chris Sharma lived. A gathering of all the top names in the sport, my old circle, my old peers. It felt both empowering and intimidating. Like I was back where I belonged, but maybe I had become both too soft and too jaded along the way.

Walking into the house was like passing through a portal into another time and place, one where only climbing mattered. Climbers were hunched over open laptops, splicing footage into clips from the day. Air beta, where you mime out the moves to each other in the air, was happening in the living room. The kitchen was filled with mounds of dirty dishes, old half-eaten boxes of cheap cookies, wine, energy bars, and protein-shake powders. There were no vegetables. There was, in fact, no fridge.

"Beth! How have you been?" Joe said as he wrapped me up in a long hug. I hadn't seen Joe since a trade show last summer. Since he'd said: "Now that you aren't the first couple of rock, do you think Colette and I can be?"

I'd laughed it off. "Are you sure that's a title you want?"

I assumed he idolized Tommy, like almost everyone else. But now, here in this frat house of sorts in an ancient village in Spain, he seemed so genuinely happy to see me.

He followed up before I could decide whether to tell him honestly how I'd been. "What do you want to climb on tomorrow? We're heading to the cave in the afternoon, sounds like everybody's going too. Want to join?"

I hadn't ever been to the cave, but I had heard so much about it and seen it everywhere in the climbing press. It was huge, intimidating, and I was pretty sure the easiest routes were 5.12.

"Um, wherever there are good warm-ups!" I laughed uncomfortably, trying to make light of my situation. Emily knew that I was injured; she knew I was always injured.

"Yeah, there are! There's this amazing 7b and another really good 7b+," he said as he poured himself a glass of wine. Europe uses a different grading system, but the routes he was describing were 5.12

and up. Those were warm-ups for this crew, and had been for me, once, too.

"Oh, um." I tried to think how to tell him I couldn't climb that grade right now. That I was hoping to get there by the end of the trip, or maybe even harder, but I needed something easier first.

Emily jumped in to rescue me. "I think we'll try and find her some 6s, you know, to get her acclimated."

My face turned red, and I stared at the empty void in the kitchen where the fridge should have been.

Joe seemed shocked, as shocked as I would have been if our positions were reversed. "Damn, you're on 6s?" he said, and we all had to laugh at the sheer absurdity of my situation.

Underneath the laughter, I felt ashamed and betrayed by my body. I was mortified, and then that kindled into a vast anger. Yes, I needed 6s. But I wanted 7s. I wanted to just go out with them and climb hard until my arms fell off. Instead, here I was. I felt weak and pathetic, like I shouldn't be sponsored; I shouldn't get money deposited into my bank account right now to be a professional climber. I knew how lame and stupid my body was, what a shadow of myself I'd become. Inwardly I seethed, furious at myself and at everyone around me. *I should be climbing 5.13 here. Hell, I should be climbing 5.14, since I hear they are so soft. But nope, I need 5.10s. And, honestly, I should probably only try 5.9s because the Valley 5.10s have been injuring me. I'm not proud of this. I'd rather be in any other body but mine.*

I knew I got stared at, at the crag, and not in the old BethandTommy way. I knew people whispered about me at the belays and on the hikes up. *There's Beth Rodden, the one who did that supposed 5.14c in Yosemite, the one who had videos and articles about her. But look at her, flailing and failing on a 5.10. I heard she left Tommy for some boulderer—look where that got her. She looks like she couldn't climb a tree if she tried.*

I tried to hide all that from Joe, plastering on a smile, squeezing out another self-deprecating laugh. "Yeah, 6s. I know, pathetic, but my body sucks right now."

"Shit, that sucks, I'm sorry," he said. "You should check out the Football crag. I've never been, but I think it has 6s. Come meet us in the afternoon at Santa Linya."

Great.

◆ ◆ ◆

Sam and Emily and I drove down from the rental house in the ancient village at the top of the hill, winding through old stone buildings and then along steep hillsides. It was so pretty, even if I was at war with my body. The stark contrast between the bright orange and red and black cliffs against the vibrant green fields and grasses. The rolling landscape stretched on for as far as the eye could see, cliffs scattering the horizon.

This was not how I had imagined the trip would be. I wanted to blend in with the crowd, hop back on the varsity team. But now they had to drive me to a separate cliff? I felt like a child ordering off a different menu. Did I also want some crayons to draw with? They were kind and set up some topropes and belayed me on 5.10s until it was time to go to the grown-up cliff, but I could tell this was not where they wanted to be either.

"I'll do one more, then we can head over to the cave for you guys," I said as I lowered down after an uninteresting but fine enough 5.10. "You sure you don't want to climb any more of these? They actually aren't terrible." I looked at the two of them, so fit and strong and happy. I remembered how nice it had been to try as hard as I could without any part of my body snapping or cracking. Back then I wouldn't have wasted my time, energy, or skin on these mediocre climbs at the JV crag. I wondered if they were being kinder than I would have been, in their position. Did they feel like every minute here, every hour, they were getting weaker by association? They didn't show it.

"We're good," Emily said. "Seriously, stay as long as you want, the cave doesn't get good until the evening."

I tied in for my next climb, feeling internally rushed. I knew they'd wait forever, but I imagined it might be with the excruciating patience of a parent waiting for a toddler to tie their own shoe.

I spent the rest of the trip worrying about what I figured people must be thinking. *Why isn't Beth trying hard anymore? She didn't break a leg or lose an arm. Look at Tommy; he free climbed El Cap six months after he literally cut off his finger. Beth says she's hurt, but she just doesn't have it in her.* The idea that people might think I wasn't trying, that I must be faking, made me seethe. I knew I wasn't making my injuries up. (I rolled my ankle to the side, to test it. Yep, it still hurt.) Who wouldn't want to climb hard? Who wouldn't want to be a race car that wins every Formula 1 race? Given the choice, I would still be the race car. Not the vehicle draped in a dusty cover, filled with broken parts, doomed never to see the asphalt again.

No one else could understand how much I wanted it. How badly I wanted to show everyone that I wasn't just half of BethandTommy; I was *Beth*. I was Beth and I pulled my weight and I could suffer and try harder than anyone. No one I saw in Catalonia had freed El Cap. No one in Spain could climb Meltdown or Magic Line. *Goddamnit, Magic Line.* If my foot hadn't slipped, if I had sent it that first time, then I wouldn't have gone on the bike ride. I wouldn't have been worried about cross-training. I wouldn't have started the cascade of injuries, and my body wouldn't have broken down. And even if it had, I would have been safe, protected by how recently I'd been in magazines and movies, celebrated for my latest send. Or if female climbers were granted multi-year contracts as freely as I'd seen them offered to Tommy, if we had been given the same degree of stability—of trust, of certainty, of commitment for the duration of our careers—I wouldn't have had to worry constantly that I was about to get dropped. I wouldn't have felt like I had to push through injury after injury, making things worse. Instead, there I was, sitting in the corner at Santa Linya, eating some stale beef jerky and watching everyone else send and smile and laugh.

I hated my body. I hated the nagging suspicion that everyone else was hating and doubting my body too.

I wound up paying $1,000 to move my flight up and leave Spain early. Everyone had been so kind, trying to include me, finding easier routes even if that meant venturing to different areas. Even so, this wasn't the place I needed to be. My new self couldn't—didn't want to—fit into my old life. I was surprised by how badly I wanted the things I had once dismissed as distractions. Good food. Conversation about more than just climbing. A fridge.

But I still wanted to find a way to climb hard.

◆ ◆ ◆

After Spain, the injuries continued. I kept trying to get healthy, kept circling back to Magic Line and throwing myself at it, trying and failing again. But I couldn't move without another vital piece of me popping, tearing, breaking. I turned down photo shoot after photo shoot, trip after trip. Nothing seemed to help. Acupuncture, massage, physical therapy, laser treatments, this new diet or that new supplement—I tried it all, emptied my bank account, but it got me nowhere. I started to think that I was being punished for my sins. Or that my body was finally revealing how tattered I felt on the inside.

Back when we first moved in together, Randy and I had adopted a dog. Max was a shy, anxious, and injured Rhodesian ridgeback who had become my constant companion. He'd been hit by a car before we got him, and he was still frightened of everything—he and I made quite the pair, perpetually rehabilitating together. But caring for him, devoting my energy to something other than my body and my career, made me feel lighter.

Phrases like *mind-body connection* were a joke to me, and I don't like being told what to do or how to think—especially when it comes to my body. It was my machine, my tool to succeed, and I knew it best. When people—like my shoulder surgeon, or my hand therapist (who lived in Colorado, and who I called *constantly* for advice), or my therapist-therapist, or even Randy—tried to suggest that maybe my anxiety and relentless self-criticism could be part of the problem, I rejected the idea. I had never been open to hearing that I might have some unresolved issues from Kyrgyzstan. (When Debbie had asked about it, I shut her down. I just needed her help with this Randy situation, I insisted.) I was no more open to being asked to relinquish my negative thoughts and obsessive habits.

Three years into my cascade of finger injuries (my left index finger for the second time, then my right index finger, then my right ring finger, then my left index finger *again*), my hand therapist, Brenda, told me that we needed to do some "brain training" and visualize how my body was going to heal from a finger injury. *Nothing else is working, might as well try this crap,* I thought. Still, even the act of accepting that suggestion, of letting in an idea that was different from my usual perspective, was a first step to letting in more. With time, and those gentle nudges from people who cared about me, I began to consider the connections between the emotional and the physical. And, perhaps even more slowly, to contemplate whether the years of strict calorie restriction, starving my body of nutrients, might have had consequences beyond my waistline. I started to understand the patterns that our minds can fall into, like the needle on a turntable dropping into a familiar groove.

◆ ◆ ◆

It had been a year and a half since Spain. I was still obsessed with Magic Line, still believed that one more win on my scorecard would be both my fairy-tale ending and my new beginning in climbing. A classic hero's journey, an easily packaged narrative to sell to my sponsors and the public: the comeback kid, can't keep her down for long. Beth triumphant. But my body, the thing that I'd counted on to produce achievement after achievement, that I knew how to manipulate and starve and punish and mold and use, couldn't even handle a month or two of rudimentary climbing before breaking down again. As crass as it sounds, I had fucked with my body for so long. Now I was getting fucked by my body.

One morning, I woke up in Berkeley to an email from my Yosemite neighbor, Tom. *Hey Beth, we were thinking about climbing Arrowhead Arête on Wednesday, would you like to join us?*

Years earlier, when Tommy and I had rented the entryway of a house full of climbers while we built our place, Tom and Theresa had also rented a room in the same house. Soon they had graduated to their own house nearby, and during my divorce they were a constant presence on my answering machine. "Hey, Beth, it's Tom, we'd love to go for a walk with you and check in, give us a call back." Click. "Hey, Beth, it's Theresa, I'm about to head out on a hike on the loop trail, would you like to join me?" Click. "Hey, Beth, we're heading to the Cookie, we'd love it if you wanted to join." Click. I never called them back. This was shortly after one of my closest friends had called me a sinner, and I was keeping to myself. I figured that Tom and Theresa knew me as BethandTommy, and I didn't think they could ever like me as just Beth.

Finally, I picked up one of their calls (by accident) and agreed to take a walk with Theresa. As we walked, she told me about how she had been with another guy when she first met Tom. She broke up with her boyfriend to pursue Tom (not the dramatic affair I had, but still), and she understood how something like that could happen. Ever since she'd made it clear that I wasn't a villain in her eyes, they had both felt safe to me.

Tom and Theresa were still good about checking in. Still good about reaching out even if I didn't reciprocate, even if I was in a lava pit of anger and sadness about my injuries. This email was their latest attempt.

I had never heard of Arrowhead Arête, and I had to go get my guidebook out of the storage room to look it up. I read about it: a 5.8, off the beaten path, beautiful views. But as I turned the page, my stubborn left index finger seared with pain. Of course I couldn't join them. Sure, maybe I could do the actual climbing, but even a 5.8 in the Valley meant belaying and rappelling and rope work, taking out gear and breaking down anchors. I picked up the phone and called Tom.

"Hey!" I said, still always needing to sound perky and optimistic. I wondered if he could tell I was faking it. "Thank you so much for the invite, but I'm still kinda dealing with this pesky finger. I don't think it'll be long now, probably next week, if not sooner, but yeah, I don't know, I don't think I can make it. But thank you again so much for the invite." I was keenly aware that if I kept turning people down, at some point they'd stop asking, and I didn't want that, even though sometimes I wanted that.

"What would be okay for you? Or what hurts it?" Tom asked, with genuine curiosity.

"Um, well, I don't know. I mean, I've found some ways to climb that don't hurt it, but belaying and rope management hurt, which is weird and annoying, and I bet taking out gear would be hard and placing it, so that basically means I'd be useless on the climb, and I know that's a burden . . ." I trailed off, depressing even myself. I tried to pull it together and added, "But it looks fun! You guys should totally do it, let me know how it is. Send pictures!"

Tom was an accomplished climber, a reliable Valley partner for anyone, though he'd never say so. He was athletically gifted but maintained a healthy relationship with climbing. He loved it, didn't obsess about it, just wanted to have fun. He had been married to Theresa for over ten years, and during that time she had endured a series of really bad injuries too. So he got it. Once, when she was two years into a terrible ankle recovery and so sad that she couldn't do anything outside or go anywhere, Tom had skied and towed her on a sled so they could go snow camping, one of her favorite things.

"So, if you just had a toprope," he asked, "and Theresa and I led everything, took out all the gear, belayed each pitch, were totally willing to bail from anywhere if it hurts, then you would come?"

It sounded so sad when he put it like that. I paused. I didn't want to say yes. I wanted to interrupt him, tell him that my finger was fine, I could handle it, I was tough. I wanted to make sure that if anyone saw me up there (oh God, I hoped no one would see me up there; the guidebook said off the beaten path, rarely climbed, and I was hanging on to that) they could go back and tell all the climbing gossips that Beth was back; she'd cruised that thing. *Yeah, it's only 5.8, but man, she walked up it like it was a sidewalk. She is definitely the queen of Yosemite granite.* I shook my head. I didn't know what to say. It sounded so nice to just go climb. No strings attached. No need to prove anything, with two people who didn't care about the endgame, just the experience.

Finally I said, "Yes, okay—really? Are you sure? But yes, that sounds wonderful. Wow, thank you, Tom." It was as though I had this sandbag of fear hanging from every decision I made, weighed down with every possible outcome and what people might think about each one. And to just make a decision, to go with it, felt like cutting a hole in that sandbag and watching it all drain out. Sweet relief.

The hike to Arrowhead Arête is steep and long for the Valley, and on top of everything else I was afraid that I wouldn't be fit enough. But halfway up the approach, T-shirt soaked in sweat, lips chapped from breathing hard, the sensation of being off the Valley floor really began to soak in. The big brown meadows that can be seen a few hundred feet up, with the low river in the fall winding through them. The top of the Ahwahnee hotel and the government buildings in the Village. It was like visiting a relative's house that I hadn't seen in a few years. Sure, I'd remember the smell and feel of their shag carpeting, but to feel it on my skin, to hug them with my own arms, brought back something that memories can't.

We got to the base of the climb, and Theresa started racking up. Nearly two decades into my climbing career, it still was rare for me to climb with other women. I thought it was so cool that she was going to lead this.

"Okay, you guys, we'll see you at the top of this pitch," she said as she started off. She climbed with grace and confidence but then wasn't afraid to yell down to Tom, on belay: "Watch me here, I'm a little scared." How impressive was that? Just admitting she was scared? No worries about it? No hesitation?

Tom and I climbed, one right after the other. I don't remember what we talked about, the jokes or the remarks we made. I don't remember if my finger hurt or if I was scared. But what I *do* remember is that my cheeks were sore at the top of the climb from smiling and laughing so much. When was the last time I'd had sore cheeks on a climbing day? I must have been a fourteen-year-old kid, in the gym with her friends. When we got to the top I stood on this tiny pillar, like a piece of Toblerone two thousand feet above Yosemite Valley, and looked around. There was Half Dome, and Glacier Point Apron, and the swallows dive-bombing behind me. I wasn't on a noteworthy climb. I wasn't even close. I was on a climb that only a couple of years ago I would have thought of as pathetic and a waste of my time. But there I was, standing on one of the most unique places I had ever been in Yosemite, after basically being guided up. Could Andre Agassi ever have felt content after winning a Ping-Pong match against a ten-year-old? That was how I felt. Happy.

CHAPTER
THIRTY-SEVEN

Tuolumne, California, Fall 2011

Through every injury and every setback, Randy was steady and unfazed. He wasn't the type to make false promises about how soon I would heal or to lay out a detailed ten-point plan to get me back on my career track—which was what I desperately wanted, at the time. I'd always been the sort of person who makes a plan and then endeavors to execute it to perfection: to fast-forward through the struggle to the solution. Randy was more likely to try to name the problem and the feelings underlying it—to spend time with the problem instead of rushing to the fix. (Which drove me crazy.)

That didn't mean things were perfect between us. In the early years of our relationship, we often fought about our social lives. It wasn't just about the Bay Crew and his breakup with Courtney. Even when I wasn't feeling ostracized, even when I was among people who made me feel safe, I still had times when I would rather be alone. It took me a long time to put a name to it, but I was truly, deeply introverted. And Randy—he loved his friends. I think his happiest place would be living in a commune with all of them. Spending time with friends wasn't just something he enjoyed; it was important to him: part of his values. As important as (or more so than) a day of climbing, which sometimes I still can't understand. It took a long time for him to understand that I need quiet and alone time to recharge.

One of the biggest tension points between us was his unwillingness to tolerate my anxieties, my need for control, the way Tommy had. Randy wasn't willing to let me build our lives, his life, around my rituals, my superstitions, my need to fast or binge on exercise on any given day. That was maddening, isolating even. Though, with time, I came to understand it as just a different kind of support.

◆ ◆ ◆

I wasn't expecting a proposal. One day in late September, after a day of climbing on the high-country knobs of Tuolumne, we stopped in our meadow. The one that we had stumbled across three years earlier, when Randy had pulled the car over without a plan. When everything was still so uncertain. We had kept coming back ever since. It was our secret spot, a refuge from the tourists and busy trails and crags. A place that we knew we'd have to ourselves, where we could just listen to the wind and the birds and soak in the solitude. We'd been there countless times, after a day's climbing or in the morning, eating breakfast. But this time was different. Randy got down on one knee, pulled out a ring, and said: "I want to do life with you, whatever that is. I love you." Somewhere between my total shock and the start of my tears, I said yes.

At first, I was embarrassed to get remarried. *Better luck this time, Beth.* Randy said he had never wanted a big wedding, or even a wedding at all. He wanted to elope, and that sounded fine to me. Less stress, fewer people. (Besides, I still wondered sometimes: Aside from our families, was anyone truly happy for us?) I had already tried to create the fairy-tale wedding, and I knew that no flower arrangements or flatware would ensure our happiness or success. That would come from us, wading through the messiness of our lives and finding ways to love each other, imperfectly but enough.

The winter bridging 2011 and 2012 was the driest in a series of dry years for California. Tioga Road stayed open through Christmas, instead of closing in November as it usually would, and it was lovely and awful to be able to drive up to our favorite place on earth when it should have been buried in snow. At New Year's we checked the forecast, and in the end we decided to include our parents and siblings rather than doing a true elopement. We gave them one week's notice, as much time as the weather forecast could predict: our wedding would be in Tuolumne, at eight thousand feet. If they'd like to join us, it would be a thirty-minute uphill hike from the parking lot. We'd all make a nice dinner afterward and have cookies and ice cream for dessert. I felt brave and decisive, for once, making a choice about how it was going to be and then letting everyone know. It's sometimes said that the wedding is for the family and the marriage is for the couple, but this time, they both felt like they were for us.

The day before the wedding, I went on a bike ride. I was beginning to hear my inner critic differently, to let go—at least a little—of my pursuit of perfection, my tight grip of control. I still thought I should be skinnier—that was a constant, ever since I'd started climbing. I'd been taught by the industry that losing weight was crucial for success. But the feeling wasn't as sharp and insistent as it had been in the past. Now it was more of a dull nagging, a chore instead of a guiding light. I pedaled harder, until my lungs burned. I still felt the tension, the inner war. *You'll look at these pictures forever.* The pain felt empowering. *Maybe next fall I'll send Magic Line.* At thirty-one years old, I was still under the old curse, or motivation. It's funny how something can be both positive and negative at the same time.

I wrote my vows that night, and Randy wrote his on the car ride up with his sister and brother-in-law. Our niece spread flower petals my mom brought from her favorite florist in Davis. I took off my down jacket and fleece pants behind a tree to reveal the dress I'd bought on sale at J.Crew earlier that week and clutched my dad's elbow as we walked from behind the tree to where Randy stood.

◆ ◆ ◆

From the very beginning of our relationship, Randy talked about having kids. He'd bring the idea up casually, mixed in with *What do you need from the grocery store?* and *I still need to train tonight.* Early on, after a dinner with friends who were expecting, he sent me a text that said, Got me psyched to see you pregnant one day. The way he mentioned it always caught me off guard, filled me with a confusing mixture of curiosity and fear. Pregnancy had never seemed like something to bring up lightly: it was something to map out in spreadsheets, with the solidity of data and comforting columns of pros and cons, so I could know exactly what would happen and how it would go. Whenever the subject came up, I always brushed it off quickly—I still needed to do Magic Line, and a lot of other hard, rad things. But each time Randy mentioned it, it made a bigger dent in my plans.

I wanted to have a baby with Randy, to see him be a dad, to grow a little family together, the way we had when we adopted Max. But I had always thought of pregnancy as something I'd do "someday." As in someday when I didn't care about climbing anymore. Someday when I didn't care about my career. The idea of trying to juggle both was impossible to me. How could I climb hard if I gained thirty pounds? How could I do a photo shoot if I couldn't fit into my sponsor's gear? I couldn't take a baby up El Cap. I had no role models for motherhood in the niche world of elite female climbers—everyone who had kids, it seemed, either retired first or got dropped by their sponsors.

Our existence as female professional climbers was already so tenuous, and so contingent on the state of our bodies. Photo shoots meant being asked to take off our shirts and suck in our stomachs—even in the middle of winter—while more often than not the men remained fully clothed. Even the very best of us, Lynn, had her signature achievement denigrated for years: after she freed the Nose, plenty of people claimed she'd only been able to do it—while so many men failed—because of her tiny fingers. (Never mind that Tommy's sausage fingers didn't stop him from repeating it.) Our arms were too skinny, or our stomachs were too soft. We were valued for our hotness, or we weren't hot enough. Climbers' salaries are typically low to begin with, but the women earned even less than the men. And, collectively, we put up with it all. There were just so few of us, and so very few slots for us to fit into: too often it came down to one all-female climbing expedition each season, one woman-focused film at each festival, or one woman added to the team on a high-profile trip. We were all vying to be the token—to be the check in the designated box.

For a decade and a half I had clung to the space I'd been able to carve out for myself. I had no margin for maternity leave.

There was this particular way I always heard people in the climbing world talk about pregnant women and their bodies—with a *despite* hovering between their words. It was always: *Did you see how hard she's still climbing? Did you hear how far she ran? Can you believe how many pull-ups she can do, even with all that extra weight?* (Once, I told a friend that a mutual friend of ours was pregnant, and he responded: "Oh, shit.") Pregnancy was a blip to bounce back from as quickly as possible rather than something to be celebrated.

Well into my fourth year of constant, degrading injuries, contemplating having a baby felt like admitting that I was done. That everything I'd worked for was over, that I would never climb hard and send again. That these injuries weren't a detour but a dead end. It felt like I'd be admitting defeat, and losing me.

But every time we talked about my hesitations, Randy made it clear that he didn't *need* me to be a pro climber. For him, there wasn't only one acceptable outcome. In fact, that was what made life exciting for him: its endless menu of possibilities, all the detours and different paths to wander down. There was so much more to life than climbing hard—a reminder I needed, even if right then I just wanted my body back. From injury to injury, I had already lost so much control over my body. The idea of pregnancy felt like a leap off a cliff, and I didn't know how far I would fall—or what I would hit at the bottom. Could I really plunge my career, my life, into that much uncertainty? Did Randy understand the enormity of what he was suggesting? Sometimes I wanted to take that leap with him. Occasionally it felt exciting. But most of the time the idea was just terrifying, and I resented him for being so nonchalant about it.

◆ ◆ ◆

One evening in August 2013, I sat outside a vegan restaurant in Salt Lake City with Steph Davis. The summer sun had dipped behind the horizon, but the air was still hot.

After that phone call during my divorce, we'd continued to grow closer. She was maybe the only person in the world who really understood my position: a woman in the public eye of the climbing community, in a public marriage with another professional climber, who'd initiated her split. I started to confide in her about a lot of things, even about contracts and sponsorships—which felt so taboo, but once we started talking openly, so much of my competitiveness fell away. Even though I knew she'd never wanted kids, she was the obvious person to talk to about the possibility of pregnancy.

"It really sucks," I said to her on that darkening restaurant patio about my most recent finger injury. "I don't know what is wrong with my body. I know I can do Magic Line—I basically have done it twice now—but I keep getting broken." I paused. "Randy thinks we should just have a kid." I laughed and coughed at the same time, to make sure it sounded like I thought it was a bad idea. But her reaction was the opposite of what I'd expected.

"You should!" she said. "You should totally have a kid, and then do Magic Line. You should show that you can be a badass and a mom; there's not enough of that out there."

"I'll get dropped," I said. The same old fear that had always driven me. Even though it had been years since Meltdown, most of my sponsors hadn't dropped me yet, but some of them had cut my salary completely and paid me only in free gear—the kind of B-team sponsorship that had thrilled me when I was young.

"That's bullshit. You should tell your sponsors you are going to continue your career."

I couldn't believe what she was saying—Steph, of all people. One of the few women on the planet who understood the implicit conditions of our job and our bodies.

Why *did* all the women think they had to retire or move on before having kids? Yet the men could just keep on with their careers. Men would gallivant off on expeditions across the world, while their wives stayed at home with the babies. Maybe I wanted to gallivant across the world while my husband stayed home with our baby.

I had put so much pressure on Magic Line. First, it had been the climb that would prove I could make it without Tommy. Now it was the climb I had to do before having a child—one last hit before I gave it all up. But Steph had me thinking: maybe I could step away, have a baby, and then come back.

◆　◆　◆

After so much indecision, I got pregnant as soon as we started trying. The first few weeks were surreal. Our dog Max had died unexpectedly, just before I found out I was pregnant, and it felt impossible to grieve him and to look forward to this new expansion of our little family at the same time. I needed Max with me, for this. My sadness over his loss amplified my natural pessimism: I wanted to be sure the baby would be healthy, that everything would be okay, before I celebrated too much.

We tracked the baby's progress using a website—*Now he's the size of a peanut; now he's the size of a cherry.* In the mornings Randy would ask, "Do you feel different? Can you tell?" He was filled with so much curiosity and excitement, while for the first few months I was mainly filled with nausea and uncertainty. Was I eating the right things? How soon should we tell our families? Were the schools good in our neighborhood?

Should I climb today? Should I have climbed yesterday? I used exercise as a deterrent, a way to suppress my spinning mind, but I was too sick and tired to make that work. And yet those early months were a tender secret, an adventure, just between us, new and uncharted.

I found that I got attached early. I wanted, needed, a plan for what our life would be like, and it was fun to daydream about something different. I'd only had one vision of my life for so long: my climbing, my control, my way of walking through this world. I imagined at first that having a baby wouldn't be so different from having a dog. I pictured my parents coming to Yosemite often. Randy and I would leave the baby with them all day, take long runs, go up to Tuolumne, maybe even climb El Cap together. We'd come home to a sleeping infant, to eager parents willing to do it all again the next day, and the next week. I assumed I would lose the extra weight with ease, my body returning to its previous form within a week or two. Nothing much would really change.

What I didn't anticipate was the way pregnancy unraveled my mind. Though I'd never been able to make the connection or say the words out loud, I had been an anxious person since Kyrgyzstan, inclined to see threats all around me. In my life with Tommy I had created a bubble where I could cope. Where I felt safe, or at least safe enough. When we traveled, I'd ask him to keep his eyes open for any "bad people" who might want to hurt us. He didn't question me, he just said: *Of course.*

Randy was different. He was never unkind, but he wasn't willing to just go along with my paranoia either. He was willing to say what almost no one else had ever said to me since Kyrgyzstan: *This isn't normal. Your fear has led you into some wrong turns. This isn't okay.*

Once, I'd gone with him to a party at his work and met one of his colleagues, Sameer. He had dark skin, dark hair, and when he shook my hand, he said, "I've heard so much about you. It's nice to finally meet you."

I froze, stomach in knots, looking around the room for Randy. When I spotted him, I smiled at Sameer and extricated myself, walking away. Then I pulled Randy rudely from his own conversation. "Did you tell Sameer about me? Do you know where he's from? What his story is? Do you know if he's safe or not? Where does he live? Does he know where *you* live?"

Randy looked confused, then disgusted.

"We pair together all the time," he said. "So, yes, he knows all about you. He's awesome. He's not dangerous. No one here is. You aren't in danger, Beth. You are safe. These are good, kind people I work with. This is you having an irrational fear."

I'd been outraged, then dismissive. *He has no idea what I've been through,* I thought. He didn't know what he was talking about.

But Randy had a way of nudging me toward my own conclusions, my own solutions. Back in the spring of 2009, we were bouldering together in Yosemite. I was trying a hard highball (boulderer-speak for a tall problem) that no woman had ever done. Fifteen feet above my pads, I could feel my arms getting heavy with fatigue. I looked down at my potential fall. I looked up at the last move. Neither seemed like a good option, so I yelled down to Randy, "I can't do it, I can't do the last move. Can you run around and grab my hand?" I was frozen, but I knew I could hold that position long enough for him to rescue me.

It was the kind of moment when Tommy would have raced around to the sloping back of the boulder, scrambled up to the top, and reached down over the edge to pull me to safety. He wouldn't have hesitated. But when I asked Randy to do the same, he said, "You've got this. I've got you spotted. The pads are good. Trust yourself, you can do it." Part of me wished he would just rescue me, but I could feel my hands quivering, and I didn't have time to argue. With no other choice, I tried the move—and I did it. Gently, kindly, but firmly, he had pushed me to grow through my fear.

He was like that in all sorts of ways, and with him my life became wider, warmer, less narrowly focused. On our climbing trips overseas, we went sightseeing on our rest days. We went on a real honeymoon, ate meals in restaurants, and had friends who never climbed—who made conversation about everything but climbing. Still, the core of my anxiety was untouched: I didn't trust the world. And the years of injuries had also eroded any trust I once had in my body. I experienced a growing fear of sickness—I became a germaphobe, and cultivated rituals to manage that paranoia, like always opening the gym door with my sleeve pulled down over my hand or holding my breath every time I passed someone else on the sidewalk.

Once I was pregnant, all of that was heightened. I was in survival mode, not on a sabbatical, and now I had a new constellation of hazards to avoid. The internet was a yawning chasm of terrifying medical information, ready to swallow me whole. Randy would come home from work to find me sobbing about whether or not I should get a flu shot or whether I had driven too closely behind a diesel truck. Some days he was able to respond gently to my neuroses, and some days I overwhelmed us both. He started to encourage me more and more frequently to talk to someone.

I had long since stopped seeing Debbie, my therapist in Davis. Randy and I had seen a counselor when we got engaged—my idea, for once. I had seen the triggers and places where we got stuck in our relationship, and after going through a divorce, I could see how things that began as no big deal could turn into larger problems. But this? My urgent sense of the threats that surrounded me? My commitment to keeping our family, our baby, safe? I wasn't willing to accept that it was a problem.

CHAPTER
THIRTY-EIGHT

Berkeley, California, April 2014

The night before my due date, Randy and I went out to Penrose, my favorite restaurant in Oakland. We arrived just before they stopped seating people, at 8:55 p.m.—a far cry from my old habits: dinner at four thirty and bed before nine. We split two appetizers and two entrées and a dessert. I had already eaten five bagels that day, each one a pause in my frenzied pre-baby cleaning of the house. Each one a small slice of relief.

Pregnancy had loosened the invisible handcuffs that had gripped my eating since I was a teenager. I felt like I could let myself breathe and eat without guilt or shame or a forced ten-mile run the next day. At first, I had justified every calorie: *You are growing another human, so you can eat this.* But over the months, that need to rationalize it had faded away. Slowly, it became almost normal for me to just eat what I wanted, without any mandatory calculations about matching my output to input.

Over cups of tea and conversation, my friend and midwife Jaime had managed to plant the seed that food was nourishing and healthy and a positive thing, for bodies and me and our baby. That seed grew as my body changed, as it built and nurtured another body. When my body showed me what miracles it could work, I started to believe that eating wasn't a test I had to pass each day. That a body wasn't just an instrument used to accomplish objectives. There was enjoyment and fulfillment in knowing that eating was normal and healthy and beneficial, and in listening to my body, not fighting it, not being constantly at war with it. But first I had to figure out how to actually be *in* my body in new and different ways. If I could get used to being in this body, without treating it as a vessel that defines me, then perhaps I could start to tackle one of the most important things in life: to know myself, to trust myself. (Even now, writing that feels perilous, admitting that I actually might know what's right for myself.)

After we got home from dinner, I lay on my side, trying and failing to get comfortable, listening to Randy breathing deeply in his sleep. I started to feel some cramping, like a period cramp but slightly different. At first it seemed like one more item on a list of discomforts I'd been living with for nine months. But as the cramps started to intensify and get closer together, I let myself think, *Could this really be it?*

No, doubtful. Suck it up, Rodden. And then I tossed and turned some more. It couldn't be real: I was convinced that our baby would be two weeks late. I was resigned to it. I had been two weeks late, and so had my brother, my niece, my nephew. After an hour I finally got up and went into the bathroom to pee. When I was on the toilet, I looked down and saw bright red blood in the bowl, something I hadn't seen in nine glorious months of not having a period. I remembered Jaime saying something about the "bloody show" that can happen during the beginning of labor. I looked over into the darkness of our bedroom, at the lump that was Randy sleeping, and wondered if I should wake him up. This could go on for hours, even days. So I sat there, reeling at each contraction as it built, pressing my head into the towel bar during each wave of pain.

Each contraction seemed to last for an age, but the hours shrank down as they passed, compressing into a single long moment. At some point in the night I called for Randy, whispering at first and eventually shouting his name to wake him. At some point, he called Jaime. And at some point after that, we decided it was time to drive across the Bay

Bridge, through the morning traffic, to the hospital. I sat in the back of our white Prius, next to the newly installed car seat, clutching the headrest behind Randy's ears, groaning and screaming every time a contraction came.

Arriving at the hospital felt like being seated at a not-very-attentive restaurant. They put a band around my wrist and told me what room I'd be in and sent me on my way, saying someone would check on me soon.

A while later a nurse walked in, asked me the most mundane questions, wrote down my answers, and then told me to lie down. I looked at the bed and then looked at her. Another contraction was coming on, and I knew I had to be upright or squatting for those. Every movie I'd ever seen with a birth scene showed a woman lying on a bed, but that seemed like torture, just fundamentally wrong for what my body wanted to do. Like telling someone to eat their food through their nose; it just wouldn't work. I looked at her again and then at the bed. I almost always followed instructions and never made a scene. But there was no way I was getting in that bed.

"Um, I don't want to lie in that bed," I said in a hushed voice, looking at my feet.

She looked at me and said, "I'm sorry, what?"

I felt my face flush even more, if that's possible for a woman a handful of hours before pushing a human out of her. But something primal came up in me, a confidence that felt like a muscle I'd always had but rarely used. "I'm not lying down in that bed, I'm going to stand. I've been standing or squatting for ten hours, and that's what I'm going to do." I winced after I said it, so averse to confrontation. Still, I knew I was right. It felt strange, and lovely, to be sure of myself.

We compromised: I lay down, my pain intensifying, while she inserted an IV port in case I wanted an epidural, and then I got back onto my feet again. I held on to the side of the bed until the next contraction passed and then looked around the room. I needed something taller, something I didn't have to bend over as far to lean on, like the height of my towel bar at home. I spotted the sink in the room's small bathroom: that was where I wanted to be. I waddled over, with Randy rubbing my back, and spent the next five hours bent over the sink. I clutched Randy's hand the entire time, wondering if I was breaking his thumb with each contraction. But he just stood there, patiently, lovingly, talking to me when I wanted conversation and rubbing my back in between.

Eventually, Jaime came in and said, "Beth, I'm wondering if we should have you switch positions. You've been in here for five hours."

I wondered how much longer it would be. I was good at suffering, really good at it. But even on El Cap, in a storm, I had a general idea how long it would take to get to the top or bottom, and that was always comforting. One of the worst things about Kyrgyzstan had been the open-endedness of it. Would we be hostages for another day? Another week? Month? Year? It was maddening not to be able to see the end—to envision the moves it would take to get there. The same was true for labor. Was I going to be in this bathroom for another hour? Three? Seven? Was there going to be a C-section? Should I get the epidural? Should I try the bathtub full of water? If someone could just tell me how much longer, I would know what to do.

Finally, I said, "I'll move to the door handle." There was a pause.

"The door handle?" Jaime asked.

"Yes, it's about the same height as here. I'll move there." I motioned three feet away to the bathroom door.

The doctor came in and told me to lie down because it was almost time to start pushing. I still felt certain that my body didn't want to be prone.

"No. I'm standing and squatting. I can't get into that bed, it's too painful, it doesn't feel right," I said, still hanging on to the bathroom door. "I'm sorry," I added, always wanting to make sure people weren't too mad.

He paused. "Elizabeth, we deliver babies lying down here, so I need you to lie down so we can safely deliver your baby."

Another contraction came, and a guttural scream came out of me. I felt that strange, familiar strength rise up in me again, surprising me with its force.

"I know that babies get delivered every second of every day in many different ways, and right now I want to be standing and squatting. If that is not okay, then I will walk out right now and Jaime can deliver the baby in my car," I said in a very firm but feeble voice, since I felt another contraction starting.

I heard him whisper something to the nurse and then to Jaime. Then he said, "Give us a second, Elizabeth," and everyone left the room except for me and Randy.

I looked over at the bed, and my body shuddered at the thought of going horizontal. But the railing at the foot of the bed looked like a nice height. I waddled over with Randy and went through another contraction, a huge scream, and a desire to push. Randy looked down and said, "I can see his head!"

Then everyone filed back in, and the doctor said, "Okay, Elizabeth, you can squat. I haven't delivered a baby in that position before, but I'll get on the ground and we'll do it."

Had he really wanted me to lie down because he didn't want to sit on the floor? "Thank you," I said, wanting to stay on his good side.

I pushed for two hours, naked and screaming and, somehow, not caring at all who saw or heard me. My body, some instinct in it, took over, and my usual self-consciousness, my need to plan and game out my options, fell away. The doctor said, "One more and he'll be here," and then there he was: Theo.

I finally allowed myself to be guided into the bed. The doctor placed a brand-new Theo in my hands and then onto my bare chest. He was so warm and wrinkly and perfect in my trembling arms. I held him tight, but not too tight, against my skin and bare breast. My mind spun with elation and pride and love and responsibility, all mixed up together. I wanted to feel it all. Babies are born every second of every day, but what my body had just done, what Randy and I had been through, how our lives had now been set on a new path, was the most extraordinary thing for us, unlikely to ever be surpassed. I felt like I was a part of something enormous, transcendent: millions and billions of births stretching back through human history and ahead through millions and billions more in the future. The most meaningful moment of my life would be repeated across the hallway in a few minutes, maybe, and again tomorrow, and the next day.

Randy was on my left side, stroking my head. One of the nurses started talking to me, squeezing my arm with each sentence. I was smiling and nodding, trying to listen to what she said, but I couldn't take my eyes off of Theo. He had the longest fingernails and eyelashes that I'd ever seen. His slow growth inside me was no longer abstract, imagined, or tracked on an app.

The nurse had just helped me get him to latch on to my nipple, telling me that my milk would take a little while to come in but the colostrum I was producing was all he needed until then. I felt her squeeze my forearm extra tight, until I looked up into her eyes. Tears welling up, she said, "You did it, Beth. I'm so proud of you. You knew what you needed, and you stuck to it. You showed us all that you knew what was best for you, and you didn't let us tell you otherwise. I see some of people's most vulnerable moments in here, and it was a privilege to watch you today."

I started crying, unsure if it was from what she'd said or the ocean of emotions that my mind and body were swimming through. Randy gave me a kiss, and I looked at him and Jaime and gave them the most heartfelt thank-you that I have ever said.

The nurse walked over to her chart to start filling out more paperwork. I tried to let what she had said sink in, tried to understand what had just happened. Watching Randy hold Theo, I wanted to etch into my mind the look on his face, how sincere and vulnerable and full of love it was. We had forgotten the camera, but pictures and video couldn't capture all of this anyway.

CHAPTER
THIRTY-NINE

Berkeley, California, May 2014

I tried to hang on to that strange power I had felt during my labor. That absolute certainty that I knew what I needed, what was best for my body and my baby. I could already feel some anxiety starting to seep in through the bliss and euphoria. The sour worry and dread that I would do something wrong, make a bad decision that would endanger my child. It was no longer just me or Randy or our new dog, another rescued ridgeback named Bodie, who I had to take into account. I had to protect my baby.

Everything was a threat. A well-meaning doctor would say something like *It would be pretty serious if Theo got a fever in the first month*, and I would spiral into paranoia about visitors, people we loved and who loved us, bringing sickness with them. I considered making them wear medical masks and gloves if they came over. I was scared to take Theo outside; I saw every mosquito as a potential carrier of West Nile virus. Soon after we brought him home, I became fixated on our furniture. It was older, and I worried that toxic flame retardants built into the couch, the mattress, the cushions would hurt our son. I bought new ones, changed out our dish and laundry soaps too. In those early weeks, I felt charged with an electric current of fear for my baby. I was desperate to protect him and overwhelmed by the danger I saw all around me. Where was the Beth who could sleep in a portaledge two thousand feet off the ground?

My body was failing me too. Everything I thought was supposed to be natural was hard and complicated instead. Breastfeeding was incredibly painful and difficult; I endured three acute rounds of mastitis before we figured out that Theo had serious tongue-tie and wasn't latching correctly. For weeks after delivery, I couldn't stand upright for more than a minute without extreme pain—I had a bladder prolapse, and I felt like my insides were going to fall out. Between the physical and the mental toll, nothing about early parenthood resembled the rosy dreams I'd had back when I was pregnant.

Randy would find me lying in bed with Theo, crying. Once, when he asked me what the tears were for, the only answer I could find was "Everything."

The breaking point came shortly after Theo turned two. I knew my paranoia was out of hand, knew I was exasperating myself and Randy. He'd been willing to go along with things for the first couple months: the new furniture, the new dish soaps. But after a while, he cracked and started challenging me. "We can't raise him in a bubble, Beth," he'd say. "He has to be exposed to the real world." I told myself, and Randy, that I would ease my grip on Theo's life in just a little while—after he turned three, after he started school, after he learned subtraction . . . Soon, Randy's once-gentle suggestions that I should go to therapy started to feel like hounding. I had always told myself that he hadn't been in Kyrgyzstan and had no idea what we'd been through. But I started to realize that maybe he was right.

One foggy morning, I was playing with Theo in a park near our house in Berkeley. We went there most days, after Randy left for work, and stayed until it was time for Theo's—okay, our—morning nap. We'd been digging in the sandbox when I heard the park's gate squeak. Another family had arrived, a mom and dad with a little boy just about Theo's age. The mom, carrying a lunch box for the child, wore a hijab.

I felt my stomach twist and my heart start to race with memories of Su. *Do these three know him? Have they found me?*

I knew I wasn't being rational. I tried to push down the feelings, tried to reason with myself, but I couldn't. I shoved Theo's things into our backpack and picked him up as he started to toddle toward the new arrivals. "Maybe another day, it's nap time now," I said in an anxious, laughing voice. I glanced at the parents, wondering how transparent I was. They smiled briefly, and I turned and hurried out of the park. Theo protested, but I kept saying, "It's nap time, it's nap time," as I rushed back home.

Years later, I still think about that woman, smiling at me as I hurried away. She was just one mother of a toddler smiling at another as we crossed paths in the park. Did she understand the effect she'd had on me? Did she know that I viewed her as a threat—did she understand that her safety, and that of her own son's, could be threatened if she was perceived as dangerous? Did she smile to make herself seem safe and nice and harmless, as I had so often done in my life? I'd like to believe she was just smiling, mom to mom. But maybe that's naive. More likely, she understood the forces that shaped my fear, the way our society primed me to respond to her, far more clearly than I did. These are power dynamics that I am still working to understand.

After I put Theo down to sleep, I sat and watched his breathing. I felt awful and embarrassed. I didn't want to raise my son that way. I didn't want to pass my behavior on to him, like tarnish on the family silver. I was finally starting to understand why Randy had pushed me so hard to face those buried memories. Motherhood was holding up a mirror to my psyche, and I was repelled by my reflection. That night, I told him I would try to talk about Kyrgyzstan in therapy. I didn't know if I could change, but I had to try.

The next day I called our old therapist, Susan, the one we'd seen before we got married. Going back to her sparsely decorated office felt safe. But sitting across from her in our new session, I had no idea how to start. How could I begin to talk about something that defined me—but that I had boarded up and cemented over more than fifteen years ago?

"I'm so scared of everything," I told her. "I'm scared of everything for Theo."

"I can appreciate how scary this must feel," Susan said. "I've worked through trauma with a lot of people, and there are ways that we can safely do it and make sure that you get back to a safe place before you walk out that door."

Somehow, I believed her. I had to.

Starting therapy with Susan around Kyrgyzstan felt different than the other therapy I'd done. In Davis, soon after Kyrgyzstan, I'd shown up to sessions just looking to get them over with. With Tommy, during the divorce, I wanted Debbie and Dan to either present me with a fix for my marriage or prove to me that it was irreparably broken. I wanted a safe place to explain my side to Tommy in hopes that he'd understand and give me his blessing to leave. And when Randy and I had seen Susan before we got married, we'd had particular triggers and sticking points to tackle: his resentment of my need for control, my resentment of his friends who had shunned me, our ongoing struggle to reconcile his extroversion and my introversion.

But this time I had no specific expectations. I couldn't imagine what healing, true healing, would be like. Did it exist? I was skeptical, but I wanted to try. I wanted to remember who I'd been before, and see who I could be now.

We took a couple of sessions to let me settle in, skirting around the edges of the memories I had sealed away before we really dove in. At first, I felt like I couldn't let myself feel and experience those dark emotions. I had walled them off so securely for sixteen years that I couldn't go there. I had never allowed myself to think too hard about the soldiers I'd seen on the far side of the valley, falling and dying in the firefight. I couldn't think of them as real people, couldn't imagine their families. Turat's family.

Susan suggested I start by sharing a moment or two from Kyrgyzstan that stuck out in my memory most clearly. I had a polished three-minute summary that I used when I gave speeches, and I wasn't sure I knew how to go any deeper. I stared at my feet, reflexively pinched the skin on the back of my wrist. My armpits started to sweat. I had trained myself for more than a decade not to go any deeper, not to venture past those high walls—and I am very, very good at training. I felt out of control. But I had to do it.

"I guess the night that Tommy pushed Su stands out," I said as I pinched my skin harder.

I smelled the musty brown grass on the edge of the cliff that night. I remembered the brightness of the moon, the smell in the air that the weather was changing. The crispness of it all. I remembered my ribs and hip bones jutting out, that fast-paced flywheel of anxiety constantly turning in my stomach and mind. I remembered Tommy's face, his long nose, his soft eyes. Feeling like I had told Tommy to do it. That I was responsible.

I felt these thoughts surface like tiny bubbles. Right away, I went in and popped each of them. It was second nature, not to let myself think any more about them.

But then I remembered the sound. That sound I had drowned out for sixteen years. Su hitting the ledge. The air deflating from his body. The crack of his spine. My stomach churned and my ears rang. I felt so hot. I shut my eyes, willed it to go away. But still I heard it: the crack, the crunch, the exhale.

Susan asked me what I was seeing and hearing, where I felt it in my body. *It's in my head, it's in my chest, it's in my throat, it's tight and hot and loud and sour.* I clenched my abs, still pinching myself, the skin on my wrist red and raw. I kept talking, not thinking, just reciting the sensations in my body as I experienced them. My hands shook; my vision was fuzzy. My thoughts were racing, screaming. I had to talk more and more quickly to keep up with them. Susan tried to slow me down. But everything was so hot, so fast, so loud. I was melting. I wanted to melt onto her floor and stay there forever.

I started to forget where I was. I was both staring at Susan and losing track of her at the same time, who she was in relation to me. "Beth?" I heard her say. Slowly, I started to feel pain on the skin of my left wrist. I looked down and saw that it was close to bleeding. Through the fog that had come over me, I wondered what had happened to it.

"Beth? Beth."

I looked up again. This kind woman with curly salt-and-pepper hair was speaking to me. She looked like a stranger. I saw her mouth move and heard words come out of it, but I couldn't piece them together. I felt the way I had after my first concussion, like the world was shimmering just out of my reach.

"Beth? Beth? We need to stop and get you back so you can bike home," Susan said.

I looked at her and nodded. I could still hear the crunch and the thud, echoing in my head. We talked a little more. I have no idea what we talked about. The weather? Randy? But my lips moved and I heard words come out of them.

After another few minutes I started to feel more normal. I could understand what Susan was saying, what I was saying. That I needed to bike home, that it was time for me to go. When I walked outside, the sun was blinding. I promised her I would walk around the block before I rode home.

After that, each time I went back, Susan would ask me: "Which memory makes you the most nervous to think about, to talk about? What's the biggest sticking point?" Some of them were external: the sound of a mortar flying through the air, and the terrible unknowability of where it would land. A memory from the firefight: a soldier across the valley, running and then suddenly dropping, midstride, like a puppet whose strings had been sliced clean through. Turat, trying to tell us what had happened to his friends. His resignation, his fear and dignity, knowing that he was going to die.

Other memories were internal. For so long I had buried the feelings of shame and guilt about some of my actions, my thoughts, during our final escape. Now I had to face the silent message I had given Tommy—the moment I had offered him my blessing to push Su off the cliff. Years earlier, learning that Su had survived his fall had eased Tommy's conscience. But it hadn't done anything to relieve my own sense of culpability. Then there was the moment, during our mad run to safety, when I had asked Jason to follow Tommy, to bring up the rear. Understandable, maybe: Tommy had just pushed Su. He was a wreck. But I knew I'd done it so that if one of them got shot, it would be Jason. That was an almost unforgivable thought to face.

Some days, we burrowed so deeply into those feelings and memories that my brain short-circuited and I lost track of my words, Susan's words, of names and time and place. Other days I couldn't face that depth of sensation, and we skated over the surface instead. Over the course of two years, and maybe three dozen sessions, Susan helped me excavate the kidnapping from my mind and release it from my body.

I had trained myself to lock Kyrgyzstan away, and facing those memories one by one felt like a kind of training project too. Each sound, each smell, that I allowed myself to feel again was a piece of the puzzle falling into place. But instead of finding a sequence that successfully led up a blank rock wall, instead of the immediate gratification of a send, a magazine cover, or a raise from a sponsor, the gains were gradual, less tangible. I began to be less afraid of my own thoughts. And as my thoughts became less frightening to me, less shameful, that meant I could loosen my rigid control over them. I could be kinder to myself. I could *be* myself. I could begin to trust that if I showed the thoughts and feelings I had always hidden away, the people I cared about would still stay.

Letting go of the fear and shame from Kyrgyzstan, learning to face those uncomfortable memories, changed my relationship to other moments of fear and shame too. I carried the lessons from those sessions with me: that it was better to find the sticking points, to face them, instead of burying them in shame or with hours of training. To trust that therapy is a safe place to unpack my hardest feelings. That understanding, that shift, helped me to start to quiet the inner critic who was always in my ear, and in my head.

If I was no longer at war with myself—or at least less so—then I didn't have to be at war with the world either. Slowly, I started to feel a little bit safer—to trust the world again. In my marriage, in motherhood, in my growing network of friendships—I began to relax into a new version of me.

CHAPTER FORTY

November 2018

The Great Escape is a popular route on the south side of Yosemite Valley. The area is shady, with dark-gray granite and tiered walls that are less continuous than Yosemite's best-known big rock races. The route itself is four or five pitches, or about four hundred and fifty feet high, and it's a sport climb, which is rare in Yosemite. Before Theo was born, back when I was still hoping to have another shot at Magic Line, I had climbed it a couple of times with Randy, swapping leads as we went. But on this chilly day, in early November 2018, I planned to climb it with Becca Caldwell—Tommy's wife.

The route is rated 5.11, and I thought we could handle it, but I was still nervous. Mostly, Becca and I bouldered together. She'd been a casual, beginner climber when she and Tommy met, a few months after our split. She'd gained a ton of skill since then, but she still didn't have a lot of experience leading or placing gear. Meanwhile, I hadn't done much rope climbing since Theo had been born four and a half years earlier. In a strange way, I felt some of those same nerves I'd felt a decade earlier, leading Randy up Astroboy. Could I really do this? Could I be the one who led us up the route?

After our divorce and our finances were sorted out, things between Tommy and me had settled into a kind of cordial awkwardness. We'd say hello when we saw each other, at a crag or a trade show, and then go our separate ways. I built my life with Randy, and he started a family with Becca. He didn't let me know when he was coming to Yosemite. It felt weird and sad, sometimes. In walking away from our marriage, I had also lost the closest friend I'd ever had, and a partnership that had defined my life up to that point. But it wasn't something I felt able to complain about to anyone.

It was Randy who'd suggested I reach out to Becca, several years earlier. "Try to forge a relationship with just her," he'd said. I was still raw from the experience with the Bay Crew, and part of me was uncertain that *anyone* would want to be my friend, let alone Tommy's wife. But in a weird way, while Tommy and I had so much history, Becca and I had a blank slate. She was smart and fun and easy to talk to, with an ability to put everyone around her at ease. I wondered: Despite the strange, intimate intersection of our lives, could she like me?

Before that conversation with Randy, Becca and I had bouldered together once or twice; the Yosemite climbing community is too small for people to really avoid each other even if they want to. After her and Tommy's son, Fitz, was born, I'd sent Becca a package of herbal soups. And during my pregnancy, a few months later, she'd sent me an adorable onesie and a couple of other things for the baby. We'd started texting more frequently—she'd made a point of checking in.

After Theo was born, as I struggled to navigate the mental and physical fallout of early motherhood, I didn't know who to lean on. Most of my climbing friends didn't really know how to respond to a desperate text message about how my nipples wouldn't stop bleeding. But if I texted Becca to say that I couldn't stand upright without feeling like my insides might fall right out of me, she understood. She'd say something like *Isn't the beginning of motherhood wild?* Or *I can't believe this is how babies come into the world.* And I would feel so much less like an outcast with a strange, unruly body. I felt so much less alone.

During Theo's first fall season, I spent most of my time with him in Yosemite, while Randy worked five days a week in the Bay and joined us on weekends. During the turmoil of early motherhood, I wanted the slower pace and the clean air—to be able to lie in a meadow all day, as restful as a person can be with an infant, instead of constantly scanning the busy city for threats. Plus, staying in the mountains let me hang on to at least some sense that I was still a climber.

Becca and Fitz were in the Valley for the season too, while Tommy was climbing. Since there weren't many other babies around, we naturally moved beyond texting and started spending time together. It felt unexpectedly easy to let down my guard around her. It was as though we'd skipped over years of small talk and gone straight to the real stuff, the deep stuff. But even as comfortable as I felt sharing all the indignities of postpartum life with her, part of me remained wary. Surely Tommy didn't have many good things to say about me—how could his wife really like me? I still felt that scarlet letter on me, sometimes. *Don't get too comfortable, Beth,* a voice in my head would say. The one that taught me to always expect the worst from the world, the one that told me I was safer inside my shell. *The other shoe will drop soon.*

But I never detected any judgment from her. Our shared motherhood blurred the awkward edges of our other shared connection, and I loved that I didn't need to explain myself. We talked about houses, mortgages, remodeling, and refinancing. Postpartum recovery, family drama. Early on, she told me she envied Randy's safe job in the Bay; she was always wondering about Tommy up in his portaledge, or in a tent on some frozen faraway peak. Her confession was a relief, like someone showing you their cards first. I let out a sigh. Randy wasn't climbing big walls, but I'd had those same fears for him—and, of course, for Tommy when we had been together. "I totally do that too," I confessed. "Randy rides a motorcycle to work each day. If I don't hear from him, or if he's late, I check the accident log online." It was the kind of anxious behavior I didn't normally admit to: hypervigilance had penetrated so many aspects of my life for so long that I could no longer discern paranoia from normal worry. And yet somehow, with this woman whose life overlapped with mine in what could be the most awkward way, I was able to let go of my usual self-consciousness.

On an early section of the Great Escape, I struggled on a hard move, and my fragile confidence wobbled. Then, on the third pitch, I got stuck. It was cold and windy—in the short November days, the north-facing route was in full shade. I kept falling in the same spot, fingers numb, getting more and more frustrated. I waited for the sense of humiliation to creep up alongside the frustration—*Beth Rodden, stalled out on a 5.11,* a very small voice inside me sneered—but somehow, it didn't really come through this time. "Why didn't we stick to bouldering?" I called down to Becca, and heard her laugh float up to me. I was too high up to see it, but I could picture her flashing her wide, bright smile. She wasn't mad. She wasn't disgusted with my performance. Maybe I didn't need to be either.

I lowered down to where she was belaying and admitted I didn't really want to keep going. Did she? We had nothing to prove to anyone, no mandate to keep suffering up there. She said she'd rather be bouldering, and so we just bailed: off the wall, out of the wind, back to our snacks and our jackets.

◆ ◆ ◆

Over the years, our families formed other bonds too. Randy and Tommy started climbing together again, picking up their friendship where it had been interrupted. Theo formed his own relationship with the Caldwells. When they came down to Yosemite, usually twice a year for the prime climbing seasons, our kids played together; for years, Tommy and Becca were the only people besides my parents who Theo felt comfortable being left alone with. We'd take turns watching the kids while the other set of parents got away for a climb. The boys would rampage in the forest: running free, using their imaginations with sticks, rocks, leaves, playing hard until the sun fell. Their faces covered with dirt, fingernails black on the tips with untold amounts of the Valley scraped into them. No walls to contain their enthusiasm, no desks to keep them in a lane, just nature and everything it had to offer.

The power of our friendship, its strength in my life, surprised me. Friendships weren't something I had prioritized in my life. It wasn't just that I had felt out of place in groups of girls when I was younger. To be honest, I had tended to write off friendships that weren't perfect. I had been hard on those relationships in some of the same ways I was hard on myself. But now I was beginning not only to value my friendships more highly but to give them grace and room to breathe too.

One night, after a hike with Becca, I told Randy about our day and our latest conversation. "Do you think that she appreciates our relationship like I do?" I asked him. I wanted Randy to have some sort of inside information, to confirm or assuage my insecurities.

But as usual, he didn't offer a quick fix, an easy reassurance. "Does that matter to you?" he asked instead.

I thought about it. I could feel my doubts and questions hovering— but then something, a more confident voice, took over. "No," I said, "I guess not. It only really matters how I feel." This wasn't a competition, I decided. Just an unexpected blessing.

CHAPTER
FORTY-ONE

Yosemite Valley, California, November 2018

I was partway through Theo's nightly routine, on a winter evening in 2018, when my phone whistled with an incoming text. His hands were on my head, balancing while I put his feet into his pajama pants. Usually I'm quick to my phone, but getting through bedtime is a master class in perseverance and patience. I couldn't wait to crawl into the solace of my bed each night.

I glanced at my phone between pajamas and teeth-brushing and saw the first couple lines of a text from Carlo Traversi, a strong young professional climber who'd been working on Meltdown for the past few seasons: Hey Beth, hope you're well. I finished off Meltdown this morning . . . I didn't react at first—maybe because I'd been bracing for the inevitable second ascent for almost eleven years. Or because I was in the midst of my nightly back-and-forth with Theo and I didn't have energy to spare. Or maybe it didn't mean what it used to for me?

More than a decade after I sent Meltdown, I was still a sponsored professional climber. But my climbing life was so different. I had stopped promising my sponsors that I was nearly back to my old form, no longer desperate, no longer dangling that carrot the way I had during my years of injuries. They had found a new way to gauge my value: my writing about pregnancy and early motherhood had gained an audience that was, just like me, hungry for community and an honest conversation about our bodies. And while I still sometimes dreamed of climbing hard again, I was content with my new schedule, my new pace. Instead of three or four days each week of full-day training and projecting, I managed a couple of hours here and there while Theo was at preschool. After preschool, we'd wander together through all the places that I used to think weren't worth my time. (Why waste time going anywhere but El Cap?) Walking around with a little human, who was awed by anything and everything, was eye-opening. We'd stop and blow milkweed seeds for an hour. We'd throw sticks into the river, or rocks, or a blade of grass. That time with Theo slowed me down and sped me up at once, since everything is always at least a little bit frantic with a child. He opened my eyes wider to Yosemite than any pitch or crack or route ever could. I still worried about whether I was doing enough and when the ultimate ax from my sponsors might fall. But parenthood was teaching me to value my time in a new way.

I tucked Theo into bed and read *Perfect the Pig*, his book of choice that night—and every other night for the previous three weeks. It was a hand-me-down that my parents had saved from my own childhood. The pages were falling out, and a couple of them were missing.

After I finished the story, I gave Theo a kiss. Randy finished the dishes and turned out the light, and we lay in our bed in the darkness, waiting for Theo to fall asleep. Living in a three-hundred-square-foot apartment, as we do when we are in Yosemite, doesn't provide for a ton of separation. I put my head on Randy's chest and turned on my phone to read the rest of Carlo's text.

Hey Beth, hope you're well. I finished off Meltdown this morning. Just want to thank you for bringing that incredible line to life. Probably one of the hardest things I've ever climbed. Massive respect for the first ascent over 10 years ago. Hope to see you in the Valley soon!

As I read it, tears began to swell in my eyes. I had a funny feeling, the one I get when I'm overwhelmed by happiness or flattery:

almost a tingling, and a nervousness pulsing through my arms and legs. It's strange how much emotion can be drawn out of a person with a six-sentence text. But those six sentences represented the closing of a long, lingering chapter in my life. I felt like a different person, living a vastly different life, driven by different values: quiet, privacy, joy. Now, I lay there with Randy, Theo breathing his way into sleep nearby, in the basement suite of the house Tommy and I built together. My fingers throbbed from a climbing day with Becca, failing on a climb that would have been an afterthought to me during my days on Meltdown.

Lots of climbers had attempted Meltdown in the nearly eleven years since I'd established it. Until that day, all of them had failed. I'd expected to have more conflicted feelings about it all. Should I be crying for the loss of that status, my unrepeated hardest crack climb in the world? I knew Carlo had climbed harder grades than the 5.14c I'd assigned it, but then, he'd been working on Meltdown since 2015. My ego couldn't help wondering if that meant anything. Could it *actually* be 5.14d? Some people had suggested it might be, over the years. Wouldn't that mean I'd been the first American woman to climb that grade—and on a first-ascent trad climb, making the accomplishment even worthier? I felt myself wandering back to a previous mindset, when everything hinged on climbing accomplishments, when my sense of my own value was an extension of how hard I climbed, or how hard other people thought I climbed, or how impressive that was to them.

Randy heard me sniffle. He put his hand on my shoulder and squeezed. Theo was tossing and turning in his bed—still too early for us to talk. I read Carlo's text again, thinking maybe I'd feel something different, something profound, something life-changing. I smiled at his flattery. I smiled knowing that he had put three years of intermittent effort into this route. I remembered how happy I was when I climbed it. How relieved I was. How proud. I sat there waiting for grief to come, but it didn't. I felt the weight of Randy's hand on my shoulder, a small hug. Theo's breathing became constant and heavy. He was asleep.

"Carlo did Meltdown today," I said in a very flat, monotone whisper.

"Really?" Randy replied softly, in case Theo wasn't fully in his deep sleep yet. "How does that make you feel?"

I tried to listen to what was happening in my body, to understand what I was really feeling rather than leaping ahead to what I thought I should feel, the way Susan had helped me learn to do. There were no expectations here, just me and my husband. I could have said anything: been spiteful or petty or angry. But my feelings were surprisingly mild. I had loved so much about my old life. I loved dreaming up big projects, using my body as a vessel to reach my hopes and desires, seeing how high and far I could push myself and our sport. Learning about my drive and dedication.

But I had never really loved the aftermath. The wave of accolades and acknowledgment. The interviews, the videos, the pictures, the magazine covers, the raises from sponsors. It had felt great, but it was like a high, addicting. I didn't like to remember how much I'd relied on people liking me for climbing hard. How that made me feel worthy. And all of those feelings had started to infiltrate how I climbed, what I searched for—and then it all dissipated. The climbing world will always move on to the next accomplishment or athlete, and it's over for any climber until they do something to make them worthy again. I had become so entangled in that. My love for climbing had become entangled in that external validation.

When Carlo sent Meltdown and said it was really hard, I felt that outside acknowledgment again. It felt good. Carlo's praise was genuine—I had talked to him about the route over the years. But I realized I didn't need or want the more superficial or insincere praise as much anymore, the fleeting attention. None of that had helped me in my hardest times. External praise was a Band-Aid, easily ripped away. I still have an ego, but I'm trying to value being settled from within. To realize that building my own resilience feels good and nourishing, whereas the outside noise was only a tenuous prop holding me up. Maybe that comes easily for some people, but for me it is a hard thing to hold on to.

Randy's hand was still on my shoulder when I responded. "I actually don't know. I thought I would have a clear feeling, but I don't. I think I need to sit with it for a little bit."

He kissed the top of my head. "That makes total sense."

I thought back on my day, climbing with Becca, both of us not really enjoying the route. How refreshing it had been to commiserate with someone and say, "I'd rather be bouldering in the sun." I hadn't felt like I had to tough it out, to pretend I wasn't cold or scared or uncomfortable. So often, with Tommy, I had stuffed my complaints down until I burst into tears—not because he forced me to, but there was something in our dynamic that made me default to hiding my feelings. I really loved climbing with Becca. I could be myself, all of myself, and not hide it.

My fingers throbbed as I texted Carlo back. I had crimped harder that day than I had in many, many months, and the tips were a little swollen. I congratulated him, told him I was really excited for him and that I'd love to hear more about it.

CHAPTER
FORTY-TWO

Fontainebleau, France, April 2019

It was a crisp, fresh spring day in the magical forest of Fontainebleau. The kind of day where you can see your breath in the morning, but by afternoon the sun warms the air enough to make it T-shirt weather. Randy, Theo, and I were visiting the area for the fifth year in a row. We always made the trip to France in tandem with other friends and families, often including the Caldwells. My self-consciousness about climbing in a group had faded, and while I still mostly prefer a quiet scene to a crowd, the mix of families was a key ingredient to our joy in the forest. The kids running around with sticks and *pains au chocolat* and building forts while the parents played in their own way. We'd climb on the boulders and talk on the ground and occasionally pause to mediate an argument over the sacred stick of the day. Getting everyone out of the house and into the forest took hours, even though we were never able to sleep in. The days were filled with laughter and skinned knees, tears, hunger, and chaos, the adults vacillating between *This is the best thing in the world* and *What the hell were we thinking?* It was a glorious junk show.

The climbing in Fontainebleau is known for its beauty and subtle technique. The rock is some of the best sandstone in the world, a tight, fine grain. It slowly files the skin off fingertips, often leaving me bleeding or raw at the end of the day. The holds are slopey, which means they are big and not positive. Grasping them is like trying to palm a beach ball or a volleyball. Even with a whole hand, it is hard to get much purchase. It requires good footwork, a discerning eye, and a thoughtful mind: everything I love in climbing.

I'd come there for the first time with Tommy, in the spring of 2003, a few months before our wedding. We'd intended to make just a brief stop in the forest on our way to the sport-climbing paradise of Céüse. I'd agreed to the trip mostly because I felt trapped in a cycle of cake tastings and dress fittings: I wanted to escape to the simplicity of sleeping in a tent, climbing, and eating off a camp stove. (The trip did its job, and I was skinny and "perfect" looking in my wedding dress, just the way I imagined I should be.) But Fontainebleau grabbed me and held me from the start. There, even the easy climbs were fun. The hard climbs were fun. And there were so many of them: I felt like a kid in the candy store. That first time, we ended up staying for three weeks, half of our entire trip.

When I started coming back each year with Randy (who had lived in the area for two years around the same time Tommy and I first visited) and our friends, I really fell in love with the climbing, the forest, the pace of life. It was so fresh, so free of judgment or the old ghosts of my past achievements and failures.

Fontainebleau has a system of "circuit problems" that have painted numbers at the beginning of each climb. The color indicates the difficulty, yellow usually being the easiest and black the hardest. We warmed up on oranges, the second-easiest climbs, and talked about why it takes so long to get a child to put on a T-shirt or eat a bite of banana. Remember when we could fit into those pants? Our banter was easy, constant. Becca and I started trying Red 3, which looked at first to be a simple mantle—a move that looks a little like hoisting yourself out over the lip of a swimming pool. But it was harder than it looked to climb up and over the top.

There's a moment with some mantles where, even though your upper half has made it over, you are still precarious, fighting gravity, struggling to get your legs and feet back under you. It's a special type of struggle that is neither graceful nor pretty and is often referred to as a beached whale. Fontainebleau is known for these. And Red 3 was the epitome of a beached-whale problem.

After an hour, I noticed that each time I crested the lip of the boulder, my stomach would start slipping on my T-shirt, wedged between my skin and the warm sandstone rock. The shirt was hindering the friction I needed to get over the boulder. Finally I realized: *If my stomach was bare, it would be like another appendage, with skin and friction that I could use to my advantage.* But that thought put a tiny pit in my gut. To gain that advantage, I would have to bare my stomach to Becca and our other friends. My stomach, which was saggy and soft and had stretch marks. The rolls I couldn't seem to get rid of anymore. The body part that inspired adoration and awe during pregnancy but now felt like a sad, deflated balloon that I—that society—expected to be tight and taut.

I hadn't shown my bare stomach to anyone except Randy and Theo in almost five years. As Becca struggled and fell again at the same spot, my mind went back and forth, playing out each scenario, wondering how terrible I would feel, how much other people would want to stare or turn their eyes away. But then I remembered all the other conversations I'd had with my friends. We'd talked about bleeding nipples, about hemorrhoids, about sex after birth. And I wanted to send this problem.

"I'm going to try climbing in a sports bra. I think the friction of my belly will help on the top out," I said. "Apologies to your eyes for having to see my mom belly, but maybe the extra chunk will help on this problem!" I half-laughed, reaching for that old familiar tool, self-deprecation.

I tried not to give air to all the fears and worries that were swirling. *Do I gross them out? Do they think less of me? I should have done more sit-ups. I should have added another mile to my morning run. I really should give up breakfast.* I shook my head, shook those thoughts away, and tried to just focus on the climb. I pulled on, grabbed the right hand over the lip, lifted my hips up, and plopped my stomach on the sandstone. It stuck. It actually stuck! There was no slipping. My skin wrapped around the rock like cling wrap on a chocolate-chip cookie. I tried to move my left hand, but before I could, my right arm got too tired and let go. I scraped down and fell onto the pads.

"That was incredible!" Becca shouted.

I sat there laughing, feeling relieved that it had kind of worked. I felt liberated, somehow. I felt lighter.

"I'm going full mama belly too," Becca said, taking off her T-shirt as I got back to my feet.

A few tries later I stood on top of the boulder, chafed stomach and all. The dads walked up with the kids.

"Whoa, must be hot today to be climbing in a sports bra!" someone said.

"I just need to figure out how to get rid of this!" I said, laughing and clutching fistfuls of skin on my stomach. Trying to play it off as my next not-too-important task, rather than a tangle of shame and frustration. An *I'll get to this after I pack the lunches* type of thing. All the grown-ups laughed. But then I looked over at the kids and realized they were standing there absorbing it all. Theo's big brown eyes were like a sponge soaking up a cup of spilled milk. Just doing his job, observing the world and learning from his parents.

An alarm, small but loud, went off inside of my head. I hated this dark thread that was woven through me, the dangerous idea that my body was a tool, a vehicle to manipulate and use as a pathway to success. I felt like I had a spotlight on me and I was showing my worst self. I was showing Theo and all his friends that this was normal.

I didn't know how to silence the alarm. I had no tools to fix the situation. So instead I just kept laughing through my fear.

◆ ◆ ◆

A few weeks went by. I was having my best climbing trip—and my most successful, by the numbers—since well before my pregnancy. Each time I stood on top of a boulder that I'd never thought I could climb, I said something to write off the accomplishment. *It was soft. I got lucky. These boulder problems aren't actually hard, or cutting-edge, far from it. It was just because Lyn gave me good beta.* Anything to distract from the truth that I was climbing things I'd never thought I could.

Why was it still so hard to accept a compliment? Or, even worse, to compliment myself?

I was sitting on the crash pad, eating leftovers from the night before, when Randy walked up to me.

"I really think you should try El Poussif; it is such a Fontainebleau classic."

I looked up at him. Everyone was always describing him as a ninja, when he climbed and in his normal life—so smooth, so meticulous, always up to try anything even if it seemed hard. He would encourage anyone in any realm; just like he helped open my mind to parenthood, and to therapy. But the idea that I should try El Poussif? I started laughing.

"I couldn't touch that thing when I was in fighting shape in 2003. There's no way I can do it now." I silently added: *Fifteen pounds heavier.*

"I know, but it doesn't hurt to try," he said. "No one is over there. We could just go play on it for a while." He knew how to get to me. I packed up my shoes, ate the last spoonful of leftovers, and headed over.

The holds felt nonexistent. I slipped, stared at Randy with a silent *See, I told you so.* He didn't flinch.

"Try to grab it this way. And look at that right-hand pinch up there—isn't that the most amazing hold you've ever seen?" His enthusiasm for this place, his favorite place, was contagious. Half of my love for this magical forest was because of Randy and his unending devotion to climbing here. He made it fun for everyone.

I smiled, pulled on again. Stood on my right foot, straightened my leg, and reached up to the right-hand pinch. Damn, Randy was right: it was such an incredible hold, my fingers wrapping around a tiny groove that looked like elephant skin. A stray thought: *Isn't it so weird how we can find beauty and awe in a four-inch ripple of rock?* I squeezed my fingers toward my thumb, and my foot slipped off the terrible smear. I landed with a thud on the pad, a smile across my face.

I remembered trying El Poussif when I was twenty-three. I remembered that I'd never gotten that far before. I remembered how weak my arms had felt, how wobbly my body felt. But it seemed different. My body felt more familiar. I knew how it worked, even with its folds and quirks. I looked up at Randy, beaming. "I never thought I'd hit that hold."

It was startling to realize I could still perform in my body with all its changes. The one that ate actual food at the crag, not just my preportioned, prepackaged bar. The one that bumbled through the warm-ups and hung over my pants. I had convinced myself that this body would never be able to climb hard. Maybe that had been an easier story to tell myself, so I could let go of the dream of climbing hard, let go of any goals and expectations around climbing. So I could grieve.

I got even higher my next try, and then higher after that. I paused, sat on the pads, and stretched my forearms. I breathed deep breaths. I took sips of water. I laughed at the kids running like feral animals in the forest. Becca strolled over and started working on it with me. We talked things over as we worked: how to move our hips this way or that, when to use a pinky, when to high step. I wondered if this was like the magic that musicians felt when they played together, with nothing but their instruments and their creative minds.

My last try of the day, I held the pinch on the arête, and somehow my arms felt fresh. I grabbed the left hand around the corner and hoisted my body up as much as I could. I was at the tipping point now: I needed to release my left hand and reach the top hold before I toppled off. I hung there, pulling with my left toe, pinching with my right hand, pushing with my right leg, and thought about it.

I wanted a sign. I wanted to feel more solid. But as I balanced there, precarious, I realized that wasn't going to happen. There were no guarantees; I just had to try it. I took a deep breath and went for it. My hand released the wall next to my foot and, like a shot of lightning, reached for the top hold. It felt like hard-grit sandpaper that grabbed my fingers, and I pulled over, ecstatic.

The physical act of succeeding with a different, heavier body, one that I had resented for so long, created a small shift in my thinking. I'd known that the way I talked about and thought about my body wasn't healthy. I knew I had absorbed this perspective from the people around me when I was younger, and I didn't want to perpetuate that cycle. I dug through the mountains of casual comments I'd heard, the things I'd read and seen: the climbers at the gym who muttered *Nobody wants to see that* when someone without perfectly toned abs took their shirt off; the competitor who told me she always lost five pounds before each competition. I began to realize just how toxic and harmful this community, that thought of itself as progressive and compassionate, could so often be. But it was as though I'd needed proof: proof that this body was okay. Now I had it, and I could start to think differently about my body, how it felt, how I felt about living in it. To really dismantle the patterns I had inherited and lived by.

It hasn't been quick work to untangle all my old habits. I didn't just turn around and see my body differently. There are still nights when I grab my stomach rolls and wish they would disappear. But once I started to understand where that chatter came from, and how restricting it is on a human life, I found the shift I needed to start to disarm that voice, instead of trying to change myself to fit its demands.

After Kyrgyzstan, I had thought that talking about what happened would only make things worse. Eventually, through therapy, I learned to put words to the experiences that still haunted me—but that was a private thing, in a safe space. I have always gained so much from hearing other people be open and vulnerable; it makes me feel less alone. So in the months after El Poussif, I began to write about my changing experience in my body on social media, in articles, and in interviews, and—as I had when I spoke out about pregnancy and early parenthood—I found a community that valued what I had to say. Maybe not surprisingly, I also heard from certain sponsors and companies who hadn't been in touch for years. Who suddenly understood that the old climbing myths of bravado and machismo, of beautiful strong hotshots, were beginning to come apart. But while finding a new way to continue my career has been validating, I just want to shine a light on things that have often felt taboo. The things I needed to hear, and didn't, at so many stages of my life. And, so, I keep talking.

These are just steps, I know, moves in a long sequence that I am still working to unlock.

CHAPTER FORTY-THREE

November 2020

Randy and I had driven into the parking lot at the Ahwahnee hotel so many times. Years ago, we'd parked there to climb Astroboy: the early non-date, of sorts. But for the past decade, we'd almost always gone there to boulder. This day was no different—at least, that was what I tried to tell myself.

Theo was six years old and asking questions in the back seat. *How far of a walk is it? Will there be sticks there?* I answered each of his questions as they came, feeling a little tingling in my stomach, one or two small butterflies where there used to be thousands working their wings.

The three of us started the short walk out to Raggedy Anne. *No expectations,* I reminded myself.

I had never tried Magic Line, or any other big project, again after Theo was born. The relentless negative thoughts that used to occupy my brain weren't swirling like they used to, but sealing them away most of the time had left scars that I didn't want to pick open. After so many years of frustration, I had achieved what felt like a delicate but healthy balance. I still dreamed about Magic Line, of course, but I also felt at peace with letting it go. That was a hard thing to explain to others, so I only offered canned responses when people asked if I would climb hard again: *Maybe when Theo is older. Maybe if my body ever lets me. I'm happy where I'm at with climbing now; it's time to let the younger generation take over.*

I didn't really want to let the younger generation fully take over. I was forty, but I knew I still had it in me. I could stand on Yosemite granite with the best of them. Still, I pushed down that thought. Yes, lately I had been succeeding on boulders that I hadn't been able to climb even in the peak of my career. But bouldering had always been a weak discipline for me, and these weren't groundbreaking achievements. And yet some part of me wondered: If I could now boulder harder than I ever had, would some of that newfound power take me up hard routes too?

I squashed that line of thinking. I didn't want to weigh the day down with all my baggage. El Poussif had been spontaneous, a surprise same-day send. But I had put several days of work into today's planned climb. I wanted to challenge myself without losing the joy that I had rediscovered in climbing. I wanted to have fun *and* climb hard.

The butterflies inside me grew heavier, fluttered faster.

Could I find my drive while still limiting my expectations for the day? Chase a small goal while also keeping it at arm's length? I'd learned that planning with a child was like having a balloon party in a cactus garden—sure, the balloons might survive, but best not to count on it. I had already warmed up in the garage at home, in the sweet silence that was now my preferred workout soundtrack. I carried two pads, one big and one small, and Randy did the same. I smiled, remembering how I used to think boulderers were lazy. My load was more awkward than anything I used to carry up the East Ledges to the top of El Cap.

Theo's curious mind never stopped racing ahead of us. *How much farther? Dad, can you carry me? Do you think this stick looks more like a light saber, or this one? How long was Luke's? What shape was Hermione's wand?* I tried to remind myself that I would miss this, one day.

Twenty minutes later, we got to the boulder. The sun didn't reach Raggedy Anne in late November; the south rim of the Valley was too tall. It was cold enough that I could see my breath, and I wished I had brought my warmer mittens.

Raggedy Anne is tall, light gray, and gorgeous. It sits on the Valley floor, a stone's throw from the popular climbing trail up to Washington Column, and yet no one had climbed it until 2009, and only a handful of people have repeated it since. Most climbers come to Yosemite to route climb, not to boulder. The boulders here are literally and figuratively in the shadows of the famous big walls, but Yosemite bouldering on its own could be a world-class destination. The problems are hard and stiff for their grades. Bouldering in the Valley makes a person earn it, just like the routes up the big walls. Maybe some of what drove me was ego, knowing the extra respect that comes with success in Yosemite. But I always loved being forced to work hard for it.

Raggedy Anne epitomizes Valley bouldering. It's not one of these modern "pull hard on small holds to show off those gym skills" type of climbs. The holds are hardly noticeable. The boulder is a slopey, slanting arête that gently moves up and left as you climb, forcing you to find the faintest bumps and crevices to nestle your fingertips over. Sometimes it's a small crystal just one quarter the size of a pushpin head. Sometimes it's an indent in the rock so slight that it can't be seen but only felt with fingertips. The footholds are small and precarious, just what I love, sometimes only an edge as thick as a few sheets of paper. It makes the climber think, not just pull.

I set my pads down underneath the boulder and arranged them next to Randy's. Randy went over to help Theo find sticks. My phone started whistling with texts from the other moms who were coming out. I responded before getting on my shoes: Just got to the boulder, no rush, Theo is loading the base with weaponry now. Looking forward to seeing you.

I hadn't seen my lucky sending long underwear in over a decade. It might have been entombed in the Magic Line box in the garage, full of two dozen perfectly broken-in pairs of Miuras (each one worn precisely on seven different boulder problems in the garage), the rack of gear clipped in order on a faded yellow sling, and anything else that I'd been convinced would help with my inevitable send eleven years earlier.

That day, I just wore my usual yoga pants and non-color-coordinated layered jackets stained with olive oil and old sunscreen.

I took my shoes out from inside my jacket, where they had been warming before I put them on my icy feet. I felt those two butterflies stir a little. Sure, I had worked out the moves on this, I understood what to do in theory, but I hadn't been able to do Raggedy Anne in the spring of 2009, when I was still strong and light from my Meltdown and Magic Line seasons.

I put on my shoes and chalk bag. I reached in, finding way less than I usually liked. Back at home I had told myself to refill it, but then I'd remembered that I needed to put the lid on our lunch box and grab Theo's fleece pants, and the thought about the chalk had vanished, along with a million others. I shook my head. I wiped my feet on my shins and pulled on. The rock was cold. I could feel my skin harden and lose friction. I slipped off just as I was readjusting my hands.

I chalked up again, blowing on my hands for a little warmth and moisture, and wiped my feet once again on my calves. I could hear Theo's distant screams of joy when he saw his friends Miles and Judy pull up on their bikes. A smile spread across my face. I made it two moves higher and fell with a thud onto the pads. I took off my shoes, put them back in my jacket, and walked over.

"Can I see your base?" I asked Theo and the crew. They ran to the top of a boulder, something that might terrify most parents but was normal for our kids. Melis and Jen asked me how it was going. It was fine, cold, but fine. I didn't think I would do it that day, but it was fun to try. The chorus of the kids screaming and running and moms talking continued as I laced up my shoes again. Randy walked over; more parents and kids meant he could forgo his playmate duties briefly and come spot me. I smiled but didn't talk. Those two little butterflies took flight again in my stomach.

If someone had told me in my twenties that I would feel more alive being a mom, or being in love, or having a day out with my girlfriends, than I did while I was freeing a route on El Cap, I would have nodded and smiled and walked away thinking they had no idea what they were talking about. Why would I pursue some normal, boring, run-of-the-mill life when I was seeking and achieving excellence? Did they know what it was like to hang off a cliff three thousand feet up in the air? Did they know what it was like to travel to the far corners of the earth and climb a mountain, to have companies pay them to do what they loved most? Did they know how to suffer to become extraordinary?

But I had surprised myself so much, in the past decade. I was learning that life wasn't an equation to be solved, that it wasn't a matter of controlling all the pieces—my body, my eating, my training, my social circle, my marriage—and putting them in the correct places to achieve the desired result. I had treated myself like a robot for so long, thinking my discipline made me better than regular people. I finally understood that pursuing "greatness" didn't fill me the way a "normal" life did. If I wanted to have a big life, I needed to live a smaller one.

I got back on the wall. It felt stickier. I stood on the good left foot and brought my right foot up to my armpit again. It stuck like glue. I reached my left hand higher on the sloping lip of the boulder, nestled my index finger onto the sharp divot on the edge. My skin caught a tiny crystal in the rock and hung there, draped like a sheet over a lamp. I could feel my stomach start to get excited; I leaned into it, almost curious to see what would happen if I did. I felt myself entering that old hallway. I stepped into it, but my mind wandered—to the kids, to their snacks and games. To granola bars and wizard wands. It's those subtle moments that make up the greatest grief and joy in life: the lingering in bed a little longer, the laughter with my friends when I should be training, the deep, aching grief I felt when our dog died. The painful vulnerability of loving deeply, of truly and honestly valuing a friendship over some arbitrary marker of success. The shame or guilt I feel when I know I messed up, the courage to admit it and try to repair it. All the things that remind me I'm not a machine.

My feet moved to another position, right foot still high just below the arête and left foot to a small fragile edge. My hands moved to the next slopers as I thought about wands versus light sabers. I heard the kids laughing and running, and then, before I even realized it, I was falling onto the pads.

"Good try!" Randy said as I sat with my hands shaking on my knees. I looked up and saw that I'd been just two moves away from the rock-over to the precarious high slab, fifteen feet off the ground.

I laughed. I had forgotten how good it felt to do well on a physical challenge. The quickness of breath, the burning in my forearms, the racing heart. How addicting it was. My dozen years with Randy and all the therapy I'd gone through had showed me other paths to being human, to being happy, to being okay, but in that moment, I realized, maybe this path was valid too. I took off my shoes and climbed on top of the boulder with the kids. Randy climbed, making things look easy as always, letting out the magnetic, perfect laugh that had drawn me in forever ago.

I shared some snacks with Theo and then made my way back to the climb. I was nervous. My failure on Magic Line still haunted me, if I let myself dwell on it. I wasn't sure I wanted to invite that feeling into my life. Should I just walk away right now with the upper hand, knowing I'd made progress and that was good enough? If I tried again and couldn't do it, the climb would hold the power, not me. I shook my head, jammed my feet back into my shoes. Why not? It didn't have to hold the power if I failed. It could just be. But I could want this at the same time.

At some point, I imagined therapy as a task I could complete, like another dream climb checked off my list: mission accomplished. I was surprised to realize that I would need to keep going back—that I would *want* to keep going back, from time to time, to work through something, one of those sticking points in my mind. I don't want to sound like I have it all figured out. It's more like: Now I understand that it's okay to *have to* figure things out—that the figuring out is the point, in the end. That constantly fighting to keep the freight train of your life on a specific, rigid track means missing all those little derailments— the heartbreaks and surprises and delights and aches that make up the human experience.

Randy stepped onto the pads to spot me. Once again I wiped my shoes against my shins and calves. I dipped my hands into my chalk bag, first left, then right. Even less chalk now, but it didn't matter.

I stepped onto the left foothold yet again. My right foot went back up to armpit level. My left hand shuffled up the slanted lip of the boulder. It felt even stickier, like my skin was more cling wrap than cotton sheet. I moved my left foot to the friable hold, and the butter-flies started to flutter. My mind opened a door into the hallway; my breathing became audible and rhythmic. I tensed my core with each foot movement. I crimped the tiny jagged crystal with my cling-wrap pointer finger, feeling the rock jut into my skin but not caring.

I tensed my left shoulder, the once-good one that had since become the bad one. I matched my hands, moving one left-hand finger off at a time to make room for my right-hand fingers. I moved my feet up onto the high holds. I was getting to the point where I knew I didn't want to fall, more than ten feet off the ground. I shook the thought away, reached my hand to the crimp before the big move to the bad hold at the lip. I could feel every part of my body working in unison, like a sports car that had been in the garage, still faster than most if given the chance. It didn't feel effortless. There is a myth in climbing that it feels like floating when you send. I've always thought that was bullshit, just climbers trying to seem enlightened, zen. Climbing near my limit always feels hard to me. It's just that sometimes hard gets me to the top, and other times it doesn't.

I set my feet on higher holds, readjusted my right hand when it slipped slightly. I heard one of the kids yelling. It was like I'd opened a window. I was still in the hallway, but there was real life happening just outside the walls: Randy cheering, Theo lost in play with his friends, and people we loved, people who loved and supported us in turn, people who didn't expect perfection every time, climbing or lounging and chatting together. I held on tighter with my right hand and pulled up. I let my body out from the wall ever so slightly, then generated momentum upward and inward to the next hold. My left hand targeted and stuck it. I felt all four fingers land where they were supposed to. I'd never hit that hold so cleanly before. I bore down, fifteen feet off the ground, but I didn't let any doubts or worries enter. I knew I could do this.

ACKNOWLEDGMENTS

These acknowledgments are for the people who have helped me along the way, who have offered guidance, support, and encouragement to keep going even when I thought this entire book was one of my worst ideas and that I should just can it and move on. (The jury is still out on whether this was a good idea or not.) I'll try to keep it concise, but anyone who knows me knows that is not my strong point, so bear with me.

First and foremost, to my parents: I can think of no greater gift than giving someone the freedom and grace to bumble through life, trying things that you yourself might never do, and somehow still having the wherewithal to support them along the way. Thank you for doing the best you knew how with the tools you had at the time. I know that at times I was so steadfast in my belief that I knew better than you, that I'd rather be anywhere in the world but in your home, but you continually gave me a place I could come back to again and again, where I felt loved and accepted. I can think of nothing more powerful in the world than offering that. I can only hope to be half the parent you both have been.

To my husband, who I know won't read this for years, if at all: Thank you for being the shift, for planting the seed that maybe the world could be a bigger yet a smaller, richer place to explore, that life is not all black and white, that so much of the richness of being a human lives in the gray; and for igniting a curiosity in me that I am still surprised by. Most importantly, thank you for being my Jell-O. I love you.

To our kiddo: I love you beyond measure and beyond words.

To Steffi, Max, and Bodie, my four-legged family members: You have been some of the greatest loves of my life.

Now to the actual book. I did not write this book by myself, I could not have written this book by myself, and to even suggest that doesn't do justice to the vast network and expertise of people whose ideas and words and scenes appear on these pages.

First and foremost, this book would not have been possible without the constant patience, wisdom, and brilliance of Eva Holland. Eva, you came to this project when I was drowning in my own thoughts and hundreds of pages of journal entries. I was lost and sad and wanting to shelve the whole project. I'm confident that I would still be in that perilous state without your presence. You have shown compassion and kindness and a clear and direct path to getting my babbling to a concise place, which is no easy feat. I count my lucky stars each day that you still return my texts and offer exemplary advice even when you could draw the line and say, *We are DONE, Beth.* I don't know what title to give you, because how do you give just one title to someone who has done so much? Yes, a lot of these words are mine, but I'd venture to say that even more of them are yours and your ability to distill down my rambling thoughts to words and passages that actually make sense. You are a gift and a treasure and smart, and there is no way I can possibly say thank you enough in my lifetime, so I'll just be annoying and keep saying it.

Mark Lotto: I was blown away and completely intimidated when you originally agreed to take this project on. From day one, I have been nervous and dumbfounded that you were working on it, especially when you could have taken the clear and easy path to gracefully back out when you had the chance; but you stayed. Thank you for staying. Thank you for being our guiding light when we were lost in the vast sea of Beth. For championing the thoughts that I believed to be pointless and bluntly dismissing things that I was so certain deserved real estate in the book. I'm still nervous each time I get on the phone with you that I will be a doofus and say something that doesn't make sense or leads you to second-guess your decision to work with me, but somehow you just redirect those thoughts to a kind place. This book would be so inferior without your intelligence, talent, and candor. Thank you, thank you, thank you, over and over again.

To Liz and Dan: I don't really know how to sum up my appreciation for you two, and anything I say will be a poor representation of how I feel, but I'll try. This book would not be a book without you. From the earliest beginnings around your kitchen table to meetings at Pinhole to Yosemite—thank you for even entertaining the idea of a book with me. You two are some of the brightest people I know, and for both of you to take time out of your careers to show me kindness and help guide me through the early years was more than gracious. Liz, your expertise and writing wizardry still blow me away each day. The first part of this book would not be what it is without you and your words; I am forever grateful and indebted. And, Dan, your gift with the written word and ability to see the big picture gave me solace over the years and the idea that maybe, just maybe, this whole thing was worth pursuing. Your kindness and willingness to lend an ear and your time was, and is, beyond generous. I'm lucky to be able to call you both friends.

To Andrew Bisharat: Your compassion and patience and gentle nudging to lean in to things that I thought were taboo and not worth my time so long ago started this entire process. You helped me see the value in telling a story from my heart, and I'd still be stuck on my old narrow path of thinking if it weren't for you. You are a gem.

To my editor, Laura Van der Veer: Wow, I can't believe you didn't can this book when I was a year, two years, six years past deadline. Thank you for giving me the kindness to go at my own pace (with some gentle nudging) and to find and tell a story that felt true to me. This book would be so different if not for your guidance. Thank you, thank you.

To Danielle Svetcov: Thank you for showing excitement about and belief in a book long before I could ever imagine it.

To Tenyia Lee: Thank you so much for your early guidance and suggestions, from big-picture stuff to down in the weeds.

To Omar Mouallem: For reading and helping and giving advice in the most sensitive of areas, thank you.

Now to a few important people this would not have been possible without.

To Jeni: Thank you for being a constant source of contemplation and the calm yet thought-provoking friend who I could bounce ideas off of for years, even long before the book. For agreeing to read it in such an early and fragmented state. Somehow, you still provided feedback with compassion and understanding on where I wanted to go, even when it was just broken paragraphs and run-on sentences. This book and my life would be so much less without you and your love. I am the luckiest. And for all those dinners so long ago. They were a highlight of our weeks and months, and I can't wait for the next one.

To Sanni and Sandy: Thank you for being the first readers of the finished manuscript. At a time when I was still so unsure it should ever be seen, you two graciously offered your time and energy to read it. I know I never would have leaned into the parts where I still feel shame had it not been for your gentle encouragement and excitement to hear things I thought people never wanted to hear. Thank you for accepting all of me and showing me love and compassion. I am so grateful to have you in my life.

To Becca: It's impossible to say how much I treasure our relationship in a quick paragraph, and you know that brevity is not my strong suit. I could never have imagined having such an unlikely yet rich and valued friendship as I have with you. You are a light in my life and in the lives of so many others. I am confident I would not be who I am today without your tenderness and kindness and vulnerability during those early years of motherhood, all the way through to today. You are an incredible advocate for your friends and things that are important to us (including this book), and you have a way of making us feel seen, even in the most awkward (vulnerable?) of times. Thank you for showing me that love and friendship know no bounds and can come in many forms and places. I cherish our time together and look forward to much more in the years to come.

To my girlfriends, all of you: Thank you for loving me and accepting me where I am. For continuing to invite me to things even when I turn you down at least half the time because I want to be home and in bed by 9:00 p.m. I never would have imagined I'd have such a breadth of women who mean so much to me. I appreciate you all: Lyn, Nora, Becky, Rebecca, Jessica, Jen, Jill, Jen, Emily, Marina, Melis, Em, Steph, Stephanie, Theresa, Kathryn, Jess, Katie, Caitlin, Sharon . . . I know I am forgetting some of you, but please know that that doesn't mean you aren't important to me, it's just because my son lovingly stole my memory back in 2014 and I have yet to find it again.

To my sponsors: I know things ebb and flow in this very volatile world of professional climbing and the outdoor community, and there's a chance we won't be working together even by the time this book comes out. But, during this period of my life, you have been with me, and I wouldn't be where I am today without your trust and confidence and support in my career and beliefs—and whatever form those have taken. So thank you to: Outdoor Research, Yeti, Metolius Climbing, Touchstone Climbing, La Sportiva, BlueWater Ropes, and EXPED.

I wrote the majority of this book in various parking lots of Yosemite Valley, from the back seat of my car (the back seat just felt more comfortable than the front). I now know the best shady spots when it's warm and sunny spots in the depths of winter, the spots that get the best reception. It is fascinating to see and hear all the people who visit our national park, never assuming there's someone inches away, typing on their laptop. And so for all that writing and thinking time, I'd like to thank the custodial staff of Yosemite NPS. I used your bathrooms each and every day. It's a thankless task, cleaning bathrooms that hundreds, maybe thousands, of people use each day, and to have toilet paper and soap restocked each day was a gift. Thank you for doing what you do.

ABOUT THE AUTHOR

Photo © 2023 Ryan Moon

Beth Rodden has been climbing for thirty years, and she hopes to be climbing for thirty more. She lives with her family in California.